# Effect Sizes for Research

## A Broad Practical Approach

# Effect Sizes for Research

## A Broad Practical Approach

**Robert J. Grissom**
**John J. Kim**
*San Francisco State University*

**LEA**

LAWRENCE ERLBAUM ASSOCIATES, PUBLISHERS
2005    Mahwah, New Jersey                    London

Lawrence Erlbaum Associates, Inc., Publishers
10 Industrial Avenue
Mahwah, New Jersey 07430

Cover design by Sean Trane Sciarrone

**Library of Congress Cataloging-in-Publication Data**

Grissom, Robert J.
  Effect sizes for research : a broad practical approach / Rob-
ert J. Grissom, John J. Kim.
      p.  cm.
  Includes bibliographical references and index.
  ISBN 0-8058-5014-7 (alk. paper)
    1. Analysis of variance. 2. Effect sizes (Statistics) 3. Exper-
  imental design.   I. Kim, John J.   II. Title.

QA279.F75 2005
519.5'38—dc22                                          2004053284
                                                           CIP

Books published by Lawrence Erlbaum Associates are printed
on acid-free paper, and their bindings are chosen for strength
and durability.

Printed in the United States of America
10  9  8  7  6  5  4  3  2

This book is dedicated to those scholars, amply cited herein, who during the past three decades have worked diligently to develop and promote the use of effect sizes and robust statistical methods and to those who have constructively criticized such procedures.

# Contents

# Preface

Emphasis on effect sizes is a rapidly rising tide as over 20 journals in various fields of research now require that authors of research reports provide estimates of effect size. For certain kinds of applied research it is no longer considered acceptable only to report that results were statistically significant. Statistically significant results indicate that a researcher has discovered evidence of a real difference between parameters or a real association between variables, but it is one of unknown size. Especially in applied research such statements often need to be supplemented with estimates of how different the average results for studied groups are or how strong the association between variables is. Those who apply research results often need to know more, for example, than that one therapy, one teaching method, one marketing campaign, or one medication appears to be better than another; they often need evidence of how much better it is (i.e., the estimated effect size). Chapter 1 provides a more detailed definition of effect size, discussion of those circumstances in which estimation of effect sizes is especially important, and discussion of why a variety of measures of effect sizes is needed.

The purpose of this book is to inform a broad readership (broad with respect to fields of research and extent of knowledge of general statistics) about a variety of measures and estimators of effect sizes for research, their proper applications and interpretations, and their limitations. There are several excellent books on the topic of effect sizes, but these books generally treat the topic in a different context and for a purpose that is different from that of this book. Some books discuss effect sizes in the context of preresearch analysis of statistical power for determining needed sample sizes for the planned research. This is not the purpose of this book, which focuses on analyzing postresearch results in terms of the size of the obtained effects. Some books discuss effect sizes in the context of meta-analysis, the quantitative synthesizing of results from an earlier set of underlying individual research studies. This also is not the purpose of this book, which focuses on the analysis of data from an individual piece of research (called *primary research*). Books on meta-analysis are also concerned with methods for approximating estimates of effect size indirectly from reported test statistics because raw data from the underlying primary research are rarely available to meta-analysts. However, this book is concerned with direct estimation of effect sizes by primary researchers, who can estimate effect sizes directly because they, unlike meta-analysts, have access to the raw data.

The book is subtitled *A Broad Practical Approach* in part because it deals with a broad variety of kinds of effect sizes for different types of variables, designs, circumstances, and purposes. Our approach encompasses detailed discussions of standardized differences between means (chaps. 3, 6, and 7), some of the correlational measures (chap. 4), strength of association (chaps. 6 and 7), confidence intervals (chap. 2 and thereafter), other common methods, and less-known measures such as stochastic superiority (chaps. 5 and 9). The book is broad also because, in the interest of fairness and completeness, we respectfully cite alternative viewpoints for cases in which experts disagree about the appropriate measure of effect size. Consistent with the modern trend toward more use of robust statistical methods, the book also pays much attention to the statistical assumptions of methods. Also consistent with the broad approach, there are more than 300 references. Software for those calculations that would be laborious by hand is cited.

The level and content of this book make it appropriate for use as a supplement for graduate courses in statistics in such fields as psychology, education, the social sciences, business, management, and medicine. The book is also appropriate for use as the text for a special-topics seminar or independent-reading course in those fields. In addition, because of its broad content and extensive references the book is intended to be a valuable source for professional researchers, graduate students who are analyzing data for a master's or doctoral thesis, or advanced undergraduates. Readers are expected to have knowledge of parametric statistics through factorial analysis of variance and some knowledge of chi-square analysis of contingency tables. Some knowledge of nonparametric analysis in the case of two independent groups (i.e., the Mann–Whitney $U$ test or Wilcoxon $W_m$ test) would be helpful, but not essential. Although the book is not introductory with regard to statistics in general, we assume that many readers have little or no prior knowledge of measures of effect size and their estimation.

We typically use standard notation. However, where we believe that it helps understanding, we adopt notation that is more memorable and consistent with the concept that underlies the notation. Also, to assist readers who have only the minimum background in statistics, we define some basic statistical terms with which other readers will likely already be familiar. We request the forbearance of these more knowledgeable readers in this regard. Although readability was a major goal, so too was avoiding oversimplifying.

To restrain the length of the book we do not discuss multivariate cases (some references are provided); we do not present equations or discussions for all measures of effect size that are known to us. We present equations, worked examples, and discussions for estimators of many measures and provide references for others that are sufficiently discussed elsewhere. Our discussions of the presented measures are also intended to provide a basis for understanding and for the appropriate use of those other measures that are presented in the sources that we cite.

Criteria for deciding whether to include a particular measure of effect size included its conceptual and computational accessibility, both of which relate to the likelihood that the measure will find its way into common practice, which was another important criterion. However, we admit to some personal preferences and perhaps even fascination with some measures. Therefore, at times we violate our own criteria for inclusion. A few exotic measures are included.

Readers should be able to find in this book many kinds of effect sizes that they can knowledgeably apply to many of their data sets. We attempt to enhance the practicality of the book by the use of worked examples involving mostly real data, for which the book provides calculations of estimates of effect sizes that had not previously been made by the original researchers.

## ACKNOWLEDGMENTS

We are grateful for many insightful recommendations made by the reviewers: Scott Maxwell, the University of Notre Dame; Allen Huffcutt, Bradley University; Shlomo S. Sawilowsky, Wayne State University; and Timothy Urdan, Santa Clara University. Failure to implement any of their recommendations correctly is our fault. We thank Ted Steiner for clarifying a solution for a problem with the relative risk as an effect size. We also thank Julie A. Gorecki for providing data, and for her assistance with wordprocessing and graphics. The authors gratefully acknowledge the generous, prompt, and very professional assistance of our editor, Debra Riegert, and our production editor, Sarah Wahlert.

# Chapter 1

# Introduction

## REVIEW OF SIMPLE CASES
## OF NULL-HYPOTHESIS SIGNIFICANCE TESTING

Much applied research begins with a research hypothesis that states that there is a relationship between two variables or a difference between two parameters, often means. (In later chapters we consider research involving more than two variables.) One typical form of the research hypothesis is that there is a nonzero correlation between the two variables in the population. Often one variable is a categorical independent variable involving group membership (called a *grouping variable*), such as male–female or Treatment *a* versus Treatment *b*, and the other variable is a continuous dependent variable, such as score on an attitude scale or on a test of mental health or achievement. In this case of a grouping variable there are two customary forms of research hypotheses. The hypothesis might again be correlational, positing a nonzero point-biserial correlation between group membership and the dependent variable, as is discussed in chapter 4. More often in this case of a grouping variable the research hypothesis posits that there is a difference between means in the two populations.

Readers who are familiar with the general linear model should recognize the relationship between hypotheses that involve either correlation or the difference between means. However, the two kinds of hypotheses are not identical, and some researchers may prefer one or the other form of hypothesis. Although a researcher may prefer one approach, some readers of a research report may prefer the other. Therefore, researchers should consider reporting results from both approaches.

The usual statistical analysis of the results from the kinds of research at hand involves testing a null hypothesis ($H_0$) which conflicts with the research hypothesis either by positing that the correlation between the two variables is zero in the population or by positing that there is no difference between the means of the two populations. The $t$ statistic is usually used to test the $H_0$ against the research hypothesis. The significance level ($p$) that is attained by a test statistic such as $t$ represents the probability that a result at least as extreme as the obtained result would occur if the $H_0$ were true. It is very important for applied researchers to recognize that this attained $p$ value primarily indicates the strength of the evidence that the $H_0$ is wrong, but the $p$ value does not by itself indicate sufficiently how wrong the $H_0$ is.

Observe in Equation 1.1 that, for $t$, the part of the formula that is usually of greatest interest in applied research is the overall numerator, the difference between means (a value that is a major component of a common estimator of effect size). However, Equation 1.1 reveals that whether $t$ is large enough to attain statistical significance is not merely a function of how large this numerator is, but it depends on how large this numerator is relative to the overall denominator. Equation 1.1 and the nature of division reveal that for any given difference between means an increase in sample sizes will increase the absolute value of $t$ and, thus, decrease the magnitude of $p$. Therefore, a statistically significant $t$ may indicate a large difference between means or perhaps a less important small difference that has been elevated to the status of statistical significance because the researcher had the resources to use relatively large samples. Larger sample sizes also make it more likely that $t$ will attain statistical significance by increasing degrees of freedom for the $t$ test. Large sample sizes are to be encouraged because they are more likely to be representative of populations, are more likely to produce replicable results, increase statistical power, and also perhaps increase robustness to violation of statistical assumptions.

The lesson here is that the result of a $t$ test, or a result using another test statistic, that indicates by, say, $p < .05$ that one treatment is statistically significantly better than another, or that the treatment variable is statistically significantly related to the outcome variable, does not sufficiently indicate how much better the superior treatment is or how strongly the variables are related. The degree of superiority and strength of relationship are matters of effect size. (Attaining statistical significance depends on effect size, sample sizes, variances, choice of one-tailed or two-tailed testing, the adopted significance level, and the degree to which assumptions are satisfied.)

In applied research, particularly when one of the treatments is actually a control or placebo condition, it is very important to estimate how much better a statistically significantly better treatment is. It is not enough to know merely that there is evidence (e.g., $p < .05$), or even stronger evidence (say, $p < .01$), that there is some unknown degree of difference in mean performance of the two groups. If the difference between two population means is not 0, it can be anywhere from nearly 0 to far from 0. If two treatments are not equally effective, the better of the two can be anywhere from slightly better to very much better than the other.

For an example involving the $t$ test, suppose that a researcher were to compare the mean weights of two groups of overweight diabetic people who have undergone random assignment to either weight reduction Program $a$ or Program $b$. Typically, the difference in mean post program weights would be tested using the $t$ test of a $H_0$ that posits that there is no difference in mean weights, $\mu_a$ and $\mu_b$, of populations who undertake Program $a$ or $b$ ($H_0$: $\mu_a - \mu_b = 0$). The independent-groups $t$ statistic in this case is

$$t = \frac{\overline{Y}_a - \overline{Y}_b}{\left[\dfrac{s_a^2}{n_a} + \dfrac{s_b^2}{n_b}\right]^{1/2}}, \tag{1.1}$$

where $\overline{Y}$ values, $s^2$ values, and $n$s are sample means, variances, and sizes, respectively. Again, if the value of $t$ is great enough (positive or negative) to place $t$ in the extreme range of values that are improbable to occur if $H_0$ were true, the researcher will reject $H_0$ and conclude that it is plausible that there is a difference between the mean weights in the populations.

Consider a possible limitation of the aforementioned interpretation of the statistically significant result. What the researcher has apparently discovered is that there is evidence that the difference between mean weights in the populations is not zero. Such information may be of use, especially if the overall costs of the two treatments are the same, but it would often be more informative to have an estimate of what the amount of difference is than merely learning that there is evidence of what it is not (i.e., not 0). (In this example we would recommend constructing a confidence interval for the mean difference in population weights, but we defer the topic of confidence intervals to chap. 2.)

## STATISTICALLY SIGNIFYING AND PRACTICAL SIGNIFICANCE

The phrase "statistically significant" can be misleading because synonyms of *significant* in the English language, but not in the language of statistics, are *important* and *large*, and we have just observed with the $t$ test, and could illustrate with other statistics such as $F$ and $\chi^2$, that a statistically significant result may not be a large or important result. "Statistically significant" is best thought of as meaning "statistically signifying." A statistically significant result is signifying that the result is sufficient, according to the researcher's adopted standard of required evidence against $H_0$ (e.g., $p < .05$), to justify rejecting $H_0$.

Examples of statistically significant results that would not be practically significant would include statistically significant loss of weight or blood pressure that is too small to be medically significant and statistically significant lowering of scores on a test of depression that is insufficient to be reflected in the clients' behaviors or self-reports of well-being (clinical insignificance). Another example would be a statistically significant difference between schoolgirls and schoolboys that is not large enough to justify a change in educational practice (educational insignificance). In chapter 5 we report actual statistically significant differences between cultural groups that may be too small to support stereotypes or to incorporate into training for diplomats, results that may be called *culturally insignificant*. Note that the quality of a subjective judgment about the practical significance of a result is enhanced by expertise in the area of research. Although effect size, the definition of which we discuss in the next section, is not synonymous with practical significance, knowledge of a result's effect size can inform a judgment about practical significance.

## DEFINITION OF EFFECT SIZE

We assume the case of the typical null hypothesis that implies that there is no effect or no relationship between variables—for example, a null hypothesis that states that there is no difference between means of populations or that the correlation between variables in the population is zero. Whereas a test of statistical significance provides the quantified strength of evidence (attained *p* level) that a null hypothesis is wrong, an effect size (*ES*) measures the degree to which such a null hypothesis is wrong. Because of its pervasive use and usefulness, we use the name effect size for all such measures that are discussed in this book. Many effect size measures involve some form of correlation (chap. 4) or its square (chaps. 4, 6, and 7), some form of standardized difference between means (chaps. 3, 6, and 7), or the degree of overlap of distributions (chap. 5), but many measures that are discussed do not fit into these categories. Again, we use the label effect size for measures of the degree to which results differ from what is implied for them by a typical null hypothesis.

Often the relationship between the numerical value of a test statistic (*TS*) and an estimator of *ES* is $ES_{EST} = TS / f(N)$, where f(N) is some function of total sample size, such as degrees of freedom. Specific forms of this equation are available for many test statistics, including $t$, $F$, and $\chi^2$, so that reported test statistics can be approximately converted to indirect estimates of effect size by a reader of a research report without access to the raw data that would be required to estimate an effect size directly. However, researchers who work with their own raw data (primary researchers), unlike researchers who work with sets of previously reported test statistics (meta-analysts), can estimate effect sizes directly, as can readers of this book, so they do not need to use an approximate conversion formula.

## CONTROVERSY ABOUT NULL-HYPOTHESIS SIGNIFICANCE TESTING

Statisticians have long urged researchers to report effect sizes, but researchers were slow to respond. Fisher (1925) was an early, but not the first, advocate of such estimation. It can even be argued that readers of a report of applied research that involves control or placebo groups, or that involves treatments whose costs are different, have a right to see estimates of effect sizes. Some might even argue that not reporting such estimates in an understandable manner to those who might apply the results of research in such cases (e.g., educators, health officials, managers of trainee programs, clinicians, and governmental officials) may be like withholding evidence. Increasingly editors of journals that publish research are recommending, or requiring, the reporting of estimates of effect sizes. For example, the American Psychological Association recommends, and the *Journal of Educational and Psychological Measurement* and at least 22 other journals as of the time of this writing require, the reporting of such estimates. We observe later in this book that estimates of effect size are also being used in court cases involving, for example, alleged discriminatory hiring practices (chap. 4) and alleged harm from pharmaceuticals or other chemicals (chap. 8).

There is a range of professional opinions regarding when estimates of effect sizes should be reported. On the one hand is the view that null-hypothesis significance testing is meaningless because no null hypothesis can be literally true. For example, according to this view no two or more population means can be exactly equal when carried to many decimal places. Therefore, from this point of view that no effect size can be exactly zero, the task of a researcher is to estimate the size of this "obviously" nonzero effect. The opposite opinion is that significance testing is paramount and that effect sizes are to be reported only when results are found to be statistically significant. For discussions relating to this debate, consult Fan (2001), Hedges and Olkin (1985), Hunter and Schmidt (2004), Knapp (2003), Knapp and Sawilowsky (2001), Levin and Robinson (2003), Onwuegbuzie and Levin (2003), Roberts and Henson (2003), Robinson and Levin (1997), Rosenthal, Rosnow, and Rubin (2000), Sawilowsky (2003), and Sawilowsky and Yoon (2002).

As we discuss in chapters 3 and 6, many estimators of effect size tend to overestimate effect sizes in the population (called *positive* or *upward bias*). The major question in the debate is whether or not this upward bias of estimators of effect size is large enough so that the reporting of a bias-based nonzero estimate of effect size will seriously inflate the overall estimate of effect size in a field of study when the null hypothesis is true (i.e., actually zero effect in the population) and results are statistically insignificant. Those who are not concerned about such bias urge the reporting of all effect sizes, significant or not significant, to improve the accuracy of meta-analyses. Their reasoning is that such reporting will avoid the problem of meta-analyses inflating overall estimates of effect size that would result from not including the smaller effect sizes that arise from primary studies whose results did not attain statistical significance.

Some are of the opinion that effect sizes are more important in applied research, in which one might be interested in whether or not the effect size is estimated to be large enough to be of practical use. In contrast, in theoretical research one might only be interested in whether results support a theory's prediction, say, for example, that Mean *a* will be greater than Mean *b*. For references and further discussion of this controversy, consult Harlow, Mulaik, and Steiger (1997), Markus (2001), Nickerson (2000), N. Schmidt (1996), and the many responses to Krueger (2001) in the Comments section of the January 2002 issue of the American Psychologist (vol. 57, pp. 65–71). Consult Jones and Tukey (2000) for a reformulation of null-hypothesis testing that attempts to accommodate both sides in the dispute. For a review of the history of measures of effect size refer to Huberty (2002).

## THE PURPOSE OF THIS BOOK AND THE NEED
## FOR A BROAD APPROACH

It is not necessary for this book to discuss the controversy about null-hypothesis significance testing further because the purpose of this book is merely to inform readers about a variety of measures of effect size and their proper applications and limitations. One reason that a variety of effect size measures is needed is that different kinds of measures are appropriate depending on whether variables are scaled categorically, ordinally, or continuously (and also sometimes depending on certain characteristics of the sampling method and the research design and purpose that are discussed where pertinent in later chapters). The results from a given study often lend themselves to more than one measure of effect size. These different measures can sometimes provide very different, even conflicting, perspectives on the results (Gigerenzer & Edwards, 2003). Consumers of the results of research, including editors of journals, those in the news media who convey results to the public, and patients who are giving supposedly informed consent to treatment, often need to be made aware of the results in terms of alternative measures of effect sizes to guard against the possibility that biased or unwitting researchers have used a measure that makes a treatment appear to be more effective than another measure would. Some of the topics in chapter 8 exemplify this issue particularly well. Also, alternative measures should be considered when the statistical assumptions of traditional measures are not satisfied.

Data sets can have their own personalities—that is, their individual complex characteristics. For example, traditionally researchers have focused on the effects of independent variables on just one characteristic of distributions of data, their centers, such as their means or medians, representing the effect on the typical (average) participant. However, a treatment can also have an effect on aspects of a distribution other than its center, such as its tails. Treatment can have an effect on the center of a distribution and/or the variability around that center. For example, consider a treatment that increases the scores of some experimental group participants and decreases the scores of others in that group, a

Treatment × Subject interaction. The result is that the variability of the experimental group's distribution will be larger or smaller (maybe greatly so) than the variability of the control or comparison group's distribution. Whether there is an increase or decrease in variability of the experimental group's distribution depends on whether it is the higher or lower performing participants who are improved or worsened by the treatment. In such cases the centers of the two distributions may be nearly the same, whereas the treatment in fact has had an effect on the tails of a distribution. It is quite likely that a treatment will have an effect on both the center and the variability of a distribution because it is common to find that distributions that have higher means than other distributions also have the greater variabilities.

As demonstrated in later examples in this book, by applying a variety of appropriate estimates of measures of effect size to the same set of data researchers and readers of their reports can gain a broader perspective on the effects of an independent variable. In some later examples we observe that examination of estimates of different kinds of measures of effect size can greatly alter one's interpretation of results and their importance. [Also refer to Levin and Robinson (1999) in this regard.] Note that as of the time of this writing the editors of journals that recommend or require the reporting of an estimate of effect size do not specify the use of any particular kind of effect size. Note also that any appropriate estimate of effect size that a researcher has calculated must be reported to guard against a biased interpretation of the results. However, we acknowledge, as shown from time to time in this book, that there can be disagreement among experts about the appropriate measure of effect size for certain kinds of data (Levin & Robinson, 1999; also consult Hogarty & Kromrey, 2001).

There are several excellent books that treat the topic of effect size. Although our book frequently cites this body of work, these books generally treat the topic in a different context and for a purpose that is different from the purpose of this book, as we briefly discuss in the next two sections of this chapter. Note also that our book does not discuss effect sizes for single-case designs. For discussions of competing approaches for such designs, consult Campbell (2004) and the references therein.

## POWER ANALYSIS

Some books consider effect sizes in the context of preresearch power analysis for determining needed sample sizes for the planned research (Cohen, 1988; Kraemer & Thiemann, 1987; Lipsey, 1990; K. R. Murphy & Myors, 2003). The power of a statistical test is defined as the probability that use of the test will lead to rejection of a false $H_0$. Because statistical power increases as effect size increases, estimating the likely effect size, or deciding the minimum effect size that the researcher is interested in having the proposed research detect, is important for researchers who are planning research. Taking into account power-determining factors such as the projected effect size, the researcher's adopted alpha level, likely variances, and available sample sizes, books on power analysis are very useful for the planning of research. The report by Wilkinson and the American Psychological Association's Task Force on Statistical Inference (1999; referred to hereafter as APA's Task Force) urges researchers to report effect sizes to facilitate future power analyses in a researcher's field of interest.

## META-ANALYSIS

Several books cover estimation of effect sizes in the context of meta-analysis. Meta-analytic methods are procedures for quantitatively summarizing the numerical results from a set of research studies in a specific area of research. *Meta* in this context means "beyond" or "more comprehensive." Synonyms for meta-analyzing such sets of results include *integrating, combining, synthesizing, cumulating,* or *quantitatively reviewing* them. Each individual study in the set of meta-analyzed studies is called primary research. Among other procedures, a common form of meta-analysis includes averaging the (weighted) estimates of effect size from each of the underlying primary studies. The Wilkinson and the APA's Task Force (1999) report also urges primary researchers to report effect sizes for the purpose of comparing them with earlier reported effect sizes and to facilitate any later meta-analysis of such results. Meta-analyses that use previously reported effect sizes that had been directly calculated by primary researchers on their raw data will be more accurate than those that are based on effect sizes that had to be retrospectively estimated by meta-analysts using approximately accurate formulas to convert the primary studies' reported test statistics to estimates of effect size. Meta-analysts typically do not have access to raw data.

For an early example of a meta-analysis and the customary rationale for such a meta-analysis, consider a set of separate primary studies in which the dependent variable is some measure of mental health and the independent variable is membership in either a treated group or a control group (Smith & Glass, 1977). Such individual studies of these variables yield varying estimates of the same kind of effect size measure. Most of these studies yield a moderate value for estimated effect size (i.e., therapy usually seems to help, at least moderately), some yield a high or low positive value (i.e., therapy seems to help very much or very little), and a very small number of studies yield a negative value for the effect size (indicating possible harm from the therapy). No one piece of primary research is necessarily definitive in its findings.

The varying results are not surprising because of sampling variability and possibly relevant factors that vary among the individual studies—factors such as the nature of the therapy, diagnostic and demographic characteristics of the participants across the studies, kind of test of mental health, and characteristics of the therapists. A common kind of meta-analysis attempts to extract from the individual studies information about variables, called *moderator variables*, that account for the varying estimates of effect size. For example, if the effect of a treatment were different in a population of women and a population of men, gender would be said to be a moderator variable. Effect sizes are often not reported in older articles or in articles that are published in journals that do not require such reporting. Therefore, as we previously mentioned, books on meta-analytic methods include formulas for approximately converting the results of statistical tests that primary researchers typically do report, such as the value of *t* or *F*, into individual estimates of effect size that a meta-analyst can then average.

Because the focus of this book is on direct estimation of effect sizes from the raw data of a primary research study, we include only occasional discussion of meta-analysis when it is pertinent to primary research. Also, it is beyond the scope of this book to discuss limitations of meta-analysis or alternative rationales for it. Moreover, this book has no need to present formulas for approximately converting statistical results, such as *t* or *F*, into indirect estimates of effect size. Again, primary researchers can directly calculate estimates of effect size from their raw data using the formulas in this book. Because the archiving of raw data is still rare in most areas of research, meta-analyses, and applied science in general, would benefit if primary researchers, where appropriate, would routinely report estimates of effect size such as those covered in this book.

There are several approaches to meta-analytic methods. Books that cover these methods include those by Cooper (1989), Cooper and Hedges (1994), Glass, McGaw, and Smith (1981), Hedges and Olkin (1985), Hunter and Schmidt (2004), Lipsey and Wilson (2001), and Rosenthal (1991b). The approach of Hunter and Schmidt (2004) is distinguished by its purpose of attempting to estimate effect sizes from which the influences of artifacts (errors) have been removed. Such artifacts include sampling error, restricted range, and unreliability or imperfect construct validity of the independent and dependent variables. Some of these topics are discussed in chapter 4. Cohn and Becker (2003) discussed the manner in which meta-analysis increases the statistical power of a test of a null hypothesis regarding an effect size and shortens a confidence interval for it by reducing the standard error of a weighted average effect size. Confidence intervals are discussed in chapter 2 and thereafter throughout this book where they are applicable.

## ASSUMPTIONS OF TEST STATISTICS AND EFFECT SIZES

When statisticians create a new test statistic or measure of effect size, they often do so for populations that have certain characteristics. For the *t* test, *F* test, and some common examples of effect sizes, two of these assumed characteristics, called *assumptions*, are that the populations from which the samples are drawn are normally distributed and have equal variances. The latter assumption is called *homogeneity of variance* or *homoscedasticity* (from Greek words for *same* and *scatter*). When data actually come from populations with unequal variances this violation of the assumption is called *heterogeneity of variance* or *heteroscedasticity*. (Because normality and homoscedasticity are the assumptions that are more likely to be violated, we do not yet discuss the usually critically important assumption that scores are independent.) Throughout this book we will observe how violation of assumptions can affect estimation and interpretation of effect sizes, and we will discuss some alternative methods that accommodate such violations.

Often a researcher asserts that an effect size that involves the degree of difference between two means is significantly different from zero because significance was attained when comparing the two means by a $t$ test (or an $F$ test with 1 degree of freedom in the numerator). However, nonnormality and heteroscedasticity can result in the shape of the actual sampling distribution of the test statistic departing sufficiently from the theoretical sampling distribution of $t$ or $F$ so that, unbeknownst to the researcher, the actual $p$ value for the result is not the same as the observed $p$ value in a table or printout. For example, an observed $p < .05$ may actually represent a true $p > .05$, an inflation of Type I error. Also, violation of assumptions can result in lowered statistical power. For references and further discussions of the consequences of and solutions to violation of assumptions on $t$ testing and $F$ testing, consult Grissom (2000), Hunter and Schmidt (2004), Keselman, Cribbie, and Wilcox (2002), Sawilowsky (2002), Wilcox (1996, 1997), and Wilcox and Keselman (2003a).

Huberty's (2002) article on the history of effect sizes noted that heteroscedasticity is common but has been given insufficient attention in discussions of effect sizes. We attempt to redress this shortcoming. The fact that nonnormality and heteroscedasticity can affect estimation and interpretation of effect sizes is of concern in this book because real data often exhibit such characteristics, as is documented in the next section.

## VIOLATION OF ASSUMPTIONS IN REAL DATA

Unfortunately, violations of assumptions are common in real data, and they often appear in combination. Micceri (1989) presented many examples of nonnormal data, reporting that only about 3% of data in educational and psychological research have the appearance of near symmetry and light tails as in a normal distribution. Wilcox (1996) illustrated how two distributions can appear to be normal and appear to have very similar variances when in fact they have very different variances, even a ratio of variances greater than 10:1. Refer to Wilcox (2001) for a brief history of normality and departures from it.

In a review of the literature Grissom (2000) noted that there are theoretical reasons to expect and empirical results to document heteroscedasticity throughout various areas of research. When raw data that are amounts or counts have some zeros (e.g., the number of alcoholic drinks consumed by some patients during an alcoholism rehabilitation program), group means and variances are often positively related (Emerson & Stoto, 1983; Fleiss, 1986; Mueller, 1949; Norusis, 1995; Raudenbush & Bryk, 1987; Sawilowsky & Blair, 1992; Snedecor & Cochran, 1989). Therefore, distributions for samples with larger means often have larger variances than those for samples with smaller means, resulting in the possibility of heteroscedasticity. (Again, homoscedasticity and heteroscedasticity are characteristics of populations, not samples.) These characteristics may not be accurately reflected by comparison of variances of samples taken from those populations because the sampling variability of variances is high. Refer to Sawilowsky (2002) for a discussion of the implications of the relationship between means and variances, including citations of an opposing view. Also, sample distributions with greater positive skew tend to have the larger means and variances, again suggesting possible heteroscedasticity. Positive skew roughly means that a distribution is not symmetrically shaped because its right tail is more extensive than its left tail. Examples include distributions of data from studies of difference thresholds (sensitivity to a change in a stimulus), reaction time, latency of response, time to complete a task, income, length of hospital stay, and galvanic skin response (emotional palm sweating). Wilcox and Keselman (2003a) discussed skew and nonnormality in general. For tests of symmetry versus skew, consult Keselman, Wilcox, Othman, and Fradette (2002), Othman, Keselman, Wilcox, Fradette, and Padmanabhan (2002), and Perry and Stoline (2002).

There are reasons for expecting heteroscedasticity in data from research on the efficacy of a treatment. First, a treatment may be more beneficial for some participants than for others, or it can be harmful for others. If this variability of responsiveness to treatment differs from Treatment Group *a* to Treatment Group *b* because of the natures of the treatments that are being compared, heteroscedasticity may result. For example, Lambert and Bergin (1994) found that there is deterioration in some patients, usually more so in treated groups than in control groups. Mohr (1995) cited negative outcomes from therapy for some adults with psychosis. Also, some therapies may increase violence in certain kinds of offenders (Rice, 1997).

Second, suppose that the dependent variable does not sufficiently cover the range of the underlying variable that it is supposed to be measuring (the latent variable). For example, a paper-and-pencil test of depression might not be covering the full range of depression that can actually occur in depressives. In this case a ceiling or floor effect can produce a greater reduction of variabilities within those groups whose treatments most greatly decrease or increase their scores.

A ceiling effect occurs when the highest score obtainable on a dependent variable does not represent the highest possible standing with respect to the latent variable. For example, a classroom test is supposed to measure the latent variable of students' knowledge, but if the test is too easy, a student who scores 100% may not have as much knowledge of the material as is possible and another student who scores 100% may have even greater knowledge that the easy test does not enable that student to demonstrate. A floor effect occurs when the lowest score obtainable on a dependent variable does not represent the lowest possible standing with respect to the latent variable. For example, a particular screening test for a memory disorder may be so difficult for the participants that among those senile patients who score 0 on the test there may be some who actually have even a poorer memory than the others who scored 0, but they cannot exhibit their poorer memory because scores below 0 are not possible.

Heteroscedasticity can also result from *outliers*, which are defined (roughly for now) as extremely atypically high or low scores. Outliers may merely reflect recording errors or another kind of research error, but they are common and should be reported as possibly reflecting an important effect of a treatment on a minority of participants or as an indication of an important characteristic of a small minority of the participants. Precise definitions and rules for detecting outliers vary (Brant, 1990; Davies & Gather, 1993; Staudte & Sheather, 1990). Wilcox (2001, 2003) discussed a simple method for detecting outliers and also provided an S-PLUS software function for such detection (Wilcox, 2003). This method is based on the median absolute deviation (*MAD*). The *MAD* is defined and discussed as one of the alternative measures of variability in the last two sections of this chapter. Wilcox and Keselman (2003a) further discussed detection and treatment of outliers and their effect on statistical power. For additional discussion of outliers consult Barnett and Lewis (1994) and Jacoby (1997). Researchers should reflect on the possible reasons for any outliers and about what, if anything, to do about them in the analysis of their data. No single definition or rule for dealing with outliers may be applicable to all data. If one has access to a program of data entry that cross checks and reports inconsistent entries, one can protect against outliers that merely reflect erroneous entry of data (and non-outlying erroneous entries as well) by entering all data in two files to be cross checked.

Again, we are concerned about outliers here because of the possibility that they may result in heteroscedasticity that may make the use of certain measures of effect size problematic. Evidence supports the theoretical expectation that heteroscedasticity may be common. Wilcox (1987) found that ratios of largest to smallest sample variances, called maximum sample variance ratios (*VR*s), exceeding 16 are not uncommon, and there are reports of sample *VR*s above 400 (Lix, Cribbie, & Keselman, 1996) and above 566 (Keselman et al., 1998). When a researcher assumes homoscedasticity, it is equivalently assumed that the population $VR = 1$. Maximum population *VR*s of up to 12 are considered to be realistic according to Tomarken and Serlin (1986). Because of the great sampling variability of variances, one can expect to find some sample *VR*s that greatly exceed the population *VR*s, especially when sample sizes are small. However, in a study of gender differences using *n*s > 100, a sample *VR* was approximately 18,000 (Pedersen, Miller, Putcha-Bhagavatula, & Yang, 2002). In psychotherapeutic outcome research with children and adolescents, variances have been found to be statistically significantly different in treatment and control groups (Weisz, Weiss, Han, Granger, & Morton, 1995). In research on treatment of phobia, when comparing a systematic desensitization therapy group to an implosive therapy group and a control group, Hekmat (1973) found sample *VR*s over 12 and nearly 29, respectively, on the Behavior Avoidance Test. Research reports in a single issue of the *Journal of Consulting and Clinical Psychology* contained sample *VR* values of 3.24, 4.00 (several), 6.48, 6.67, 7.32, 7.84, 25.00, and 281.79 (Grissom, 2000). The last *VR* involved skewed distributions of the number of drinks per day under two different treatments for depression in alcoholics (Brown, Evans, Miller, Burgess, & Mueller, 1997). When comparing a control group and two panic-therapy groups for number of posttest panic attacks, sample *VR*s of 8.02 and 6.65 were found for control $s^2$/treated $s^2$ and Therapy 1 $s^2$/Therapy 2 $s^2$, respectively (Feske & Goldstein, 1997).

Statistical tests and measures of effect size are ideally used to compare randomly formed groups to attempt to control confounding variables, but they are often necessarily used to compare pre-existing, not randomly formable, groups such as female and male participants. Groups that are formed by random assignment are expected to represent, by virtue of truly random assignment, populations with equal variances prior to treatment. However, preexisting groups often seem to represent populations with different variances. For example, volunteers and risk takers are less variable than comparison groups on measures of sensation seeking (Watson, 1985). Boys are more variable than girls on many mental tests (Feingold, 1992). Purging bulimics are less variable than nonpurging bulimics in mean percentage of deviation of their weight from normal weight (Gross, 1985, cited in Howell, 1997). Two kinds of closed-head injury patients have significantly different variances with respect to five measures of verbal learning (Wilde, Boake, & Sherer, 1995). Other cases of heteroscedasticity should be expected. For example, in research using self-reporting of anxiety-arousing stimuli to study perceptual defense (if it exists), perceptually defensive participants should be expected to produce more variable reports of the stimuli that they had seen than would less perceptually defensive participants.

Because treatment may affect the variabilities as well as the centers of distributions, and because changes in variances can be of as much practical significance as are changes in means, researchers should think of variances not just with regard to whether their data satisfy the assumption of homoscedasticity but as informative aspects of treatment effect. For example, Skinner (1958) predicted that programmed instruction, contrasted with traditional instruction, would result in lower variances in achievement scores. Similarly, in research on the outcome of therapy more support would be given for the efficacy of a therapy if it were found that the therapy not only results in a "healthier" mean on a test of mental health, but also in less variability on the test when contrasted with a control group or alternative therapy group. Also, a remedial program that is intended to raise all participants' competence levels to a minimally acceptable level could be considered to be a failure or a limited success if it brought the group mean up to that level but also greatly increased variability by lowering the performance of some participants. For example, a remedial program increased mean scholastic performance but also increased variability (Bryk, 1977; Raudenbush & Bryk, 1987). Keppel (1991) presented additional examples of treatments affecting variances. Finally, Bryk and Raudenbush (1988) presented methods in clinical outcome research for identifying the patient characteristics that result in heteroscedasticity and for separately estimating treatment effects for the identified types of patients.

## EXPLORING THE DATA FOR A POSSIBLE EFFECT OF A TREATMENT ON VARIABILITY

Because treatment often has an effect on variability and because this book presents a broad approach to estimating the effects of treatments, it behooves us to consider the topic of exploring the data for a possible effect of treatment on variability. Also, as we soon observe, there sometimes are limitations to the use of the standard deviation as a measure of variability, and many common measures of effect size involve a standard deviation in their denominators. Therefore, in this section we also consider the use of alternative measures of variability.

An obvious approach to determining whether a treatment has had an effect on variability would be to apply one of the common tests of homoscedasticity to determine if there is a statistically significant difference between the variances of the two samples. However, this approach is problematic because the traditional tests of homoscedasticity often produce inaccurate $p$ values when sample sizes are small (e.g., $n <$ 11 for each sample) or unequal or when distributions are not normal (De Carlo, 1997; Weston & Hopkins, 1998). These traditional tests of homoscedasticity are reported to have low statistical power even when distributions are normal (Wilcox, Charlin, & Thompson, 1986). However, Wilcox (2003) provided an S-PLUS software function for a bootstrap method for comparing two variances, a method that appears to produce accurate $p$ values and acceptable power. The basic bootstrap method is briefly described in the penultimate section of chapter 2. For references and more details about the traditional tests of homoscedasticity, refer to Grissom (2000).

Note that it is common, and facilitated by major statistical software packages, to test for homoscedasticity and then conduct a conventional $t$ test (that assumes homoscedasticity) if the difference in variances is not statistically significant. (The same sequential method is also common prior to conducting a conventional $F$ test in the case of two or more means.) If the difference in variances is significant, the researcher forgoes the traditional $t$ test for the Welch $t$ test that does not assume homoscedasticity, as discussed in chapter 2. However, this sequential procedure is problematic, but this is not only due to the possibility of inaccurate $p$ levels and low power for the test of homoscedasticity. Sawilowsky (2002) discussed and demonstrated how this sequential procedure increases the rate of Type I error. For further discussion of this problem, consult Serlin (2002) and Zimmerman (1996). As Serlin (2002) noted, such inflation of a Type I error can also result from the use of a test of symmetry to decide if a subsequent comparison of groups is to be made using a normality-assuming parametric test (e.g., the $t$ test) or a nonparametric test (e.g., the Mann–Whitney $U$ test or equivalent Wilcoxon test, as discussed in chap. 5).

Although traditional inferential methods may often not be powerful enough to detect heteroscedasticity or yield accurate $p$ values, researchers should at least report $s^2$ for each sample for informally comparing sample variabilities, and perhaps report other alternative measures of the samples' variabilities, to which we now turn our attention. These measures of variability are less sensitive to outliers and skew than are the traditional variance and standard deviation, and they can provide better measures of the typical deviation from average scores under those conditions. (We note in chap. 3 that these alternative measures of variability can also be of use in estimating an effect size.) We are not aware of professional groups or journal editors who are recommending or requiring such measures. However, these measures are receiving increasing attention in articles on new statistical methodology, attention that can be a prelude to such an editorial recommendation or requirement, and this book attempts to be forward looking.

Recall that the variance of a sample, $s^2$, is a kind of average of squared deviations of raw scores from the mean;

$$s^2 = \frac{\sum\left(Y - \bar{Y}\right)^2}{n}, \tag{1.2}$$

or, when the variance of a sample is used as an unbiased estimator of a population variance,

$$s^2 = \frac{\sum\left(Y - \bar{Y}\right)^2}{n-1}. \tag{1.3}$$

Note in this equation that one or a few extremely outlying low or extremely outlying high scores can have a great effect on the variance. An outlying score contributes (adds) 1 to the denominator while contributing a large amount to the numerator because of its large squared deviation from the mean, whereas each moderate score contributes 1 to the denominator while contributing only a moderate amount to the numerator. A statistic or a parameter is said to be *nonresistant* if it only takes one or a few outliers to have a relatively large effect on it. Thus, the variance and standard deviation are nonresistant. Therefore, although presenting the sample variances or standard deviations for comparison across groups can be of use in a research report, researchers should consider also presenting an alternative measure of variability that is more resistant to outliers than the variance or standard deviation are. Note also that the median is a more outlier-resistant measure of a distribution's center than is the arithmetic mean because the median, as the middle-ranked score, is influenced not by the magnitude of the scores above or below it, but by the ranking of scores. The mean of raw scores, as we noted is the case for the variance, has a numerator that can be greatly influenced by each extreme score, whereas each extreme score only adds 1 to the denominator.

The range is not a very useful as measure of variability because it is extremely nonresistant. The *range*, by definition, is only sensitive to the most extremely high score and the most extremely low score, so the magnitude of either one of these scores can have a great effect on the range. However, researchers should report the lowest and highest score within each group because it can be informative to compare the lowest scores across the groups and to compare the highest scores across the groups.

Among the measures of variability within a sample that are more resistant to outliers than are the variance, standard deviation, and range, we consider the Winsorized variance, the median absolute deviation, and the interquartile range. The reporting of one or more of these measures for each sample should be considered for an informal exploration of a possible effect of an independent variable on variability. However, again we note that if groups have not been randomly formed, a posttreatment difference in variabilities of the samples might not necessarily be attributable, or entirely attributable, to an effect of treatment. Although the measures of variability that we consider here are not new to statisticians, they are only recently becoming widely known to researchers through the writings, frequently cited here, of Rand R. Wilcox.

The steps that follow for calculating a Winsorized variance (named for the statistician Charles Winsor) are clarified by the worked example in the next section. To calculate the Winsorized variance of a sample:

1. Order the scores in the sample from smallest to largest.
2. Remove the most extreme .*cn* of the lowest scores and remove the same .*cn* of the most extreme of the highest scores of that sample, where .*c* is a proportion (often .2) and *n* is the total sample size. If .*cn* is not an integer round it down to the nearest integer.

3. Call the lowest remaining score $Y_L$ and the highest remaining score $Y_H$.
4. Replace each of the removed lowest scores with .$cn$ repetitions of $Y_L$, and replace each of the removed highest scores with .$cn$ repetitions of $Y_H$, so that the total size of this reconstituted sample returns to its original size.
5. Calculate the usual unbiased $s^2$ (as defined by Equation 1.3) on the reconstituted sample to produce the Winsorized variance, $s_w^2$.

Depending on various factors, the amount of Winsorizing (i.e., removing and replacing) that is typically recommended is .$c$ = .10, .20, or .25. The greater the value of $c$ that is used, the more the researcher is focusing on the variability of the more central subset of data. For example, when .$c$ = .20, more than 20% of the scores would have to be outliers before the Winsorized variance would be influenced by outliers. Wilcox (1996, 2003) provided further discussion, references, and an S-PLUS software function (Wilcox, 2003) for calculating a Winsorized variance. However, of the alternatives to the nonresistant $s^2$ that we discuss here, we believe that $s_w^2$ may perhaps be the most grudgingly adopted by researchers for two reasons. First, many researchers may balk at the uncertainty regarding the choice of a value for $c$. Second, although Winsorizing is actually a decades-old procedure that has been used and recommended by quite respectable statisticians, the procedure may seem to some researchers (excluding the present authors) to be "hocus pocus." For similar reasons some instructors may refrain from teaching this method to students because of concern that it may encourage them to devise their own less justifiable methods for altering data. For a method that is perhaps less psychologically and pedagogically problematic we turn now to the *MAD*.

The *MAD* for a sample is calculated as follows:

1. Order the sample's scores from the lowest to the highest.
2. Find the median score, *Mdn*. If there is an even number of scores in a sample there will be two middle-ranked scores tied for the median. In this case calculate *Mdn* as the midpoint (arithmetic mean) of these two scores.
3. For each score in the sample find its absolute deviation from the sample's median by successively subtracting *Mdn* from each $Y_i$ score, ignoring whether each such difference is positive or negative, to produce the set of deviations $|Y_1 - Mdn|, ..., |Y_n - Mdn|$.
4. Order the absolute deviations, $|Y_i - Mdn|$, from the lowest to the highest, to produce a series of increasing (signless) numbers.
5. Obtain the *MAD* by finding the median of these absolute deviations.

Note that the *MAD* is conceptually more similar to the traditional $s$ than to $s^2$ because the latter involves squaring deviation scores, whereas the *MAD* does not square deviations. Under normality the *MAD* = .6745*s*. Wilcox (2003) provided an S-PLUS software function for calculating the *MAD*. Manual calculation is demonstrated in the next section.

The final measure of variability that is discussed here is the interquartile range, which is based on quantiles. A *quantile* is roughly defined here as a score that is equal to or greater than a specified proportion of the scores in a distribution. Common examples of quantiles are quartiles, which divide the data into successive fourths of the data: .25, .50, .75, and 1.00. The second quartile, $Q_2$ (.50 quantile) is the overall *Mdn* of the scores in the distribution; that is, the score that has .50 of the scores ranked below it. The first quartile, $Q_1$ (.25 quantile), is the median of the scores that rank below the overall *Mdn*; that is, the score that outranks 25% of the scores. The third quartile, $Q_3$ (.75 quantile), is the median of the scores that rank above the overall *Mdn*; that is, the score that outranks 75% of the scores. The more variable a distribution is, the greater the difference there should be between the scores at $Q_3$ and $Q_1$, at least with respect to variability of the middle bulk of the data. A measure of such variability is the interquartile range, $R_{iq}$, which is defined as follows:

$$R_{iq} = Q_3 - Q_1. \qquad (1.4)$$

For normal distributions the approximate relationship between the ordinary *s* and $R_{iq}$ is $s = .75\,R_{iq}$. For an introduction to quantiles, consult Hoaglin, Mosteller, and Tukey (1985); for a technical discussion, refer to Serfling (1980). When using statistical software packages researchers should try to ascertain how the software is defining quantiles because only a rough definition has been given here for our purposes and definitions vary. To pursue this topic refer to Hyndman and Fan (1996) and the discussion and references in Wilcox (2003), who also provided a simple example of a manual calculation using a method that gives evidence of being the best for determining the interquartile range.

There are additional measures that are more resistant to outliers than are $s^2$ and *s*, but discussion of these would be beyond the scope of this book. For example, for technical reasons a measure called the *fourth spread*, which is superficially similar to $R_{iq}$, might be superior to $R_{iq}$ (Brant, 1990; Wilcox, 1996). Also, in chapter 3 we mention a somewhat exotic, but apparently very commendable, resistant alternative measure that can be used to make inferences about differences between two population's variabilities. Note that what we call a *measure of variability* in this book is also called a *measure of a distribution's scale* and that what we call a *distribution's center* is often called its *location*.

Graphical methods for exploring differences between distributions in addition to differences between their means are cited in chapter 5. One such graphic depiction of data that is relevant to the present discussion and that researchers are urged to present for each sample is a boxplot. Statistical software packages may vary in the details of the boxplots that they present (Frigge, Hoaglin, & Iglewicz, 1989), but generally included are the range, median, first and third quartiles so that the interquartile range can be calculated, and outliers that can also give an indication of skew. Major statistical software packages can produce two or more boxplots in the same figure for direct comparison. Consult Wilcox (2003) for further discussion and Carling (2000) for improvements in boxplots. Trenkler (2002) provided software for a more detailed comparison of two or more boxplots. For a general method for detecting outliers using boxplots refer to Schwertman, Owens, and Adnan (2004).

## WORKED EXAMPLES OF MEASURES OF VARIABILITY

Consider the following real data that represent partial data from research on mothers of schizophrenic children (research that will be discussed in detail where needed in chap. 3): 1, 1, 1, 1, 2, 2, 2, 3, 3, and 7. The possible scores ranged from 0 to 10. Note in Fig. 1.1 that the data are positively skewed.

Standard software output, or simple inspection of the data, yield for the median of the raw scores, $Mdn = 2$. As expected, because positive skew pulls the very nonresistant mean to a value that is greater than the median, $\bar{Y} > Mdn$ in the present case; specifically, $\bar{Y} = 2.3$. Note that although 9 of the 10 scores range from 1 to 3, the outlying score, 7, causes

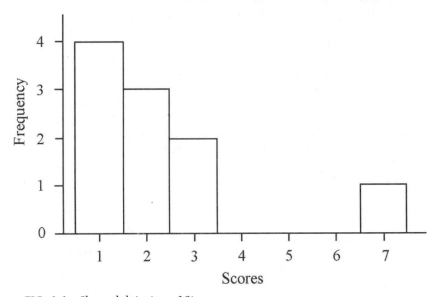

FIG. 1.1   Skewed data ($n = 10$).

the range to equal 6. Software output also yields for the unbiased estimate of population variance for these data $s^2 = 3.34$. Although the present small set of data might not be ideal for justifying the application of the alternative measures of variability, it serves to demonstrate the calculation of the Winsorized variance and the *MAD*. Several statistical software packages calculate $R_{iq}$. For this example, $R_{iq} = 2$.

Step 1 for calculating the Winsorized variance ($s_w^2$), ordering the scores from the lowest to the highest, has already been done. For Step 2 we use $c = 20$, so $.cn = .2(10) = 2$. Therefore, we remove the two lowest scores and the two highest scores, which leaves 6 of the original 10 scores remaining. Applying Step 3, $Y_L = 1$ and $Y_H = 3$. Applying Step 4, we replace the two lowest removed scores with two repetitions of $Y_L = 1$, and we replace the two highest removed scores with two repetitions of $Y_H = 3$, so that the reconstituted sample of $n = 10$ is 1, 1, 1, 1, 2, 2, 2, 3, 3, and 3. Although steps 1 through 4 have not changed the left side of the distribution, the reconstituted data clearly are more symmetrical than before because of the removal and replacement of the outlying score, 7. For step 5 we use any statistical software to calculate, for the reconstituted data, the unbiased $s^2$ of Equation 1.3 to find that $s_w^2 = .767$. (For those who need the refresher, an example of a manual calculation of $s^2$ using a raw-score computational version of Equation 1.3 can be found in the section entitled Only Classificatory Factors in chap. 7.) Observe that, because of removal and replacement of the outlier ($Y_i = 7$), as we should expect, $s_w^2 < s^2$; that is, $.767 < 3.34$. Also, the mean of the reconstituted data, $\bar{Y}_w = 1.9$, is closer to the median, $Mdn = 2$, than was the original mean, $\bar{Y} = 2.3$. The range had been 6 but it is now 2, which well describes the reconstituted data in which every score is between 1 and 3, inclusive.

To calculate the *MAD* for the original data, we proceed to Step 3 of that method because Step 1, ordering the scores from the lowest to the highest, was previously done, and for Step 2 we have already found that $Mdn = 2$. For Step 3 we now find that the absolute deviation between each original score and the median is $|1-2| = 1$, $|1-2| = 1$, $|1-2| = 1$, $|1-2| = 1$, $|2-2| = 0$, $|2-2| = 0$, $|2-2| = 0$, $|3-2| = 1$, $|3-2| = 1$, and $|7-2| = 5$. For Step 4 we order these absolute deviations from the lowest to the highest: 0, 0, 0, 1, 1, 1, 1, 1, 1, and 5. For Step 5 we find by inspection that the median of these absolute deviations is 1; that is, the *MAD* = 1.

With regard to the usual intention that the standard deviation measure within what distance from the mean the typical below–average and typical above–average scores lie, observe the following facts about the data. Nine of the 10 original scores ($Y_i = 7$ being the exception) are within approximately 1 point of the mean ($\bar{Y} = 2.3$) but the standard deviation of these skewed data is $s = (s^2)^{1/2} = 1.83$, a value that is nearly twice as large as the typical distance (deviation) of the scores from the mean. In contrast the Winsorized standard deviation, which is $s_w = (s_w^2)^{1/2} = .876$, is close to the typical deviation of approximately 1 point for the Winsorized data and for the original data. Finally, note that the *MAD* too is more representative of the typical amount of deviation from the original mean than the standard deviation is; *MAD* = 1. Of course, the demonstration of the methods in this section with a single small set of data does not constitute mathematical proof or even strong empirical evidence of their merits. Interested readers should refer to Wilcox (1996, 1997, 2003) and the references therein. In the boxplots in Fig. 1.2 for the current data, the asterisk indicates the outlier, the middle horizontal line within each box indicates the median, the black diamond within each box indicates the mean, and the lines that form the bottom and top of each box indicate the first and third quartiles respectively. Note that because of the idiosyncratic nature of the current data set (many repeated values) the interquartile range for the Winsorized data (2) happens to be equal to the range of the Winsorized data.

## QUESTIONS

1. List six factors that influence the statistical significance of *t*.
2. What is the meaning of *statistical significance*, and what do the authors mean by *statistically signifying*?
3. Give an example, not from the text, of a statistically significant result that might not be practically significant.
4. Define effect size in general terms.
5. In what circumstances would the reporting of effect sizes be most useful?

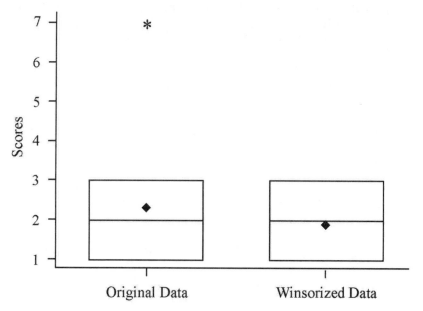

FIG. 1.2.   Boxplots of original and Winsorized data.

6. What is the major issue in the debate regarding the reporting of effect sizes when results do not attain statistical significance?
7. Why should a researcher consider reporting more than one kind of effect size for a set of data?
8. What is often the relationship between a treatment's effect on means and variances?
9. Define *power analysis*.
10. Define *meta-analysis*.
11. What are two assumptions of the *t* and *F* tests on means?
12. Define *heteroscedasticity*.
13. Is hereoscedasticity a practical concern for data analysts, or is it merely of theoretical interest?
14. Discuss two reasons to expect heteroscedasticity.
15. Contrast a ceiling effect and a floor effect, providing an example of each that is not in the text.
16. Define outliers and provide two possible causes of them.
17. Discuss whether the use of preexisting groups or randomly formed groups impacts the possibility of heteroscedasticity differently.
18. Discuss the usefulness of tests of homoscedasticity in general.
19. Why is it problematic to precede a test of two means, or a test of more than two means, with a test of homoscedasticity?
20. What effect can one or a few outliers have on the variance?
21. Define *nonresistance*.
22. How resistant to outliers is the variance? In general terms, compare its resistance to that of four other measures of variability.
23. Define *MAD*.
24. Provide rough definitions of *quantile* and *quartile*.
25. Define *median*.
26. Define *interquartile range*.
27. Which characteristics of data do boxplots usually provide?

# Chapter 2

# Confidence Intervals for Comparing the Averages of Two Groups

## INTRODUCTION

Although the topics of this chapter are generally not considered to be examples of effect sizes, and they might not be expected by some readers to be found in a book on effect sizes, this section and chapter 3 demonstrate that there are connections between confidence intervals and effect sizes, both of which can provide useful perspectives on the data. The confidence intervals that are discussed in this chapter and the effect sizes in chapter 3 all provide information that relates to the amount of difference between two populations' averages, including means. When the dependent variable is a commonly understood variable that is scaled in familiar units, such as weight in research that compares two weight-reduction programs, a confidence interval and an effect size can provide useful and complementary information about the results. Note that some authors do consider confidence intervals to be estimates of effect size (Fidler, Thomason, Cumming, Finch, & Leeman, 2004).

Additional examples of familiar scales include ounces of alcohol consumed, milligrams of drugs consumed, and counts of such things as family size, cigarettes smoked, acts of misbehavior (defined), days absent, days abstinent, dollars earned or spent, length of hospital stay, and relapses. Confidence intervals in terms of such familiar measures are readily understood because such measures are widely encountered outside of a specialist's research setting. Bond, Wiitala, and Richard (2003) argued for the use of simple differences between means as effect sizes for meta-analysis when the dependent variable is measured on a familiar scale, and they presented a method for doing so.

Confidence intervals can be informative when sample sizes are large enough to cause a relatively small difference to attain statistical significance. On the other hand, when samples are their usual small or moderate size, resulting in large sampling error, apparently inconsistent results in the literature may be revealed later by the use of a confidence interval for each study to be more consistent than traditional analyses originally seemed to indicate. Such confidence intervals might well show substantial overlap, as was discussed and illustrated by Hunter and Schmidt (2004). Also, by being introduced to the concept of confidence intervals in this chapter those readers who are not very familiar with the topic should better understand the topics of confidence intervals for effect sizes that are presented in chapter 3 and thereafter. Unfortunately, the topics of this chapter are often not covered in statistics textbooks.

Wilkinson and the American Psychological Association's Task Force on Statistical Inference (1999) called for the greater use of confidence intervals, effect sizes, and confidence intervals for effect sizes; the fifth edition of the *Publication Manual of the American Psychological Association* (American Psychological Association, 2001) strongly recommended the use of confidence intervals. Many additional endorsements of confidence intervals can be cited, including those in Borenstein (1994), Cohen (1994), Fidler et al. (2004), Harlow et al. (1997), Hunter and Schmidt (2004), and Kirk (1996, 2001). Confidence intervals are frequently reported in medical research. Nonetheless, as we note later in this chapter and thereafter, with regard to confidence intervals in general or specific kinds of confidence intervals, the method can have limitations and interpretive problems. Its merits notwithstanding, we do not assert that the method is always the method of choice.

## CONFIDENCE INTERVALS FOR $\mu_a - \mu_b$: INDEPENDENT GROUPS

Especially for an applied researcher in areas in which studies use the same familiar dependent variable, the practically most important part of the formula for the $t$ statistic that tests the usual null hypothesis about two population means is the numerator, $\overline{Y}_a - \overline{Y}_b$. Using $\overline{Y}_a - \overline{Y}_b$ to estimate the size of the difference between $\mu_a$ and $\mu_b$ can provide a very informative kind of result, especially when the dependent variable is measured by a commonly understood variable such as weight. Recall the example from chapter 1 in which we were interested in comparing the mean weights of diabetic participants in weight-reduction Programs a and b. It would be of great practical interest in this case to gain information about the difference in mean population weights. The procedure for constructing a confidence interval uses the data from Groups *a* and *b* to estimate a range of values that is likely to contain the value of $\mu_a - \mu_b$ within them, with a specifiable degree of confidence in this estimate. For example, a confidence interval for the difference in weight gain between two populations of anorectic girls who are represented by two samples who have received either Treatment *a* or Treatment *b* might lead to a reported result such as: "One can be approximately 95% confident that the interval between 10 pounds and 20 pounds contains the difference in mean gain of weight in the two populations."

Theoretically, although any given population of scores has a constant mean, equal-sized random samples from a population have varying means (sampling variability). Therefore, $\overline{Y}_a$ and $\overline{Y}_b$ might each be either overestimating or underestimating their respective population means. Thus, $\overline{Y}_a - \overline{Y}_b$ may well be larger or smaller than $\mu_a - \mu_b$. In other words, there is a margin of error when using $\overline{Y}_a - \overline{Y}_b$ to estimate $\mu_a - \mu_b$. If there is such a margin of error it may be positive, $(\overline{Y}_a - \overline{Y}_b) > (\mu_a - \mu_b)$, or negative, $(\overline{Y}_a - \overline{Y}_b) < (\mu_a - \mu_b)$. The larger the sample sizes and the less variable the populations of raw scores, the smaller the absolute value of the margin of error will be. That is, as is reflected in Equation 2.1, the margin of error is a function of the standard error. In this case the standard error is the standard deviation of the distribution of differences between two populations' sample means.

Another factor that influences the amount of margin of error is the level of confidence that one wants to have in one's estimate of a range of values that is likely to contain $\mu_a - \mu_b$. Although it might seem counterintuitive to some readers at first, we soon observe that the more confident one wants to be in this estimate, the greater the margin of error will have to be. For a very simple example, it is safe to say that we can be 100% confident that the difference in mean annual incomes of the population of high-school dropouts and the population of college graduates would be found within the interval between $0 and $1,000,000, but our 100% confidence in this estimate is of no benefit because it involves an unacceptably large margin of error (an insufficiently informative result). The actual difference between these two population means of annual income is obviously not near $0 or near $1,000,000. (For the purpose of this section, we used mean income as a dependent variable in our example despite the fact that income data are usually skewed and are typified by medians instead of means.)

A procedure that greatly decreases the margin of error without excessively reducing our level of confidence in the truth of our result would be useful. The tradition is to adopt what is called the 95% (or .95) *confidence level* that leads to an estimate of a range of values that has a .95 probability of containing the value of $\mu_a - \mu_b$. When expressed as a decimal value (e.g., .95) the confidence level of an accurately calculated confidence interval is also called the *probability coverage of a confidence interval*. To the extent that a method for constructing a confidence interval is inaccurate, the actual probability coverage will depart from what it was intended to be and what it appears to be (e.g., depart from the nominal .95). Although 95% confidence may seem to some readers to be only slightly less confidence than 100% confidence, such a procedure typically results in a very much narrower, more informative interval than in our example that compared incomes. For simplicity, the first procedure that we discuss assumes normality, homoscedasticity, and independent groups. The procedure is easily generalized to confidence levels other than the 95% level. First, we consider an additional assumption of random sampling and consider further the assumption of independent groups.

In nonexperimental research we typically have to accept violation of the assumption of random sampling. Some finesse this problem by concluding that research results apply to theoretical populations from which our samples would have constituted a random sample. It can be argued that such a conclusion can be justified if the samples that were used seem to be reasonably representative of the kinds of people to whom we want to generalize the results. In the case of experimental research random assignment to treatments satisfies the assumption (in terms of the statistical validity of the results, if not necessarily in terms of the external validity of the results). We have more to say about the possible influence of sampling method on confidence intervals later.

*Independent groups* can be roughly defined for our purposes as groups within which no individual's score on the dependent variable is related to or predictable from the scores of any individual in another group. Groups are independent if the probability that an individual in a group will produce a certain score remains the same regardless of what score is produced by an individual in another group. Research with dependent groups requires methods for construction of confidence intervals that are different from methods used for research with independent groups, as we discuss in the last section of this chapter.

Assuming for simplicity for now that the assumptions of normality, homoscedasticity, and independence have been satisfied and that the usual (central) $t$ distribution is applicable, it can be shown that for constructing a confidence interval for $\mu_a - \mu_b$ the margin of error (*ME*) is given by

$$ME = t^* \left[ s_p^2 \left( \frac{1}{n_a} + \frac{1}{n_b} \right) \right]^{1/2} . \tag{2.1}$$

The part of Equation 2.1 after $t^*$ is the standard error of the difference between two sample means. In addition to its role in confidence intervals, the standard error is used to indicate the precision with which a statistic is estimating a parameter; the smaller the standard error the greater the precision.

When Equation 2.1 is used to construct a 95% confidence interval, $t^*$ is the absolute value of $t$ that a table of critical values of $t$ indicates is required to attain statistical significance at the .05 two-tailed level (or .025 one-tailed level) in a $t$ test. For the 95% or any other level of confidence, $s_p^2$ is the pooled estimate of the assumed common variance of the two populations, $\sigma^2$. Use for the degrees-of-freedom (*df*) row of the $t$ table, $df = n_a + n_b - 2$. Because for now we are assuming homoscedasticity, the best estimate of $\sigma^2$ is obtained by pooling the data from the two samples to calculate the usual weighted average of the two samples' estimates of $\sigma^2$ to produce (weighting by sample sizes via the separate sample's *df*s):

$$s_p^2 = \frac{(n_a - 1)s_a^2 + (n_b - 1)s_b^2}{n_a + n_b - 2}. \tag{2.2}$$

Because approximately 95% of the time when such confidence intervals are constructed, in the current case, the value of $\overline{Y}_a - \overline{Y}_b$ might be overestimating or underestimating $\mu_a - \mu_b$ by the $ME_{.95}$, one can say that approximately 95% of the time the following interval of values will contain the value of $\mu_a - \mu_b$:

$$(\overline{Y}_a - \overline{Y}_b) \pm ME_{.95}. \tag{2.3}$$

The value $(\overline{Y}_a - \overline{Y}_b) - ME_{.95}$ is called the *lower limit of the 95% confidence interval*, and the value $(\overline{Y}_a - \overline{Y}_b) + ME_{.95}$ is called the *upper limit of the 95% confidence interval*. A confidence interval is (for our purpose) the interval of values between the lower limit and the upper limit. We often use *CI* for confidence interval, and to denote the 95% *CI* we use .95 *CI* or $CI_{.95}$.

Although confidence intervals for the difference between two averages are not effect sizes, they can provide (but not always) useful information about the magnitude of the results. For example, in our case of comparing two weight-reduction programs for diabetics, suppose that the lower and upper limits of the confidence interval for $\mu_a - \mu_b$ after 1 year in one or the other program were 1 lb and 2 lb, respectively. A between–program difference in mean population weights (a constant, but an unknown one) that we are 95% confident would be found in the interval between 1 and 2 lb after 1 year in the programs would seem to indicate that there is likely little practical difference in the effectiveness of the two programs, one of which seeming to be only negligibly better than the other at most. On the other hand, if the lower and upper limits were found to be, say, 20 and 30 lb, then one would be fairly confident that one has evidence (not proof) that the more effective program is substantially better.

Note in the two examples of outcomes that neither the interval from 1 to 2 nor from 20 to 30 contains the value 0 within it. It can be shown in the present case that if the 95% confidence interval does not contain the value 0 the results imply that a two–tailed $t$ test of $H_0$: $\mu_a - \mu_b = 0$ would have produced a statistically significant $t$ at the .05 significance level. If the interval does contain the value 0, say, for example, limits of $-10$ and $+10$, we would conclude that the difference between $\overline{Y}_a$ and $\overline{Y}_b$ is not significant at the two-tailed .05 level of significance. In general, if we were to adopt a significance level alpha, if the $(1 - \alpha)$ confidence interval for the difference between two populations' means does not contain zero, the confidence interval is equivalent to having found a statistically significant difference between $\overline{Y}_a$ and $\overline{Y}_b$ at the alpha significance level. Therefore, such a confidence interval not only tells us what a $t$ test of statistical significance would have told us, but the confidence interval can also provide possibly important additional information, especially if the dependent variable measure is a familiar one, such as weight.

Some have interpreted the relationship between the results from significance testing and construction of confidence intervals to mean that significance testing is not needed. Refer to Frick (1995) for a rebuttal. Also consult Knapp and Sawilowsky (2001). In chapter 8 we discuss the example of the difference between two populations' proportions, an example in which there is not a simple relationship between the two approaches to analyzing data. Another such example is the case of a single population proportion. Consult Knapp (2002) and Reichardt and Gollob (1997) for an argument justifying the use of confidence intervals in some cases and tests of statistical significance in other cases. Also refer to Dixon and Massey (1983) for a discussion of some technical differences between the two approaches. Note that apparent confidence levels may be overestimating true confidence levels when confidence intervals are only constructed contingent on first obtaining statistical significance. Consult Meeks and D'Agostino (1983) and Serlin (2002) to address this problem.

To construct a confidence interval other than the .95 CI, in general the $1 - \alpha$ CI, the value of $t^*$ that is used in Equation 2.1 is the absolute value of $t$ that a $t$ table indicates is required for two-tailed statistical significance at the alpha significance level (the same $t$ as for $\alpha/2$, one-tailed). For examples, for a .90 CI use the critical $t$ required at $\alpha = .10$ two-tailed or $\alpha = .05$ one-tailed, and for a .99 CI use $\alpha = .01$ two-tailed or $\alpha = .005$ one-tailed. However, one would likely find that a .99 CI results in a very wide, less informative interval, as was suggested in our example of income comparisons. For a given set of data, the lower the confidence level, the narrower the interval. Indeed, it has been suggested that when a statistically significant difference between means is inferred by observing a .95 CI that does not include 0 it might be proper to report an unusually narrow interval by reporting a .80 or even .70 CI together with the traditional .95 CI (Vaske, Gliner, & Morgan, 2002). Consult Onwuegbuzie and Levin (2003) for a contrary view, and also refer to Kempthorne and Folks (1971). Note in this regard that criterion probability levels in the field of statistical inference are not always conventionally .95 (or the related .05). For example, statistical power levels of .95 are typically unattainable, and power = .80 is considered by some to be an acceptable convention for minimum acceptable power (Cohen, 1988).

Recall that the 95% CI is also called the .95 CI. Such a confidence interval is often mistakenly interpreted to mean that there is a .95 probability that $\mu_a - \mu_b$ will be one of the values within the calculated interval, as if $\mu_a - \mu_b$ were a variable. However, $\mu_a - \mu_b$ is actually a constant in any specific pair of populations (an unknown constant), and it is each confidence limit that is actually a variable. Theoretically, because of sampling variability, duplicating a specific example of research by repeatedly randomly sampling equal-sized samples from two populations will produce varying values of $\overline{Y}_a - \overline{Y}_b$, whereas the actual value of $\mu_a - \mu_b$ remains constant for the specific pair of populations that are being repeatedly compared via their sample means. In other words, although a researcher actually typically samples Populations $a$ and $b$ only once each, varying results are possible for $\overline{Y}_a$, $\overline{Y}_b$, and, thereby, $\overline{Y}_a - \overline{Y}_b$, in any one instance of research. Similarly, sample variances from a population would vary from instance to instance of research, so the margin of error is also a variable. Therefore, instead of saying that there is, say, a .95 probability that $\mu_a - \mu_b$ is a value within the calculated interval, one should say that there is a .95 probability that the calculated interval will contain the value of $\mu_a - \mu_b$. Note that we quite intentionally used the future tense (i.e., "will") in the previous sentence because the probability relates to what *might* happen if we proceed to construct a confidence interval, and assumptions are satisfied; the probability does not relate to what *has* happened after the interval has been constructed. Once an interval has already been constructed it must simply be the case that the interval includes $\mu_a - \mu_b$ (i.e., probability of inclusion = 1) or does not include $\mu_a - \mu_b$ (i.e., probability of inclusion = 0). For example, if the actual difference between $\mu_a$ and $\mu_b$ were, say, exactly 10 lb, when constructing a .95 CI there would be a .95 probability that the calculated interval will contain the value 10. Stated theoretically, if this specific research were repeated an indefinitely large number of times, approaching infinity, the percentage of times that the calculated .95 CIs would contain the value 10 would approach 95% (if assumptions are satisfied). It is in this sense that the reader should interpret any statement that is made about the results from construction of confidence intervals in worked examples in this book.

The game of horseshoe tossing provides an analogy of the proper interpretation of confidence intervals. In this analogy the targeted spike fixed in the ground represents a constant parameter (e.g., the difference between two populations' means), the left and right sides of the tossed horseshoe represent the limits of the interval, and an expert player who can surround the spike with the horseshoe in 95% of the tosses represents a researcher who has actually attained a .95 CI. What varies in the sample of tosses is not the location of the spike, but whether or not the tossed horseshoe surrounds it. For a listing of the common and the precise varying definitions of confidence intervals, refer to Fidler and Thompson (2001).

## WORKED EXAMPLE FOR INDEPENDENT GROUPS

The following example illustrates the aforementioned method for constructing a .95 CI for $\mu_a - \mu_b$, assuming normality and homoscedasticity.

In an unpublished study (Everitt, cited in raw data published by Hand, Daly, Lunn, McConway, & Ostrowski, 1994) that compared Treatments $a$ and $b$ for young girls with anorexia nervosa (self-starvation) and used weight as the dependent variable, we find that the data yield the following statistics: $\overline{Y}_a = 85.697$, $\overline{Y}_b = 81.108$, $s_a^2 = 69.755$, and $s_b^2 = 22.508$. The sample sizes were $n_a = 29$ and $n_b = 26$, so $df = 29 + 26 - 2 = 53$. Many statistical software packages will construct a confidence interval for the present case, but we illustrate a manual calculation to facilitate understanding the present procedure and those to come.

A problem with a manual calculation with the current set of data is that the $t$ tables in statistics textbooks do not provide the needed $t^*$ value for Equation 2.1 when $df = 53$. Therefore, using a $t$ table that provides critical values of $t$ for $df = 50$ and $df = 55$ (Snedecor & Cochran, 1989), we linearly interpolate three fifths of the way between 50 and 55 to estimate the critical value of $t$ at $df = 53$; $t^* = 2.006$. (A more precise method of interpolation is available, but it would result in little if any difference in $t$ in this case because there is not even very much difference in critical values of $t$ at $df = 50$ and $df = 55$.)

Now applying the required values, which were just reported, to Equation 2.2 we find that

$$s_p^2 = \frac{\left[(29-1)69.755 + (26-1)22.508\right]}{29+26-2} = 47.469.$$

Applying the needed values now to Equation 2.1 we find that

$$ME_{.95} = 2.006\left[47.469\left(\frac{1}{29} + \frac{1}{26}\right)\right]^{1/2} = 3.733.$$

Therefore, the limits of the .95 $CI$ given by Equation 2.3 are

$$CI_{.95}: (85.697 - 81.108) \pm 3.733.$$

The interval is thus bounded by the lower limit of $4.589 - 3.733 = .856$ lb and the upper limit of $4.589 + 3.733 = 8.322$ lb. The difference between the two sample means, 4.589 lb, is called a *point estimate of the difference* between $\mu_a$ and $\mu_b$. The interval from .856 to 8.322 does not include the value 0, so this confidence interval also informs us that the difference between $\overline{Y}_a$ and $\overline{Y}_b$ is statistically significant at the two-tailed .05 level. We conclude that there is statistically significantly greater weight in the girls who underwent Treatment $a$ compared to the girls who underwent Treatment $b$. We are also 95% confident that the interval between .856 lb and 8.322 lb contains the difference in weight between the two treatment populations. Note that the sample sizes are not equal ($n_a = 29$, $n_b = 26$), which is not necessarily problematic. However, if the smaller size of Sample $b$ resulted from participants dropping out for a reason that was related to the degree of effectiveness of a treatment (nonrandom attrition), then the confidence interval and a test of significance would be invalid. The point estimate and the limits of the interval are depicted in Fig. 2.1.

Again, the practical significance of the just-noted result would be a matter for expert opinion in the field of study—medical opinion in this case—not a matter of statistical opinion. Similarly, suppose that the current confidence limits, .856 and 8.322, had resulted not from two treatments for anorexia nervosa but from two programs intended to raise the IQs of children who are about average in IQ. The practical significance of such limits (rounded to 1 and 8 IQ points) would be a matter about which educators or developmental psychologists should opine. In different fields of research the same numerical results may well have different degrees of practical significance.

Observe that there was approximately a 3:1 ratio of $s_a^2$ and $s_b^2$ in our example $(69.755/22.508 = 3.1)$. This ratio suggests possible heteroscedasticity, although it could also be plausibly attributable to sampling variability of variances, which can be great. However, we do not conduct a test of homoscedasticity because of the likely low power of such a test (Grissom, 2000; Wilcox, 1996). The possibility of heteroscedasticity suggests that one of the more robust methods that are discussed in later sections of this chapter may be more appropriate for the data at hand.

## FURTHER DISCUSSIONS AND METHODS

For further discussions of computer-intensive methods for constructing more accurate confidence intervals when assumptions are satisfied (including construction of confidence intervals using noncentral distributions), consult Altman, Machin, Bryant, and Gardner (2000), Bird (2002), Cumming and Finch (2001), Smithson (2001, 2003), and Tryon (2001); and, for a brief introduction, see chapter 3. Refer to Fidler and

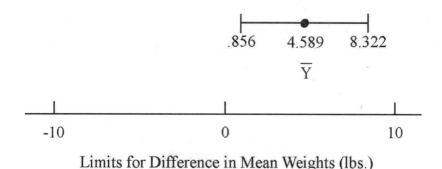

FIG. 2.1. Limits for the 95% confidence interval for the difference in mean weights of anorectic girls who had been given either Treatment a or Treatment b.

Thompson (2001) for an illustration of the use of SPSS software for the construction of a confidence interval for $\mu_a - \mu_b$. For negative or moderated views of confidence intervals we cite, for the sake of fairness and completeness, Feinstein (1998), Frick (1995), Parker (1995), and Knapp and Sawilowsky (2001). Smithson (2003), whose book is favorably disposed toward confidence intervals, also discussed their limitations.

Note that this chapter only considers the case in which the sampling distribution of the estimator (e.g., the difference between two sample means) on which a confidence interval is based is symmetrically distributed. In such cases the resulting confidence interval is said to be symmetric because the value that is subtracted from the estimate to find the lower limit of the interval is the same as the value that is added to the estimate to find the upper limit. (We call this value *the margin of error*.) Therefore, in such cases the upper and lower limits are equidistant from the estimate. However, when the sampling distribution of the estimator might be skewed (e.g., a proportion in a sample, such as the proportion of treated patients whose health improves), it is possible to construct an *asymmetric confidence interval*. An asymmetric confidence interval is one in which the value that is subtracted from the estimate is not the same as the value that is added to the estimate to find the lower and upper limit, respectively. In such cases the limits are calculated separately as values that cut off approximately $\alpha/2$ of the area of the sampling distribution. Thus, with regard to an asymmetric confidence interval, the lower limit is calculated as the value that has $\alpha/2$ of the area of the sampling distribution below it, and the upper limit is calculated as the value that has $\alpha/2$ of the area beyond it, with no requirement that these two values be equidistant from the estimate. This topic is discussed further where relevant in later chapters.

Finally, recall that most experimental research involves randomly assigning participants who have not been first randomly sampled from a large defined population to form a pool of participants. Instead, the participant pool is a local subpopulation of readily accessible prospective participants, such as college students who are available to an academic researcher. Such sampling, called *convenience sampling*, may result in a $t$-based confidence interval that is wider than it could be. For elaboration and an alternative approach, refer to Lunneborg (2001). Much of the remainder of this chapter is informed by Wilcox's (1996, 1997) research and expert reviews of confidence intervals under violation of assumptions, supplemented with more recent findings by Wilcox and others.

## SOLUTIONS TO VIOLATIONS OF ASSUMPTIONS: WELCH'S APPROXIMATE METHOD

Even if only the assumption of homoscedasticity is violated, the use of the aforementioned $t$-based procedure can produce a misleading confidence level, unless perhaps $n_a = n_b \geq 15$ (Ramsey, 1980; Wilcox, 1997). In the case of heteroscedasticity, if $n_a \neq n_b$, the actual confidence level can be lower than the nominal one. For example, a supposed .95 $CI$ may in fact be an interval that has less than a .95 probability of containing the value of $\mu_a - \mu_b$.

The least a researcher should do about possible heteroscedasticity when constructing a confidence interval for $\mu_a - \mu_b$ under the assumption of normality would be to use samples as close to equal size as is possible and consisting of at least 15 participants each. However, a long known, but little used, often more accurate approximate procedure for constructing a confidence interval for $\mu_a - \mu_b$ in this case is Welch's (1938) approximate solution. This method is also known as the Satterthwaite (1946) procedure and is related to the work of Aspin (1949) as well. The Welch procedure accommodates heteroscedasticity in two ways. First, Equation 2.1 is modified so as to use estimates of $\sigma_a^2$ and $\sigma_b^2$ (population variances that are believed to be different) from $s_a^2$ and $s_b^2$ separately instead of pooling $s_a^2$ and $s_b^2$ to estimate a common population variance. Second, the equation for degrees of freedom is also modified to take into account the inequality of $\sigma_a^2$ and $\sigma_b^2$. Thus, using the .95 $CI$ again for our example, in this method

$$ME_w = t^* \left[ \frac{s_a^2}{n_a} + \frac{s_b^2}{n_b} \right]^{1/2}, \qquad (2.4)$$

where $w$ stands for Welch and, as before, $t^*$ is the absolute value of the $t$ statistic that a $t$ table indicates is required to attain significance at the two-tailed .05 level. The heteroscedasticity-adjusted degrees of freedom for the Welch procedure, $df_w$, is given by:

$$df_w = \frac{\left[ \dfrac{s_a^2}{n_a} + \dfrac{s_b^2}{n_b} \right]^2}{\dfrac{\left( \dfrac{s_a^2}{n_a} \right)^2}{n_a - 1} + \dfrac{\left( \dfrac{s_b^2}{n_b} \right)^2}{n_b - 1}}. \qquad (2.5)$$

To find $t^*$ enter a $t$ table at the degrees of freedom row that results from Equation 2.5. You may have to interpolate between the two degrees of freedom values in the table that are closest to your calculated value, as was demonstrated earlier, or you can round your obtained degrees of freedom value down or up to the nearest value in the table. (Note that rounding down degrees of freedom can result in a larger loss of statistical power for a $t$ test than one might expect; Sawilowsky & Markman, 2002.) The limits of the confidence interval are then found using expression 2.3, with $ME_w$ replacing $ME$.

The Welch method often results in a smaller margin of error than the usual, previously demonstrated, method that pools the two values of $s^2$ and leaves degrees of freedom unadjusted. A smaller margin of error would result in a narrower, more informative, confidence interval. However, although the Welch method appears to counter heteroscedasticity well enough, it may not provide accurate confidence levels when at least one of the population distributions is not normal, especially (but not exclusively) when $n_a \neq n_b$. According to the review by Wilcox (1996), the Welch method may be at its worst when two populations are skewed differently and sample sizes are small and unequal. Bonett and Price (2002) confirmed that the method is problematic when sample sizes are small and the two population distributions are grossly and very differently nonnormal. Again, at the very least researchers should try to use samples that are as large and as close to equal in size as is possible. Using equal or nearly equal-sized samples ranging from n = 10 to n = 30 each might result in sufficiently accurate confidence levels under a variety of types of nonnormality, but a researcher cannot be certain if the kind and degree of nonnormality in a given set of data represents an exception to this conclusion (Bonett & Price, 2002). Researchers should also consider using one of the robust methods to deal simultaneously with heteroscedasticity and nonnormality when constructing a confidence interval to compare the centers of two groups. (Such methods are discussed in the two sections after the next section.)

The prevalence of disappointingly wide confidence intervals may be partly responsible for their infrequent use in the past. The application of more robust methods may result in narrower confidence intervals that inspire researchers to report confidence intervals routinely, where appropriate, as many methodologists have urged. Of course, a decision about reporting a confidence interval must be made a priori, and it should not be based on how pleasing its width is to the researcher.

Note that if $n_a > 60$ and $n_b > 60$ one may construct a satisfactory confidence interval under heteroscedasticity simply by using a table of the standardized normal curve, instead of a $t$ table, to find the appropriate $z$ value instead of a $t^*$ value to insert into Equation 2.4, thus eliminating the use of Equation 2.5 (Moses, 1986). In the case of a .95 $CI$, $z = 1.96$. In the general case of $n_a > 60$ and $n_b > 60$, for a confidence interval at the $(1 - \alpha)$ level of confidence used in place of $t^*$ in Equation 2.4 the positive value of $z$ that the table indicates has $1 - (\alpha/2)$ of the area of the normal curve below it, or $\alpha/2$ of the area of the normal curve above it.

## WORKED EXAMPLE OF THE WELCH METHOD

The following worked example of the Welch method constructs a .95 $CI$ for $\mu_a - \mu_b$ from the same data on weight gain in anorexia nervosa as in the previous example.

We first find $df_w$ so that we can determine the value of $t^*$ to use in Equation 2.4 to obtain $ME_w$. Applying the previously stated values to Equation 2.5 we find that

$$df_w = \frac{\left[\dfrac{69.755}{29} + \dfrac{22.508}{26}\right]^2}{\dfrac{\left(\dfrac{69.755}{29}\right)^2}{29-1} + \dfrac{\left(\dfrac{22.508}{26}\right)^2}{26-1}} = 45.221.$$

Rounded to the nearest integer, $df_w = 45$. Most $t$ tables in statistics textbooks do not include $df = 45$, but in the $t$ table in Snedecor and Cochran (1989) we find that for $df = 45$ the critical value of $t = 2.014$. Applying this value of $t^*$ and the other previously stated required values to Equation 2.4 yields

$$ME_w = 2.014\left[\frac{69.755}{29} + \frac{22.508}{26}\right]^{1/2} = 3.643.$$

Therefore, the limits of the .95 $CI$ are, using expression 2.3 with $ME$ replaced by $ME_w$,

$$CI_{.95}: (85.697 - 81.108) \pm 3.643;$$

$$CI_{.95}: 4.589 \pm 3.643.$$

We previously found that the point estimate of $\mu_a - \mu_b$ is 4.589 lb for the present data. Now using the Welch method we find that the margin of error associated with this point estimate is not $\pm3.733$ lb, as before, but $\pm3.643$ lb.

Observe that, as is often the case, $|ME_w| < |ME|$, $3.643 < 3.733$, but the Welch-based interval, bounded by $4.589 - 3.643 = .946$ and $4.589 + 3.643 = 8.232$, is only slightly narrower than the previously constructed interval from .856 to 8.322. Provided that a researcher has used the more nearly accurate method, it is good to narrow the confidence interval without lowering the confidence level. As before, the interval does not contain the value 0, so this interval implies that $\overline{Y}_a$ is statistically significantly greater than $\overline{Y}_b$ at the .05 level, two-tailed.

Recall that the Welch method may not yield accurate confidence intervals when $n_a \neq n_b$. However, in our example the samples sizes are not very unequal and not very small. In the next section we consider a method that addresses the problems of heteroscedasticity and skew at the same time.

## YUEN'S CONFIDENCE INTERVAL
## FOR THE DIFFERENCE BETWEEN TWO TRIMMED MEANS

Yuen's (1974) method constructs a confidence interval for $\mu_{ta} - \mu_{tb}$, in which each $\mu_t$ is a trimmed population mean. A trimmed mean of a sample ($\bar{Y}_t$) is the usual arithmetic mean calculated after removing (trimming) the $c$ lowest and the same $c$ highest scores, without replacing them. (The $\mu_t$ is defined and discussed further in the final paragraph of this section.) Choice of the optimum amount of trimming depends on several factors, the detailed discussion of which would be beyond the scope of this book. Consult Wilcox (1996, 1997, 2001, 2003), Wilcox and Keselman (2002a), and Sawilowsky (2002) for detailed discussions and references on this subject.

The reader is alerted that trimming has been recommended and is being increasingly studied by respected statistical methodologists, but the practice is not common. Many researchers and instructors of statistics may be leery of any method that alters or discards data. This issue is discussed at greater length at the end of this section.

The optimum amount of trimming may range from 0% to slightly over 25%. The greater the number of outliers, the greater the justification might be for, say, 25%, trimming. Small samples may also justify 25% trimming (Rosenberger & Gasko, 1983). For a discussion of trimming less than 20%, refer to Keselman, Wilcox et al. (2002). Also consult Sawilowsky (2002). If population distributions were normal, which is not the assumption of this section, then one would use the usual arithmetic means, which is equivalent to 0% trimming. Note that if one trimmed all but the middle-ranked score, the trimmed mean would be the same as the median. Thus, a trimmed mean is conceptually and numerically between the traditional arithmetic mean (0% trimming) and the median (maximum trimming). If one or more outliers are causing the departure from normality, then trimming can eliminate the outlier(s) and bring the focus to the middle group of scores.

Because it may sometimes be optimum or close to optimum, 20% (.2) trimming is the method that we demonstrate. In this case $c = .2n$ for each sample. If $c$ is not a whole number, then round $c$ down to the nearest whole number. For example, if $n = 29$, $.2n = .2(29) = 5.8$, and, rounding down, $c = 5$. The number of remaining scores, $n_r$, in the group is equal to $n - 2c$. In the previous example of the anorectic sample that received Treatment $a$, $n_r = n_a - 2c = 29 - 2(5) = 19$. For the sample that received Treatment $b$, $c = .2n_b = .2(26) = 5.2$, which rounds to 5. For this group, $n_r = n_b - 2c = 26 - 2(5) = 16$.

The first step in the Yuen method is to arrange the scores for each group separately in order. Then, for each group separately, eliminate the $c = .2n$ most extreme low scores and the same number (for that particular group) of the most extreme high scores. The procedure does not require that $n_a = n_b$. If $n_a \neq n_b$, it may or may not turn out that a different number of scores is trimmed from Groups $a$ and $b$, depending on the results of rounding the values of c. Next, calculate the trimmed mean, $\overline{Y}_t$, for each group by applying the usual formula for the arithmetic mean using the remaining sample size, $n_r$, in the denominator; $\overline{Y}_t = (\Sigma Y) / n_r$. Continuing in this section with the previous data on weight gain in anorexia, we remove the five highest and five lowest scores from each sample to find the trimmed means of the remaining scores, $\overline{Y}_{ta} = 85.294$ and $\overline{Y}_{tb} = 81.031$.

The next step is to calculate the numerator of the Winsorized variance, $SS_w$, for each group by applying Steps 3 through 5 for calculating a Winsorized variance that were presented in the last section of chapter 1. (Steps 1 and 2 of that procedure will already have been completed by this stage of the method.) Applying Steps 3 through 5 to calculate the numerator of a Winsorized variance we replace, in each sample, the trimmed five lowest original scores with five repetitions of the lowest remaining score, and we replace the five trimmed highest original scores with five repetitions of the highest remaining score. Because $s^2 = SS / (n - 1)$, $SS = s^2(n - 1)$. Using any software for descriptive statistics we find that for the reconstituted samples (original remaining scores plus the scores that replaced the trimmed scores) $s^2_{wa} = 30.206$ and $s^2_{wb} = 12.718$. Therefore, $SS_{wa} = 30.206(29 - 1) = 845.768$ and $SS_{wb} = 12.718(26 - 1) = 317.950$.

Next, we calculate a needed statistic, $w_y$, separately for each group, to find $w_{ya}$ and $w_{yb}$. Each sample's $w_y$ is found separately by calculating:

$$W_y = \frac{SS_w}{n_r (n_r - 1)}. \tag{2.6}$$

The $ME_y$ ($y$ stands for Yuen) for the confidence interval for $\mu_{ta} - \mu_{tb}$ is

$$ME_y = t^*(w_{ya} + w_{yb})^{1/2}, \tag{2.7}$$

and the confidence limits for $\mu_{ta} - \mu_{tb}$ become

$$(\overline{Y}_{ta} - \overline{Y}_{tb}) \pm ME_y. \tag{2.8}$$

The degrees of freedom to be used to find the tabled value of $t^*$ in Yuen's procedure, $df_y$, is

$$df_y = \frac{\left(w_{ya} + w_{yb}\right)^2}{\dfrac{w_{ya}^2}{n_{ra} - 1} + \dfrac{w_{yb}^2}{n_{rb} - 1}}. \tag{2.9}$$

Applying the previously reported required values to Equation 2.6 we find that

$$W_{ya} = \frac{845.768}{19(19-1)} = 2.473,$$

and

$$W_{yb} = \frac{317.950}{16(16-1)} = 1.325.$$

Now applying the required values to Equation 2.9 we find that

$$df_y = \frac{(2.473+1.325)^2}{\dfrac{2.473^2}{19-1} + \dfrac{1.325^2}{16-1}} = 32.$$

Most $t$ tables in statistics textbooks will provide critical values of $t$ for $df = 30$ and $df = 40$, but not for degrees of freedom between these values. However, using the $t$ table in Snedecor and Cochran (1989), we find rows for $df = 30$ and $df = 35$. Because $df = 32$ is two fifths of the distance between $df = 30$ and $df = 35$, we linearly interpolate two fifths of the way between the $t$ values at $df = 30$ and $df = 35$ to estimate that the critical value of $t^*$ is approximately 2.037. (More accurate interpolation is possible but would likely make a negligible, if any, difference in our final results.)

Now applying the obtained required values to Equation 2.7 we find that for the .95 $CI$

$$ME_{y.95} = 2.037(2.473 + 1.325)^{1/2} = 3.970.$$

Finally, applying the required values to expression 2.8 we find that the .95 $CI$ is bounded by the limits $(85.294 - 81.031 = 4.263) \pm 3.970$. Thus, the point estimate of $\mu_{ta} - \mu_{tb}$ is 4.263 lb, and the .95 $CI$ ranges from $4.263 - 3.970 = .293$ lb to $4.263 + 3.970 = 8.233$ lb. Although the Yuen method usually results in narrower confidence intervals than the Welch method (Wilcox, 1996), such is not the case with regard to these data. The Yuen-based interval from .293 lb to 8.233 lb is wider than the previously calculated Welch-based interval from .946 lb to 8.232 lb (and also wider than the confidence interval that was constructed using the traditional $t$-based method). However, it is possible that the use of an alternative to $s_w$ in the Yuen procedure may narrow the interval (Bunner & Sawilowsky, 2002).

Note that all three of the methods that were applied to the data on anorexia lead to the same general conclusions. All three methods resulted in confidence intervals that did not contain the value 0, so we can conclude that the mean (or trimmed mean) weight of girls in Sample $a$ is statistically significantly greater than the mean (or trimmed mean) weight of girls in Sample *b* at the two-tailed .05 level. Also, all three methods yielded a lower limit of mean (or trimmed mean) weight difference that is under 1 lb and an upper limit of mean (or trimmed mean) weight difference that is slightly over 8 lb. Again, a conclusion about the clinical significance of such results would be for specialists in the field of anorexia nervosa to decide.

Note in Equations 2.7 and 2.9 that the Yuen method is a hybrid procedure of countering nonnormality by trimming and countering heteroscedasticity by using the Welch method of adjusting degrees of freedom and treating sample variabilities separately instead of pooling them. Wilcox (1997) aptly called the Yuen method the Yuen–Welch method (although the names of statisticians Aspin and Satterthwaite could be added to Welch) and provided S-PLUS software functions for constructing a .95 *CI* using this method. Wilcox (1996) also provided Minitab macros for constructing the interval at the .95 or other levels of confidence. Reed (2003) provided executable FORTRAN code for Yuen's method, and Keselman, Othman, Wilcox, and Fradette (2004) are further developing Yuen's method.

Note that although the Yuen method has been known since 1974, was made accessible by Wilcox through his 1996 and 1997 books and software, and appears often to be superior to the traditional *t* procedure and the Welch procedure for constructing a confidence interval, the Yuen method is not widely used. Its lack of use may be largely attributable to a lack of awareness because it is absent from nearly all textbooks of statistics. Also, historically researchers have been slow to adopt new statistical methods and slow to forego popular methods that ultimately are found by methodologists to be problematic. Moreover, as was mentioned earlier, there may also be discomfort on the part of many researchers about trimming data in general and about lack of certainty regarding the optimum amount of trimming to be done for any particular set of data.

However, there may be an irony here. It could be argued that some researchers may accept the use of medians, which amounts, in effect, to the maximum amount of trimming (trimming all but the middle-ranked or two middle-ranked scores) but would be leery of the more modest amount of trimming (20%) that was discussed in this section. Also, as Wilcox (2001) pointed out, trimming is common in certain kinds of judging in athletic competition, such as removing the highest and lowest ratings before calculating the mean of the judges' ratings of a figure-skating performance.

Although by using the Yuen method one is not constructing a confidence interval for the traditional $\mu_a - \mu_b$, but for the less familiar $\mu_{ta} - \mu_{tb}$, the researcher who is interested in constructing a confidence interval for the difference between the outcomes for the average (typical) members of Population *a* and Population *b* should recognize that, when there is skew, $\mu_t$ may better represent the score of the typical person in a population than would a skew-distorted traditional $\mu$. Refer to Staudte and Sheather (1990) for a precise definition of $\mu_t$. For our purpose we define, say, a 20% $\mu_t$ as the mean of those scores in the population that fall between the .20 and .80 quantiles of that population. Note also that the Yuen method, when used to test the significance of the difference between two trimmed sample means, may provide good control of Type I error. However, the relative statistical power (efficiency) of the Yuen method versus the traditional $t$-test method that uses the usual means and variances may depend greatly on the degree of skew (Cribbie & Keselman, 2003a). For a negative view of trimming, refer to Bonett and Price (2002).

## OTHER METHODS FOR INDEPENDENT GROUPS

Wilcox (1996) provided discussion and a Minitab macro for constructing a .95 CI for the difference between two populations' medians to counter nonnormality, but this method is not discussed here because it may often not provide as good a solution to violations of assumptions as the Yuen method. However, there are other promising methods for constructing a confidence interval for the difference between two populations' centers. One such method is based on Harrell and Davis' (1982) improved method for estimating population medians. The sample median is a biased estimator of the population median (although, for even slightly nonnormal population distributions, a sample's median can provide a more accurate estimate of the mean of the population than does the mean of that sample; Wilcox, 2003). The Harrell–Davis estimator of a population's median appears to be a less biased estimator, and appears to have less sampling variability than does the ordinary sample median.

The use of the Harrell–Davis estimator to construct a confidence interval is too complicated to be done manually, is not widely available in software, and is not demonstrated here. However, Wilcox (1996) again provided discussion, references, and a Minitab macro for this method for constructing the confidence interval. Wilcox (2003) also provided discussion and an S-PLUS software function for a simple method for constructing a confidence interval for the difference between two populations' medians that is based on a method by McKean and Schrader (1984).

An alternative computationally simple procedure for constructing a confidence interval for the difference between two medians that modifies the McKean–Schrader method and uses manual calculation is available (Bonett & Price, 2002). Unlike the Welch method, the Bonett–Price method seems to produce fairly accurate confidence levels when sample sizes are small even under extreme nonnormality. Bonett and Price (2002) extended the method to the construction of confidence intervals for the difference between two medians at a time from multiple groups (simultaneous confidence intervals) in one-way and factorial designs. Although there are several more methods for constructing a confidence interval for the difference between two populations' centers (Wilcox, 1996,

1997, 2003; Lunneborg, 2001), only one more, the one-step $M$-estimator method, is mentioned here because it is among the methods that appear to be often (but not always) better than the traditional method.

The one-step $M$-estimator method is based on a refinement of the trimming procedure. (The letter $M$ stands for maximum likelihood.) There are two related issues when calculating trimmed means. We have already discussed the first issue, choosing how much trimming to do. Second, as we have also discussed, traditional trimming trims equally on both sides of a distribution. However, in the case of skew, traditional trimming results in trimming as many scores on the side of the distribution opposite to the skew, where trimming is not needed or less needed, as on the skewed side of the distribution, where trimming is needed or needed more. A measure of location (center of a distribution) whose value is minimally changed by outliers is called a *resistant measure of location*. $M$ estimators of location are resistant measures that can be based on determining how much, if any, trimming should be done separately for each side of a distribution (Hampel, Ronchetti, Rousseeuw, & Stahel, 1986; Staudte & Sheather, 1990).

The arithmetic mean gives equal weight to all scores (no trimming) when averaging them. However, when calculating a trimmed mean traditional trimming in effect gives no weight to the trimmed scores and equal weight to each of the remaining scores and the scores that have replaced the trimmed scores. Using $M$ estimators is less drastic than using trimmed means because $M$ estimators can weight scores with weights other than 0 (discarding) or 1 (keeping and treating equally). They calculate location by giving progressively more weight to the scores closer to the center of the distribution. Different $M$ estimators use different weighting schemes (Hoaglin, Mosteller, & Tukey, 1983).

The simplest $M$-estimation procedure is called *one-step M estimation*. Constructing a confidence interval using $M$ estimation is too complicated and laborious to do manually. Again, fortunately a Minitab macro (Wilcox, 1996) and an S-PLUS software function (Wilcox, 1997, 2003) are available for constructing a confidence interval for the difference between the locations of two populations using one-step $M$ estimation. Note that when heteroscedasticity is caused by skew, using traditionally trimmed means may be better than using one-step $M$ estimators (Bickel & Lehmann, 1975), but both methods may yield inaccurate confidence levels when sample sizes are below 20.

In general, because of the possibility of excessively inaccurate confidence levels, the original methods using one-step $M$ estimators are not recommended when both sample sizes are below 20. However, a modified version of such estimators may prove to be applicable to small samples (Wilcox, 2003, with an S-PLUS software function). Accessible introductions to $M$ estimation can be found in Wilcox (1996, 2001, 2003) and Wilcox and Keselman (2003a). Note that when a population's distribution is not normal, not only a sample's median, but also the sample's $M$ estimator, modified one-step $M$ estimator, and 20% trimmed mean can provide a more accurate estimate of the mean of the population than can the mean of that sample (Wilcox, 2003).

There are ongoing attempts to improve methods that are robust in the presence of nonnormality and heteroscedasticity. For example, research continues on the optimum amount of trimming (Sawilowsky, 2002) and on combining, in sequence, a test of symmetry followed by trimming, transforming to eliminate skew, and bootstrapping (Keselman, Wilcox et al., 2002). With regard to the construction of confidence intervals for the difference between two populations' centers, the goal is to develop methods that are more accurate under a wider range of circumstances, such as small sample sizes, than the methods that have been discussed in this and the preceding sections. One such robust method is the percentile $t$ bootstrap method applied to one-step $M$ estimators (Keselman, Wilcox, & Lix, 2003; Wilcox, 2001, 2002, 2003). There are various bootstrapping methods, to which we provide only a brief conceptual introduction.

A bootstrap sample can be obtained by randomly sampling $k$ scores one at a time, with replacement, from the originally obtained sample of scores. Numerous such bootstrap samples are obtained. A targeted statistic of interest (e.g., the mean) is calculated for each bootstrap sample. Then a sampling distribution of all of these bootstrap-based values of the targeted statistic is generated. This sampling distribution is intended to approximate more accurately the actual sampling distribution of the targeted statistic when assumptions are not satisfied, as contrasted with its supposed theoretical distribution (e.g., the normal or $t$ distributions) when assumptions are satisfied.

The goal of bootstrapping in the present context is to base the construction of confidence intervals and significance testing on a bootstrap-based sampling distribution that more accurately approximates the actual sampling distribution of the statistic than does the traditional supposed sampling distribution. Recall that what we called the margin of error is a function of the standard error of the relevant sampling distribution. Bootstrapping provides an empirical estimate of this standard error that can be used in place of what its theoretical value would be if assumptions were satisfied.

Wilcox (2001, 2002, 2003) provided specialized software for bootstrapping to construct confidence intervals. In the case of confidence intervals for the difference between two populations' locations (e.g., means, trimmed means, and medians), bootstrap samples are taken from the two original samples from the two populations. Refer to Wilcox (2003) for detailed descriptions of the applications of various bootstrap methods to attempt to improve the Welch method, Yuen method, and the median-comparison method for constructing such confidence intervals. Researchers' acceptance of such relatively new bootstrap methods will depend in part on the methods' demonstrated abilities to produce accurate confidence levels.

Note that bootstrapping is intended to deal with violations of statistical assumptions. Bootstrapping cannot rectify flaws in the design of research, such as the use of original samples that are not representative of the intended populations of interest. For criticisms of bootstrap methods for constructing confidence intervals, refer to Gleser (1996). Consult Shaffer (2002) for a strategy for constructing confidence intervals that is based on a reformulation of the null hypothesis. The noncentrality approach to constructing confidence intervals is discussed in the next chapter where it becomes appropriate.

More than a cursory discussion of bootstrap methods would be beyond the scope of this book. For nontechnical general discussions of bootstrap methods, consult Diaconis and Efron (1983), Thompson (1993, 1999), and Wilcox and Keselman (2003a). For book-length introductory treatments refer to Chernick (1999) and Lunneborg (1999). For more advanced book-length treatments consult Davison and Hinkley (1997), Efron and Tibshirani (1993), and Sprent (1998).

This book only discusses confidence intervals that have a lower and an upper limit (two-sided confidence intervals). However, there are one-sided confidence intervals that involve only a lower or only an upper limit. For example, a researcher may be interested in acquiring evidence that a parameter, such as the difference between two populations' means, exceeds a certain minimum value. In such a case the lower limit for, say, a one-sided .95 CI is found by calculating the lower limit of a two-sided .90 CI. Consult Smithson (2003) for further discussion.

## DEPENDENT GROUPS

Construction of confidence intervals when using dependent groups requires modification of methods that are applicable to independent groups. Dependent-groups designs include repeated-measures (within-groups and pretest–posttest) and matched-groups designs. It is well known that interpreting results from a pretest–posttest design can be problematic, especially if the design does not involve a control or other comparison group and random assignment to each group. (Consult Hunter & Schmidt, 2004, for a favorable view of the pretest–posttest design.) Also, the customary counterbalancing in repeated-measures designs does not protect against the possibility that a lingering effect of Treatment *a* when Treatment *b* is next applied may not be the same as the lingering effect of Treatment *b* when Treatment *a* is next applied (asymmetrical transfer of effect). We now use real data from a pretest–posttest design to illustrate construction of a confidence interval for dependent groups. Table 2.1 depicts the weights (lb) of 17 anorectic girls before and after treatment (Everitt, cited in raw data presented in Hand et al., 1994).

Assuming normality, we construct a .95 CI for the mean difference between posttreatment and pretreatment scores in the population,

### TABLE 2.1
### Differences Between Anorectics' Weights (in lbs)
### Posttreatment and Pretreatment

| Participant | Posttreatment | Pretreatment | Difference (D) |
|---|---|---|---|
| 1 | 95.2 | 83.8 | 11.4 |
| 2 | 94.3 | 83.3 | 11.0 |
| 3 | 91.5 | 86.0 | 5.5 |
| 4 | 91.9 | 82.5 | 9.4 |
| 5 | 100.3 | 86.7 | 13.6 |
| 6 | 76.7 | 79.6 | –2.9 |
| 7 | 76.8 | 76.9 | –0.1 |
| 8 | 101.6 | 94.2 | 7.4 |
| 9 | 94.9 | 73.4 | 21.5 |
| 10 | 75.2 | 80.5 | –5.3 |
| 11 | 77.8 | 81.6 | –3.8 |
| 12 | 95.5 | 82.1 | 13.4 |
| 13 | 90.7 | 77.6 | 13.1 |
| 14 | 92.5 | 83.5 | 9.0 |
| 15 | 93.8 | 89.9 | 3.9 |
| 16 | 91.7 | 86.0 | 5.7 |
| 17 | 98.0 | 87.3 | 10.7 |

*Note.* Adapted from data of Brian S. Everitt, from *A handbook of small data sets,* by D. J. Hand, F. Daly, A. D. Lunn, K. J. McConway, and E. Ostrowski, 1994, London: Chapman and Hall. Adapted with permission of Brian S. Everitt.

$\mu_a - \mu_b$. We begin by defining a difference score, $D_i = Y_a - Y_b$, where $Y_a$ and $Y_b$ are the scores (weights in this example) of the same participants under Condition $a$ (posttreatment weight) and Condition $b$ (pretreatment weight), respectively. Thus, for Participant 1 in Table 2.1 we find that $D_1 = 95.2 - 83.8 = 11.4$. Because $\overline{Y}_a - \overline{Y}_b$ estimates $\mu_a - \mu_b$, and because it can easily be shown that the mean of such a set of $D$ values, $\overline{D} = (\Sigma D)/n$, is also equal to $\overline{Y}_a - \overline{Y}_b$, $\overline{D}$ too estimates $\mu_a - \mu_b$. Therefore, because $\overline{D}$ is a point estimate of $\mu_a - \mu_b$, a confidence interval for $\mu_a - \mu_b$ can be constructed around the value of $\overline{D}$.

Recall from expression 2.3 that the limits of the confidence intervals that are discussed in this chapter are given by the point estimate plus or minus the margin of error (*ME*). In the case of two dependent groups the limits are thus:

$$\overline{D} \pm ME_{dep}, \qquad (2.10)$$

where *dep* stands for dependent, and

$$ME_{dep} = t^* \frac{S_D}{n^{1/2}}. \qquad (2.11)$$

The symbol $S_D$ in Equation 2.11 represents the standard deviation of the values of $D$, and $S_D / n^{1/2}$ is the standard error of the mean of the values of $D$. The $S_D$ is calculated as an unbiased estimate of $\sigma_D$ in the population, so first $n - 1$ is used in the denominator of $S_D$, whereas $n$ is then used in the denominator of the standard error of the mean, as shown in Equation 2.11, so as not to correct twice for the bias. The n that is used in Equation 2.11 is the number of paired observations (i.e., the number of $D$ values).

For a .95 CI we need to find the value of $t^*$ required for statistical significance at the two-tailed .05 level. The degrees of freedom for $t^*$ for the case of dependent groups is given by $n - 1$. In the current example $df = n - 1 = 17 - 1 = 16$. A row for $df = 16$ can be found in the $t$ table in most statistics textbooks. The critical value of $t^*$ will be 2.120.

Using any statistical software to calculate the needed sample statistics one finds that $\overline{D} = 7.265$ and $s_D = 7.157$. Applying the required values to Equation 2.11 we find that:

$$ME_{dep} = 2.120 \left( \frac{7.157}{17^{1/2}} \right) = 3.680.$$

Finally, applying the required values to expression 2.10 we find that the lower and upper limits of the .95 CI for $\mu_a - \mu_b$ are $\overline{D} \pm ME_{dep} = 7.265 - 3.680 = 3.6$ lb and $7.265 + 3.680 = 10.9$ lb, respectively. We are approximately 95% confident (again, assuming normality) that the interval between 3.6 and 11.0 lb would contain the mean weight gain in the population. Because this interval does not contain the value 0, the gain in weight can be considered to be statistically significant at the .05 level, two tailed. Note again that in general we cannot nearly definitively attribute statistically significant gains or losses from pretreatment to posttreatment to the effect of a treatment unless there is random assignment to the treatment and to a control or comparison group. In our example of treatments for anorexia, a control group was included by the researcher, but it would be beyond the scope of this chapter to discuss further analysis of these data (e.g., analysis of covariance).

For dependent data in which the distribution of the $D$ values is skewed there is a Minitab macro (Wilcox, 1996) and S–PLUS software functions (Wilcox, 1997) for constructing an approximate confidence interval for the difference between two quantiles. (Quantiles were defined in chap. 1

of this book and are discussed further in chap. 5.) In the case of two dependent groups Wilcox (1997) also discussed and provided S-PLUS functions for constructing a confidence interval for the difference between two trimmed means, two medians, and other measures of two distribution's locations. However, in the case of a confidence interval for the difference between means of dependent groups, for much real data skew might not greatly distort confidence levels.

## QUESTIONS

1. In what circumstance is a confidence interval most useful?
2. List three examples of familiar scales that are not listed in the text.
3. Provide a valid definition of *confidence interval*.
4. Define lower and upper confidence limits.
5. Define *confidence level*.
6. What is a common misinterpretation of, say, a 95% confidence interval?
7. To what does .95 refer in a 95% confidence interval?
8. In the concept of confidence intervals what is constant and what is a random variable?
9. Define *margin of error* in the context of confidence intervals.
10. List three factors that influence the magnitude of the margin of error, and what effect does each factor have?
11. Define *probability coverage*.
12. What is the trade-off between using a 95% or a 99% confidence interval?
13. Define *independent groups*.
14. What assumption is being made when a pooled estimate is made of population variance?
15. For tests and confidence intervals involving the difference between two means, what is the relationship between the confidence level and a significance level?
16. For all parameters is there always a simple relationship between the confidence level and a significance level?
17. Which factors influence the width of a confidence interval, and in what way does each factor influence this width?
18. In what specific ways is the game of horseshoe tossing analogous to the construction of confidence intervals?
19. Discuss the relationship between the practical significance of results in applied research and the magnitudes of the lower and upper limits of a confidence interval.
20. Define and briefly discuss the purpose of asymmetric confidence intervals.
21. Contrast random sampling and convenience sampling.
22. What is the purpose of Welch's approximate method for constructing confidence intervals, and when might a researcher consider using it?

23. What are two differences between the Welch method and the traditional method for constructing confidence intervals?
24. What is the effect of skew on the Welch method?
25. Define *trimming* and discuss its purpose.
26. What factors might influence the optimal amount of trimming?
27. What is the purpose of Yuen's method, and in what ways is it a hybrid method?
28. What is the irony if a researcher would never consider using trimmed means but would consider using medians?
29. Define a *bootstrap sample*.
30. In the context of this chapter, what is the general purpose of bootstrapping?
31. Define and state the purpose of *one-sided confidence intervals*.
32. List versions of dependent-groups designs.
33. Define difference scores and describe the role that they play in the construction of confidence intervals in the case of two dependent groups.

# Chapter 3

# The Standardized Difference Between Means

## UNFAMILIAR AND INCOMPARABLE SCALES

A confidence interval for the difference between two populations' centers can be especially informative when the dependent variable is measured on the same familiar scale across the studies in an area. However, often dependent variables are abstract and are measured indirectly using relatively unfamiliar measures. For example, consider research that compares Treatments a and b for depression, a variable that is more abstract and more problematic to measure directly than would be the case with the familiar dependent variable measures that were listed in chapter 2. Although depression is very real to the person who suffers from it, there is no single, direct way for a researcher to define and measure it as one could do for the familiar scales. There are many tests of depression available to and used by researchers, as is true for many other variables outside of the physical and biomedical sciences. (In such cases the presumed underlying variable is called the *latent variable*, and the test that is believed to be measuring this dependent variable validly is called the *measure of the dependent variable*.) For example, suppose that confidence limits of 5 and 10 points mean difference in Beck Depression Inventory (BDI) scores between depressed groups that were given Treatment a or b are reported. Such a finding would be less familiar and less informative (except perhaps to specialists) than would be a report of confidence limits of 5 and 10 lb difference in mean weights in our earlier example of research on weight gain from treatments for anorexia.

Furthermore, suppose that a researcher conducted a study that compared the efficacy of Treatments a and b for depression and that another researcher conducted another study that also compared these two treatments. Suppose also that the first researcher used the BDI as the dependent variable measure, whereas the second researcher used, for a conceptual replication of the first study, a different measure, say, the MMPI Depression scale (MMPI–D). It would seem to be difficult to compare precisely or combine the results of these two studies because the two scales of depression are not the same. One would not know the relationship between the numerical scores on the two measures. An interval of, say, 5 to 10 points with regard to the difference between means on one measure of depression would not necessarily represent the same degree of difference in underlying depression as would an interval of 5 to 10 points with respect to another measure of depression.

We need a measure of effect size that places different dependent variable measures on the same scale so that results from studies that use different measures can be compared or combined. One such measure of effect size is the standardized difference between means, a frequently used measure to which we now turn our attention.

## STANDARDIZED DIFFERENCE BETWEEN MEANS: ASSUMING NORMALITY AND A CONTROL GROUP

A standardized difference between means is like a z score, $z = (Y - \overline{Y}) / s$, that standardizes a difference in the sense that it divides it by a standard deviation. A z score indicates how many standard deviations above or below $\overline{Y}$ a Y raw score is, and it can indicate more. For example, assuming a normal distribution of raw scores so that z too will be normally distributed, inspecting a table of the standardized normal curve in any introductory statistics textbook one finds that approximately 84% of z scores fall below $z = +1.00$ (also inspect Fig. 3.1 that is displayed and discussed later). Therefore, a z score can provide a very informative result, such as indicating that a score at $z = +1.00$ is outscoring approximately 84% of the other scores. Recall that in a normal curve approximately 34% of the scores lie between $z = 0$ and $z = +1.00$, approximately 14% of the scores lie between $z = +1.00$ and $z = +2.00$, and approximately 2% of the scores exceed $z = +2.00$. Of course, because of symmetry these same percentages apply if one substitutes minus signs for the plus signs in the previous sentence. Thus, under normality, a score at $z = +1.00$ is exceeding approximately 2% + 14% + 34% + 34% = 84% of the scores.

Using z scores, or z–like measures, one can also compare results obtained from different scales, results that would not be comparable if one used raw scores. For example, one cannot directly compare a student's grade point average (GPA) with that student's Scholastic Aptitude Test (SAT) scores; they are on very different scales. The range of GPA scores is usually from 0 to 4.00, whereas it is safe to assume that anyone reading this book and who has taken the SATs scored well above 4 on them. In this example it would be meaningless to say that such a person's score on the SAT was higher than his or her GPA. Similarly, it would be meaningless to conclude that most people are heavier than they are tall when one finds that most people have more pounds of weight than they have inches of height. However, one can meaningfully compare the otherwise incomparable by using z scores instead of raw scores in such examples. If one's z score on GPA was higher than one's z score on the SAT, relative to the same comparison group, then in fact that person did perform better on GPA than on the SAT (an overachiever). By using z-like measures of effect size researchers can compare or meta-analyze results from studies that use different dependent variable measures of the same underlying variable.

Assuming normality, one can obtain the same kind of information from a z-like measure of effect size as one can obtain from a z score. Suppose that one divides the difference between a treated group's mean, $\overline{Y}_e$ (e stands for a treated or experimental group), and a control group's mean, $\overline{Y}_c$, by the standard deviation of the control group's scores, $s_c$. One then has for one possible estimator of an effect size a standardized difference between means,

$$d = \frac{\overline{Y}_e - \overline{Y}_c}{S_c}. \tag{3.1}$$

Equation 3.1 estimates the parameter:

$$\Delta = \frac{\mu_e - \mu_c}{\sigma_c}. \tag{3.2}$$

The symbol $\Delta$ is the uppercase Greek letter $D$, and it stands for difference. The $d$ version of the effect-size estimator in Equation 3.1 is attributable to Gene V. Glass (e.g., Glass et al., 1981). In Equation 3.1 the standard deviation has $n - 1$ in its denominator.

Similar to a z score, $\Delta$ estimates how many $\sigma_c$ units above or below $\mu_c$ the value of $\mu_e$ is. Again if, say, $d = +1.00$, one is estimating that the average (mean) scoring members of a treated population score one $\sigma_c$ unit above the scores of the average scoring members of the control population. Also, if normality is assumed in this example, the average-scoring members of the treated population are estimated to be outscoring approximately 84% of the members of the control population. If, say, $d = -1.00$, one would estimate that the average-scoring members of the treated population are outscoring only approximately 16% of the members of the control population.

Of course, numerical results other than $d = +1.00$ or $-1.00$ are likely to occur, including results with decimal values, and they are similarly interpretable from a table of the normal curve if one assumes normality. Figure 3.1 illustrates the example of $\Delta = +1.00$. To use Fig. 3.1 to reflect on the implication of values of $d$ that have lead to an estimate other than $\Delta = +1.00$ the reader can imagine shifting the distribution of the treated population's scores to the right or to the left so that $\mu_e$ falls elsewhere on the control group's distribution.

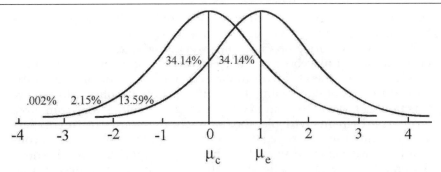

FIG. 3.1.   Assuming normality, when $\Delta = +1.00$ the mean score in the treated population will exceed approximately 84% of the scores in the control population.

Recall that the mean of $z$ scores is always 0, so the mean of the $z$ scores of the control population is equal to 0. The mean of the $z$ scores of the experimental (treated) population is also equal to 0 with regard to the distribution of $z$ scores of its own population. However, in the example depicted in Fig. 3.1 the mean of the raw scores of the experimental population corresponds to $z = +1.00$ with regard to the distribution of $z$ scores of the control population.

The $d$ estimator of $\Delta$ has been widely used since it was popularized in the 1970s (e.g., Smith & Glass, 1977). Grissom (1996) provided many references for examples in research on psychotherapy outcome, and he also provided examples of averaged values of $d$ from many meta-analyses on the efficacy of psychotherapy. These examples illustrate the use of $d$ and $\Delta$, so we consider them briefly here. Note first that when comparing various therapy groups (with the same disorder) with control groups, one should not expect to obtain the same values of $d$ from study to study because (in addition to sampling variability) therapies of varying efficacy should produce different values of $d$. Note also that sometimes the measure of the dependent variable is one in which a higher score is a "healthier" score (e.g., the measure of positive parent–child relationships in the example that will soon be discussed), but more often the clinical measure is one in which a lower score is a healthier score (e.g., a measure of depression). However, Equations 3.1 and 3.2 can be rewritten with the mean of Group c preceding the mean of Group e, so that the sign of $d$ or $\Delta$, but not their magnitudes, would change. Altering Equation 3.1 in this way when needed assures that when the treated group (Group e) has a better (healthier) outcome than the control group the value of $d$ will be positive, and when the control group has a better outcome $d$ will be negative. Altering Equation 3.1 in this way Grissom (1996) estimated that the median value of $d$ was + 0.75, with values of $d$ ranging from –0.35 to +2.47. Therefore, on the whole, therapies appear to be efficacious (median $d = +0.75$), with some therapies in some circumstances extremely so ($d = +2.47$), and very few seeming to be harmful (the rare negative values of $d$, e.g., $-0.35$).

There is a minority opinion that psychotherapies have no specific benefits, only a placebo effect wherein any improvement in peoples' mental health is merely attributable to their expectation of therapeutic success, a kind of self-healing by a self-fulfilling prophecy. To explore this point of view Grissom (1996) averaged $d$ values that compared treated participants with placebo (phony or minimum treatment) participants and then averaged $d$ values that compared placebo and control (no treatment) groups. (Note here the adaptability of Equations 3.1 and 3.2. One can use these equations to compare two groups that undergo any two different conditions. The conditions do not have to be strictly treatment vs. control.) When comparing the treatment group with the placebo group the median value of $d$ was $+0.58$, suggesting that therapy provides more than a mere expectation of improvement (placebo effect). However, when comparing placebo with control (placebo group replaces treatment group in Equation 3.1) the median value of $d$ was $+0.44$. Together these results suggest that there are placebo effects but that there is more to the efficacy of therapy than just such placebo effects. This conclusion is not necessarily definitive but these applications of standardized-difference estimators of effect size have been more informative than would have been the case if only null-hypothesis significance testing had been undertaken to compare therapy, control, and placebo. However, we are not disparaging significance testing. Often in this book there are examples of the complementary use of significance testing and effect sizes, and there are discussions of situations in which a researcher's focus might be either on significance testing or on effect sizes.

With regard to the adaptability of Equations 3.1 and 3.2, in research without a treated group (e.g., women's scores compared to men's scores) the experimental group's representation in the equations is replaced by any kind of group whose performance one wants to evaluate with regard to the distribution of some baseline comparison group. Therefore, more general forms of Equations 3.1 and 3.2 are, respectively,

$$d = \frac{\overline{Y}_a - \overline{Y}_b}{S_b}, \tag{3.3}$$

and

$$\Delta = \frac{\mu_a - \mu_b}{\sigma_b}. \tag{3.4}$$

For a real example of such an application of $d$, we use a study in which the healthy parent–child relationship scores of mothers of disturbed (schizophrenic) children (Mother Group a) were compared to those of mothers of normal children (Mother Group b), who served as the control or comparison group (Werner, Stabenau, & Pollin, 1970). In this example $\overline{Y}_a = 2.10$, $\overline{Y}_b = 3.55$, and $s_b = 1.88$. Therefore, $d = (2.10 - 3.55) / 1.88 = -0.77$. Thus, the mothers of the disturbed children scored on average about three quarters of a standard deviation unit below the mean of the comparison mothers' scores. Assuming normality for now, inspecting a table of the normal curve one finds that at $z = -0.77$ we can estimate that the average-scoring mothers of the disturbed children would be outscored by approximately 78% of the comparison mothers. Also, a two-tailed $t$ test yielded a statistically significant difference between the two means at the $p < .05$ level.

The results are consistent with three possible interpretations: (a) disturbance in parents genetically and/or experientially causes disturbance in their children, (b) disturbance in children causes disturbance in their parents, or (c) some combination of the first two interpretations can explain the results. We have assumed for simplicity in this example that the measure of the underlying dependent variable was valid and that the assumptions of normality and homoscedasticity were satisfied. Reliability of the measure of the dependent variable in the present example is not likely to be among the highest. Hunter and Schmidt (2004) discussed unreliability and provided software for the correction of a standardized difference between means for unreliability in the dependent variable (as well as correcting for other artifacts). Unreliability is discussed in chapter 4.

## EQUAL OR UNEQUAL VARIANCES

If the two populations that are being compared are assumed to have equal variances, then it is also assumed that $\sigma_a = \sigma_b = \sigma$, the common population standard deviation. In this case a better estimate of the denominator of a standardized difference between population means can be made if one pools the data from both samples to estimate the common $\sigma$ instead of using $s_b$ that is based on the data of only one sample. The pooled estimator, $s_p$, is based on a larger total sample ($N = n_a + n_b$) and is a less biased and less variable estimator of $\sigma$ than $s_b$ would be. To calculate $s_p$ take the square root of the value of $s_p^2$ that is obtained from a printout or from Equation 2.2 in chapter 2 that uses $n - 1$ in the denominator of each of the variances that is being pooled. The estimator of effect size in this case is:

$$g = \frac{\overline{Y}_a - \overline{Y}_b}{s_p}, \tag{3.5}$$

which is known as Hedges' $g$ (Hedges & Olkin, 1985), and estimates

$$g_{pop} = \frac{\mu_a - \mu_b}{\sigma}.$$ (3.6)

We always use the $g$ notation when using the standard deviation that uses $n - 1$ in the denominator of each of the variances that is being pooled. Use of the $g$ notation helps to avoid confusing Glass' $d$ (no pooling) with the estimators Cohen's $d_s$ (pooling using $n - 1$; this is the same as $g$, so $d_s$ is not used again in this book) or Cohen's $d$ (pooling using $n$ instead of $n - 1$). Throughout this book we distinguish between situations in which Hedges' $g$ or Glass' $d$ might be preferred.

When $\sigma_a = \sigma_b = \sigma$, $g_{pop} = \Delta$. However, in this case it will still be very unlikely that $s_a = s_b = s_p$ due to sampling variability of sample standard deviations, the more so the smaller the sample sizes, so it will be very unlikely that $d = g$. Similarly, differing estimates of $\Delta$ will likely result from using $s_a$ instead of $s_b$ in the denominator of the estimator even when $\sigma_a = \sigma_b$ because sampling variability can cause $s_a$ to differ from $s_b$. Research reports should clearly state which effect-size parameter is being estimated and which $s$ has been used in the denominator of the estimator.

Both Hedges' $g$ and Glass' $d$ have some positive bias (i.e., tending to overestimate their respective parameters), the more so the smaller the sample sizes and the larger the effect size in the population. Although $g$ is less biased than $d$, its bias can be reduced by using Hedges' approximately unbiased adjusted $g$, $g_{adj}$;

$$g_{adj} = g\left[1 - \frac{3}{4df - 1}\right],$$ (3.7)

where $df = n_a + n_b - 2$ (Hedges, 1981, 1982; Hedges & Olkin, 1985).

Glass' $d$ can also have its bias reduced by substituting $d$ for $g$ in Equation 3.7 and using $df = n_c - 1$, where $n_c$ is the $n$ for the sample whose $s$ is used in the denominator. The two adjusted estimators are seldom used because bias and bias reduction have traditionally been believed to be slight unless sample sizes are very small (Kraemer, 1983). Hunter and Schmidt (2004) demonstrated why they consider the bias to be negligible when sample sizes are greater than 20. [These authors also provided formulas for adjusting the point-biserial correlation for its slight bias.] However, as was discussed in the section entitled Controversy About Null-Hypothesis Significance Testing in chapter 1, regarding the debate about whether effect sizes should be reported when results are statistically insignificant, some believe that the bias is sufficient to cause concern. Consult the references that we provided in that section of chapter 1 for discussion of this issue, and also refer to Barnette and McLean (1999) for their results on the relationship between sample size and effect size.

Recall that if population means differ it is also likely that population standard deviations differ. This heteroscedasticity can cause problems.

First, because $\sigma_a \neq \sigma_b$, $(\mu_a - \mu_b) / \sigma_b \neq (\mu_a - \mu_b) / \sigma_a$. In this case the $\Delta$ parameter that is being estimated using one of the samples as the control or baseline group that provides the estimate of the standardizer will not be the same as the $\Delta$ that would be the one that is being estimated if we use the other sample as the baseline group that provides the estimate of the standardizer. Also, the formulas provided by Hedges and Olkin (1985) for constructing confidence intervals for $g_{pop}$ assume homoscedasticity. Hogarty and Kromrey (2001) demonstrated the influence of heteroscedasticity and nonnormality on Cohen's $d$ and Hedges' $g$.

To counter heteroscedasticity Cohen (1988) suggested using for $\sigma$ the square root of the mean of $\sigma^2_a$ and $\sigma^2_b$, estimated by

$$ s' = \left[ \frac{s_a^2 + s_b^2}{2} \right]^{\frac{1}{2}}. \qquad (3.8) $$

Researchers who use $s'$ (our notation, not Cohen's) as the estimator of a $\sigma$ instead of the previously discussed estimators of $\sigma_a$ or $\sigma_b$ should recognize that they are estimating the $\sigma$ of a hypothetical population whose $\sigma$ is between $\sigma_a$ and $\sigma_b$. In this case, therefore, such researchers are estimating a $\Delta$ in a hypothetical population, an effect size that we label here $\Delta'$. The burden would be on the researcher to interpret the results in terms of the hypothetical population to which this effect size relates. Researchers should also recognize that Cohen (1988) introduced $\Delta'$ originally for the purpose of conducting a power analysis for estimating the approximate needed sample sizes prior to beginning research. This purpose is different from the present purpose of using an effect size to analyze results of completed research. Huynh (1989) suggested methods for decreasing the bias and instability (variability) of Cohen's estimator of $\Delta'$ under heteroscedasticity.

## TENTATIVE RECOMMENDATIONS

When homoscedasticity is assumed the best estimator of the common $\sigma$ is $s_p$, resulting in the $g$ or $g_{adj}$ estimator of effect size. If homoscedasticity is not assumed use the $s$ of whichever sample is the reasonable baseline comparison group. For example, use the $s$ of the control or placebo group, or, if a new treatment is being compared with a standard treatment, use the $s$ of the sample that is receiving the standard treatment. It may sometimes be informative to calculate and report two estimates of $\Delta$, one based on $s_a$ and one based on $s_b$. For example, in studies that compare genders one can estimate a $\Delta_F$ to estimate where the mean female score stands in relation to the population distribution of males' scores, and one can estimate a $\Delta_M$ to estimate where the mean male score stands in relation to the population distribution of females' scores. A modest additional suggestion is to use $ns > 10$ and ones that are as close to equal as possible (Huynh, 1989; Kraemer, 1983).

One should be cautious about generalizing our suggestion to estimate two types of effect sizes on the same data because of a valid concern that stems from significance testing. In significance testing one should not conduct more than one statistical test on the same set of data unless one compensates for the capitalizing on chance that results from such multiple testing. Capitalizing on chance is a cumulation of Type I error that results from inappropriately providing more than one opportunity to obtain statistical significance within the same data set. Thus, a researcher has a greater chance of at least once attaining, say, the $p < .05$ level of statistical significance in a data set if conducting two tests of significance on those data than if conducting one test on those data. The chance probability of at least one of two such tests attaining the $p < .05$ significance level is greater than .05, just as the probability of a basketball player making one basket in either of two attempts is greater than the probability of making a basket in one attempt. The well-known and simplest (but not always optimum) solution would be to conduct the separate tests at a more stringent adopted level of significance (Bonferroni–Dunn adjustment); say, conducting each of two tests at the $p < .025$ level. Effect-size methodology is barely out if its infancy, and until some widely accepted practices develop perhaps one can be flexible about applying more than one estimator of effect sizes to the same data set (but not flexible about inflating Type I error). Indeed, as discussed later in this book, different kinds of measures of effect sizes can provide different informative perspectives on the same data set, so there will be examples in which we apply not two but several different kinds of measures of effect sizes to the same data set.

Although there are data sets for which we illustrate application of two or more measures of effect size for our pedagogical purpose, an author of a research report might choose to calculate and report only an estimator that the author can justify as being most appropriate. Nonetheless, again we state that if more than one estimator is calculated the researcher should report all such calculated estimators. It would be unacceptable to report only the effect size of which the magnitude is most supportive of the case that researcher is trying to make. Refer to Hogarty and Kromrey (2001) for further discussion. Note again that at the time of this writing editors of journals that recommend or require the reporting of effect sizes do not specify which kinds of effect sizes are to be reported. The important point is that at least one appropriate estimate of effect size should be reported whenever such reporting would be informative.

In areas of research in which the measure of the dependent variable is a common test that has been normed on a vast sample, such as has been done for many major clinical and educational tests, there is another solution to heteroscedasticity. (A normed test is one whose distribution's shape, mean, and standard deviation have already been determined by applying the test to, e.g., many thousands of people [the normative group]. For example, there are norms for the scales of the MMPI personality inventory and for various IQ and academic admissions tests, such as the SAT and Graduate Record Examination.) In this case, for an estimator of $\Delta$ one can divide $\overline{Y}_e - \overline{Y}_n$ by $s_n$, where n stands for the normative group (Kendall & Grove, 1988; Kendall, Marss-Garcia, Nath, & Sheldrick, 1999). The use of such a constant $s_n$ by all researchers who are working in the same field of research decreases uncertainty about the value of $\Delta$. This is so because when not using the common $s_n$ different researchers will find greatly varying values of $d$, even if their values of $\overline{Y}_a - \overline{Y}_b$ do not differ very much, simply due to the varying values of $s$ from study to study.

For an example of the method, suppose that for a normative group of babies $\overline{Y}_n = 100$ and $s_n = 15$ on a test of their developmental quotient, a test whose population of scores is normally distributed. Suppose further that a special diet or treatment that is given to an experimental group of babies results in their $\overline{Y}_e = 110$. In this case we estimate that $\Delta = (110 - 100) / 15 = +0.67$, with the average-scoring treated babies scoring 0.67 units above the average of the normative babies. Inspection of a table of the normal curve indicates that a $z$ of $+0.67$ is a result that outscores approximately 75% of the normative babies.

When a comparison population's distribution is not normal the interpretation of a $d$ or a $g$ in terms of estimating the percentile standing of the average-scoring members of a group with respect to the normal distribution of the baseline group's scores would not be valid. Also, because standard deviations can be very sensitive to a distribution's shape, as was compellingly illustrated by Wilcox and Muska (1999), nonnormality can greatly influence the value of a $\Delta$, $g_{pop}$, or their estimators. In chapter 5 we discuss measures of effect size (the probability of superiority and related measures) that do not assume homoscedasticity or normality.

Finally, a treatment may have importantly different effects on different dependent variables. For example, a treatment for an addiction may have a different effect on one addiction compared with another addiction in multiply addicted persons' addictions. Therefore, we should not generalize about the magnitude and sign of an effect size from one dependent variable to a supposedly related dependent variable. For example, it would be very important to know if a treatment that apparently successfully targeted alcoholism resulted in an increase in smoking.

## ADDITIONAL STANDARDIZED-DIFFERENCE EFFECT SIZES WHEN THERE ARE OUTLIERS

The previous section was entitled Tentative Recommendations because other types of estimators have been proposed for use when there are outliers that can influence the means and standard deviations. One simple suggestion for a somewhat outlier-resistant estimator is to trim the highest and lowest score from each group, replace $\overline{Y}_a - \overline{Y}_b$ with $Mdn_a - Mdn_b$, and use as the standardizer, in place of the standard deviation, the range of the trimmed data or some other measure of variability that is more outlier resistant than is the standard deviation (Hedges & Olkin, 1985). One possible such alternative to the standard deviation is the median absolute deviation from the median ($MAD$). Another alternative standardizer is $.75R_{iq}$, as proposed by Laird and Mosteller (1990) to provide some resistance to outliers while using a denominator that approximates the standard deviation. Both the $MAD$ and $R_{iq}$ were introduced in chapter 1, from which recall that $.75R_{iq}$ approximates $s$ when there is normality.

Note that, as Wilcox (1996) pointed out, using one of the relatively outlier-resistant measures of variability instead of the standard deviation does not assure us that the variabilities of the two populations will be equal when their means are not equal. Also, although at the current stage of development of methodology for effect sizes it is appropriate in this book to present a great variety of measures, eventually the field should settle on the use of a reduced number of appropriate measures. A more consistent use of measures of effect size by primary researchers would facilitate the comparison of results from study to study. Nonetheless, we briefly turn now to some additional alternatives.

### TECHNICAL NOTE 3.1: A NONPARAMETRIC ESTIMATOR OF STANDARDIZED-DIFFERENCE EFFECT SIZES

For nonparametric estimation of standardized-difference effect sizes for pretest–posttest designs consult Kraemer and Andrews (1982) and Hedges and Olkin (1985). Hedges and Olkin (1984, 1985) also provided a nonparametric estimator of a standardized-difference effect size that does not require pretest data or assume homoscedasticity. This method estimates a $\Delta_c^*$ using $d_c^*$ (our notation, not Hedges' and Olkins'), defined as

$$d_c^* = \Phi_{pc}^{-1}, \qquad (3.9)$$

where $\Phi^{-1}$ is the standard normal cumulative distribution function and the subscript $pc$ represents the proportion of control group scores that are below $Mdn_a$. Under normality $d_c^*$ estimates $\Delta_c^* = (\mu_e - \mu_c) / \sigma_c$. We do not demonstrate this method here because the sampling distribution of $d_c^*$ is not known, so methods for significance testing and for constructing a confidence interval for $\Delta_c^*$ are not known.

Recall that ideally a statistic should be resistant to outliers, as is the $MAD$, and have relatively low sampling variability to increase power and to narrow confidence intervals. Recall also from the previous section that alternatives to the standard deviation, such as the $MAD$, may provide better denominators for standardized-difference estimators of effect size than $s$ does when there are outliers. However, the biweight standard deviation, $s_{bw}$ (Goldberg & Iglewicz, 1992; Lax, 1985), appears to be superior to the $MAD$ as a measure of variability. Therefore, a more outlier-resistant alternative estimator of a standardized-difference effect size might be

$$d_{bw} = \frac{Md_e - Md_c}{s_{bwc}},$$  (3.10)

where $s_{bwc}$ is the square root of the biweight midvariance, $s^2_{bw}$, of the control group or other baseline comparison group. Lax (1985) found the biweight midvariance to be the most outlier resistant and most stable (least sampling variability) of any of the very many measures of variability that were studied. Manual calculation of $s^2_{bw}$ is laborious (Wilcox, 1996, 1997, 2003). First, calculate for each score in the control group $Z_i = (Y_i - Mdn_c) / 9MAD$. Next, set $a_i = 1$ if $|Z_i| < 1$ and set $a_i = 0$ if $|Z_i| > 1$. Then, find

$$s_{bwc} = \frac{n^{1/2} \left[ \Sigma a_i \left(Y_i - Md_c\right)^2 \left(1 - Z_i^2\right)^4 \right]^{1/2}}{\left| \Sigma a_i \left(1 - Z_i^2\right)\left(1 - 5Z_i^2\right) \right|}.$$  (3.11)

Minitab macros (Wilcox, 1996) and S-PLUS software functions (Wilcox, 1997, 2003) are available for calculating $s^2_{bw}$, for testing the significance of the difference between two groups' values of $s^2_{bw}$ (with apparently good power and good control of Type I error), and for constructing an accurate confidence interval for this difference.

## CONFIDENCE INTERVALS
## FOR A STANDARDIZED-DIFFERENCE EFFECT SIZE

Of course, the smaller the sample size, the greater the variability of the sampling distribution of an estimator. Thus, the smaller the sample size, the more likely it is that there will be a large discrepancy between a value of $d$ or $g$ and the true value of the effect size that they are estimating. (Consult Bradley, Smith, & Stoica, 2002, and Begg, 1994, for discussions of consequences of this fact.) Therefore, a confidence interval for a standardized-difference effect size can be very informative.

More accurate, but more complex methods that we prefer for constructing confidence intervals for a standardized-difference effect size are discussed later. First, a simple approximate method for manual calculation is demonstrated. This method becomes less accurate to the extent that the assumptions of homoscedasticity and normality are not met, the smaller the sample sizes (say, $n_a < 10$ and $n_b < 10$), and the more that $\Delta$ departs from 0. Note that because we are assuming homoscedasticity $\Delta = g_{pop}$, so the confidence interval that we give for $\Delta$ applies to $g_{pop}$.

An approximate 95% *CI* for Δ is given by

$$.95CI\ \Delta: d \pm z_{.025}s_d,\qquad(3.12)$$

where $z_{0.25}$ is the positive value of $z$ that has 2.5% of the area of the normal curve beyond it, namely, $z = +1.96$, and $s_d$ is the estimated standard deviation of the theoretical sampling distribution of $d$. To calculate $s_d$, following Hedges and Olkin (1985), take the square root of

$$s_d^2 = \frac{n_a + n_b}{n_a n_b} + \frac{d^2}{2(n_a + n_b)}.\qquad(3.13)$$

For example, suppose that one wants to construct a 95% *CI* for Δ when $d = +0.70$, $n_a = n_b = 20$, and we are not adjusting $d$ for bias because bias is likely very slight when each $n = 20$. In this case $s_d^2 = [(20+20) / (20\text{x}20)] + [.70^2 / [2(20+20)]] = 0.106$, and $s_d = (0.106)^{\frac{1}{2}} = 0.326$. Therefore, the limits of the .95 *CI* are $0.70 \pm 1.96(0.326)$. The lower limit for this confidence interval is 0.06 and the upper limit is 1.34 (a disappointingly wide interval). Thus, we estimate that the interval from 0.06 to 1.34 would contain the value of Δ approximately 95% of the time.

Recall from chapter 1 that there are opposing views regarding the relevance of null-hypothesis significance testing. Therefore, authors (and readers) of a research report would have varying reactions to the fact that the confidence interval from 0.06 to 1.34 does not contain 0, a result that also provides evidence at the two-tailed .05 level of significance that Δ does not equal 0. This statistically significant result would be an important perspective on the data for someone who is interested in evidence regarding a theory that predicts a difference between the two groups. This significance-testing perspective would also be important if the research were comparing two treatments of equal overall cost, so the main issue would then be which, if either, of the two treatments is more effective.

On the other hand, suppose that there are two competing treatments and that the prior literature includes an estimate of effect size when comparing one of those treatments to a control condition. Suppose further that the present research is estimating effect size when the other competing treatment is being compared to the same control condition that was used in the prior study. In this case the interest would be in the magnitudes of the currently obtained value of $d$ and of the confidence limits and in comparing the present results with the prior results as evidence regarding the competition between the two treatments.

Many meta-analyses include all available relevant estimates of effect size, including those that did not attain statistical significance in the underlying primary studies. Recall in this regard that we previously cited the results by Sawilowsky and Yoon (2002) that provided evidence of inflation of Type I error when such nonsignificant estimates are used in a meta-analysis. Recall also the finding (Meeks & D'Agostino, 1983), cited in chapter 2, that if one only constructs a confidence interval contingent on obtaining a statistically significant result, the apparent (nominal) confidence level will be greater than the true confidence level (liberal probability coverage). Perhaps a justifiable procedure for a study in which the researcher wants to report a confidence interval would be to construct a confidence interval first and then address the presence or absence of 0 in the interval from the perspective of significance testing. Nonetheless, again some believe that researchers should either conduct a test of significance or construct a confidence interval, depending on the purpose of the research (Knapp, 2002). Note in this regard that in chapter 8 we encounter a situation (the difference between two proportions) in which a test of significance and a confidence interval might produce inconsistent results.

A solution has been proposed for the issue of significance testing versus construction of confidence intervals. This solution involves a null hypothesis that posits not a single value (usually 0), as is customary for a parameter such as $\Delta$, but a range of values that would be of equal interest to the researcher, values called *good-enough values*. In this case the confidence limits are not based on the use of a distribution of a test statistic that would be used to test a traditional null hypothesis (e.g., the $t$ or normal $z$ distribution) as is done in this book. Instead, the relevant distribution is based on a test statistic that would be used to test a *range null hypothesis*. A good-enough confidence interval addresses the issue of whether an effect is large enough to be of interest. These confidence intervals can also provide evidence regarding a theory that an effect will be at least a specified size. For further discussion and references refer to the review by Serlin (2002). Steiger (2004) discussed construction of confidence intervals that are related to this approach to significance testing. The "good-enough" approach is reasonable for instances of applied research in which the researcher has a credible rationale for determining what degree of difference between two groups would be the minimum that would be of interest. The approach is also briefly mentioned in chapter 8 in the section entitled "The Difference Between Two Proportions," where the work of Fleiss, Levin, and Paik (2003) is cited.

Returning to our example, note that the confidence interval is not as informative as one would want it to be because the interval ranges from a value that would be considered to be a very small effect size (0.06) to a value that would be considered to be a large effect size (1.34). We would like to have obtained a narrower confidence interval. Recall from chapter 2 that to attempt to narrow a confidence interval some have suggested that we consider adopting a level of confidence lower than .95. The reader can try this as an exercise by constructing a $(1 - \alpha)$ *CI*, where $\alpha > .05$ to narrow the confidence interval by paying the price of having the confidence level below .95. In this case the only element in expression 3.12 that changes is that $z_{.025}$ is replaced by $z_{\alpha/2}$. This $z_{\alpha/2}$ arises, of course, because the middle $100(1 - \alpha)\%$ of the normal curve has one half of the remaining area of the curve above it; that is, it has $100(\alpha/2)\%$ above it. Note, however, that a .95 CI is traditional and that the editors and manuscript reviewers of some journals, and some professors who are supervising student research, may be uncomfortable with a result reported with less than 95% confidence.

Our current example with sample sizes of 20 each would generally be considered adequate for most experiments. Nonetheless, as a further exercise in narrowing confidence intervals (before the research is begun) by increasing sample sizes while maintaining 95% confidence, we change our example by now supposing that we had originally used $n_a = n_b = 50$ instead of 20 and that $d = +0.70$ again. Using $n_a = n_b = 50$ in Equation 3.13 and then taking the square root of the obtained $s_d^2$ one finds that now $s_d = 0.206$. The limits for the 95% $CI$ for $\Delta$ then become $0.70 \pm 1.96(0.206)$, yielding lower and upper limits of 0.30 and 1.10, respectively. This is still not a very narrow confidence interval, but it is narrower than the original confidence interval that was constructed using smaller sample sizes.

When assumptions are satisfied, for a more accurate method for constructing a confidence interval for $\Delta$ using SPSS or other software refer to Fidler and Thompson (2001) and Smithson (2001, 2003). Some rationale for this method is discussed in the next section on noncentral distributions. Additional software for constructing confidence intervals, combining them, and better understanding their meaning is Cumming and Finch's (2001) Exploratory Software for Confidence Intervals (ESCI). For an example of output from ESCI inspect our Fig. 3.2 that will be discussed shortly. ESCI runs under Excel and can, as of the time of this writing, be downloaded from http://www.latrobe.edu.au/psy/esci. This site also has useful links.

Satisfactorily narrow confidence intervals may often require impractically large sample sizes, so that a single study often cannot yield a definitive result. However, using software such as ESCI, combining a set of confidence intervals from related studies (i.e., the same variation of the independent variable and same dependent variable) may home in on a more accurate estimate of an effect size (Cumming & Finch, 2001; Wilkinson & APA Task Force, 1999). In this case of related studies the Results section of the report of a later study can include a single figure that depicts a confidence interval from its study together with the confidence intervals from all of the previous studies. Such a figure places our results in a broader context and can greatly facilitate interpretation of these results as integrated with the previous results. ESCI can produce such a figure, as is illustrated by Thompson (2002) and by our Fig. 3.2. Such a figure turns a primary study into a more informative meta-analysis.

For further discussion of confidence intervals for standardized-difference effect sizes, consult Cumming and Finch (2001), Hedges and Olkin (1985), and Thompson (2002). Hedges and Olkin (1985) provided

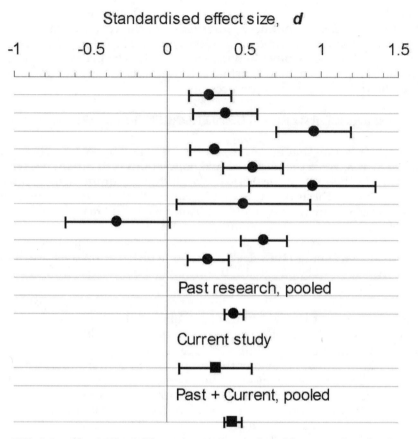

FIG. 3.2. The 95% confidence intervals, produced by ESCI, for placebo versus drug for depression. From *A Meta-Analysis of the Effectiveness of Antidepressants Compared to Placebo* by J. A. Gorecki, 2002, unpublished master's thesis, San Francisco State University, San Francisco. (British spelling per original figure.)

nomographs (charts) for aproximate confidence limits for $g_{pop}$ when $0 \leq g \leq 1.5$ and $n_a = n_b = 2$ to 10. Refer to Smithson (2003) for definitions and discussions of confidence intervals that are called exact, uniformly most accurate, and unbiased.

Figure 3.2 depicts 95% CIs for $\Delta$ that were produced by the *ESCI*'s option called MA (Meta-Analytic) Thinking. The $g$ values, calculated on real data (Gorecki, 2002), were defined as $g = (\overline{Y}_{placebo} - \overline{Y}_{drug}) / s_p$ in studies of depression. (Note that what we label "$g$" in this book the ESCI software currently labels "$d$".) The figure is intended only to illustrate an ESCI result because there were actually 11 prior studies to be compared with the latest study, but ESCI permitted depiction of confidence intervals for up to 10 prior studies, a pooled (averaged) confidence interval for those studies, a confidence interval from the current primary researcher's latest study, and a confidence interval based on a final pooling of the 10 prior studies and the latest study. The pooled confidence intervals represent a kind of meta-analysis undertaken by a primary researcher whose study has predecessors.

## CONFIDENCE INTERVALS USING NONCENTRAL DISTRIBUTIONS

The $t$ distribution that is used to test the usual null hypothesis (that the difference between the means of two populations is 0) is centered symmetrically about the value 0 because the initial presumption in research that uses hypothesis testing is that $H_0$ is true. Such a $t$ distribution that is centered symmetrically about 0 is called a *central t distribution*. (Not all central distributions are symmetrical.) However, when we construct a confidence interval for $\mu_a - \mu_b$ or for $\Delta$ there is no null hypothesis being tested at that time, so the relevant sampling distribution is a $t$ distribution that may not be centered at 0 and may not be symmetrical. Such a $t$ distribution is called a *noncentral t distribution*.

The noncentral $t$ distribution differs more from the central $t$ distribution with respect to its center and degree of skew the more $\mu_a - \mu_b$ or $\Delta$ depart from 0 and the smaller the sample sizes (or, precisely, the degrees of freedom). Therefore, if assumptions are satisfied, the more $\mu_a - \mu_b$ or $\Delta$ depart from 0, and the smaller the sample sizes, the more improvement there will be in the accuracy of confidence intervals that are based on the noncentral $t$ distribution instead of the central $t$ distribution. Thus, ESCI and much of the other modern software for the construction of such confidence intervals is based on the noncentral $t$ distribution.

It would not be possible to table useful representative values of $t$ from the noncentral $t$ distribution because its shape depends not only on degrees of freedom but also on the value of a parameter, called the *noncentrality parameter*, that is related to $\Delta$. Therefore, for example, for a given degrees of freedom the value of $t$ that would have 2.5% of the area of the distribution beyond it will typically not be the same within the central or a noncentral $t$ distribution if $H_0$ is false. Also, constructing a confidence interval for $\mu_a - \mu_b$ or for $\Delta$ using a noncentral $t$ distribution requires a procedure in which the lower limit and the upper limit of the interval have to be estimated separately because they are not equidistant from the sample value (i.e., $\overline{Y}_a - \overline{Y}_b$ or the standardized difference) in this case. Thus, such a confidence interval is not necessarily a symmetrical one bounded by the point estimate plus or minus a margin of error. The procedure is an iterative (repetitive) one in which successive approximations of each confidence limit are made until a value is found that has .025 (in the case of a 95% CI) of the noncentral $t$ distribution beyond it. Therefore, software is required for the otherwise prohibitively laborious construction of confidence intervals using noncentral distributions.

For detailed discussions of the construction of confidence intervals that are based on noncentral distributions, consult Cumming and Finch (2001), Smithson (2001, 2003), Steiger and Fouladi (1997), Thompson (2002), and the references therein. Smithson's (2001) procedure uses SPSS scripts. Additional applicable statistical packages include SAS and STATISTICA. Note that literature on the noncentral $t$ distribution often uses the symbol $\Delta$, which we use to represent the standardized difference between two population means, to represent instead the noncentrality parameter for the noncentral $t$ distribution. The noncentrality parameter is a function of how far $\mu_a - \mu_b$ is from 0, as is $\Delta$ as we use it. Note again that the noncentrality approach to the construction of confidence intervals assumes normality and homoscedasticity, whereas the bootstrap approach that was discussed in chapter 2 does not.

## THE COUNTERNULL EFFECT SIZE

Recall that a typical null hypothesis about $\mu_a$ and $\mu_b$ is that $\mu_a - \mu_b = 0$. This $H_0$ implies another; namely, $H_0$: $\Delta = 0$. In traditional significance testing if the obtained $t$ is not far enough away from 0, one decides not to reject $H_0$, and, by implication, one concludes that the $t$ test result provides insufficient evidence that $\Delta$ is other than 0. However, some consider such reasoning to be incomplete. For example, suppose that the sample $d$ is above 0 but insufficiently so to attain statistical significance. This result can be explained, as is traditional, by the population $\Delta$ actually being 0, whereas the sample $d$ happened by chance (sampling variability) to overestimate $\Delta$ in this instance of research. However, an equally plausible explanation of the result is that $\Delta$ is actually above 0, and more above 0 than $d$ is, so $d$ happened by chance to underestimate $\Delta$ here. Therefore, according to this reasoning, a value of $d$ that is beyond 0 (above or below 0) by a certain amount is providing just as much evidence that $\Delta = 2d$ as it is providing evidence that $\Delta = 0$ because $d$ is no closer to 0 (1 $d$ distance away from 0) than $d$ is to $2d$ (1 $d$ distance away from $2d$). For example, if $d$ is, say, $+0.60$, this result is just as consistent with $\Delta = +1.20$ as with $\Delta = 0$ because $+0.60$ is just as close to $+1.20$ as it is to 0. The sample $d$ is just as likely to be underestimating $\Delta$ by a certain amount as it is to be overestimating $\Delta$ by that amount (except for some positive bias as is discussed next).

In the just-given example, assuming that a $t$ test results in $t$ and, by implication, $d$ being statistically insignificantly different from 0, it would be as justifiable to conclude that $d$ is insignificantly different from $+1.20$ as it would be to conclude that $d$ is insignificantly different from 0. We must note, however, that the reasoning in this section is only approximately true because of the bias that standardized-difference estimators have toward overestimating effect size. The reasoning is more accurate when larger sample sizes or a bias-adjusted estimator are used, as previously discussed.

This reasoning leads to a measure of effect size called the *counternull value of an effect size* (Rosenthal et al., 2000; Rosenthal & Rubin, 1994). Here, we simply call this measure the *counternull effect size*, $ES_{cn}$. In the case of standardized-difference effect sizes, and in the case of some (but not all) other kinds of effect sizes that we will discuss later in this book, if one is, by implication of $t$ testing, testing $H_0$: $ES_{pop} = 0$, then

$$ES_{cn} = 2ES. \tag{3.14}$$

When null-hypothesizing a value of $ES_{pop}$ other than 0, the more general formula is

$$ES_{cn} = 2ES - ES_{null}, \tag{3.15}$$

where $ES_{null}$ is the null-hypothesized value of $ES_{pop}$. See Rosenthal et al. (2000) for an example of the use of Equation 3.15. In our example, in which the estimate of effect size (i.e., $d$) = +0.60, application of Equation 3.14 yields the estimate $ES_{cn} = 2(+0.60) = +1.20$. Therefore, the *null-counternull interval* ranges from 0 to +1.20. In other words, the results are approximately as consistent with $\Delta = +1.20$ as they are with $\Delta = 0$.

For situations in which construction of a confidence interval for an effect size would be informative but not practicable, a researcher might consider reporting instead the $ES_{null}$ and $ES_{cn}$ as limits of a null–counternull interval. In our example, the lower limit of the null–counternull interval is 0 and the estimated upper limit is +1.20. Note that Equations 3.14 and 3.15 are applicable only to estimators that have a symmetrical sampling distribution, such as $d$. For equations for application to estimators that have asymmetrical distributions, such as the correlation coefficient $r$ (discussed in the next chapter), refer to Rosenthal et al. (2000), who also discussed a kind of confidence level for a null–counternull interval.

To understand such a confidence level (perhaps better called a *likelihood level*), recall the example in which $n_a = n_a = 20$ and $d = +0.70$. In that example the estimated $ES = d = +0.70$ and, assuming the usual $ES_{null} = 0$ in this hypothetical example, using Equation 3.14 $ES_{cn} = 2ES = 2(+0.70) = +1.40$. Suppose further that the two-tailed $p$ level for the obtained $t$ in this example had been found to be, say, $p = .04$. Recall also that a $t$ test conducted at the two-tailed alpha level is associated with a confidence interval for the difference between the two involved population means, a confidence interval in which one is approximately $100(1 - \alpha)\%$ confident. Similarly, in our example one can be approximately $100(1 - p)\% = 100(1 - .04)\% = 96\%$ confident in the null–counternull interval ranging from 0 to +1.40. Note that the confidence level for a confidence interval is based on a fixed probability $(1 - \alpha)$ that is set by the researcher, typically .95, whereas the confidence level for a null–counternull interval is based on a result-determined probability, the $p$ level attained by a test statistic such as $t$.

A null–counternull interval can provide information that is only somewhat conceptually similar to and not likely numerically the same as the information that is provided by a confidence interval. Both intervals bracket the obtained estimate of effect size, but, unlike the lower limit of a confidence interval, when $ES_{null} = 0$, the lower limit of the null–counternull interval will always be 0. Confidence intervals and null–counternull intervals cannot be directly compared or combined.

We previously suggested that researchers might consider constructing a null–counternull interval in situations in which construction of a confidence interval is not practicable. However, some researchers who are conducting studies in which their focus is not on significance testing might be inclined to avoid the null–counternull approach because, like significance testing, this approach focuses on the value 0, although, unlike significance testing, it also focuses on a value at some distance from 0 (the counternull value). More information about a variety of kinds of $ES_{cn}$ can be found in Rosenthal and Rubin (1994), Rosenthal et al. (2000), and in later chapters in this book.

## DEPENDENT GROUPS

Equations 3.3, 3.4, 3.5, and 3.6 are also applicable to dependent-group designs. In the case of a pretest–posttest design the means in the numerators of these four equations become the pretest and posttest means (e.g., $\overline{Y}_{pre}$ and $\overline{Y}_{post}$ when using Equations 3.3 or 3.5). In this case the standardizer (standard deviation) in Equation 3.3 can be $s_{pre}$ or $s_{post}$ (less common). The pooled standard deviation, $s_p$, can also be used to produce instead the $g$ of Equation 3.5. Because $n_a = n_b$, $s_p$ is merely the square root of the mean of $s_{pre}^2$ and $s_{post}^2$; $s_p = [(s_{pre}^2 + s_{post}^2)/2]^{1/2}$.

The choice of a standardizer for estimation of a standardized-difference effect size must be based on the nature of the population of scores to which one wants to generalize the results in the sample. Therefore, in the case of a pretest–posttest design some have argued that the standardizer for an estimator of $\Delta$ should not be based on a standard deviation of raw scores as in the previous paragraph, but instead it should be the standard deviation of the difference scores (e.g., the standard deviation, $s_D$, of the data in column D in Table 2.1 of chapter 2). Their argument is that in this design one should be interested in generalizing to the mean posttreatment–pretreatment differences in individuals relative to the population of such difference scores. However, each standardizer has its purpose. For example, in areas of research that consist of a mix of between-group and within-group studies of the same independent variable, greater comparability with results from between-group studies can be attained when a within-group study uses a standardizer that is based on the $s$ of the raw scores. Consult the references that were cited by Morris and DeShon (2002) for discussions supporting either the standard deviation of raw scores or the standard deviation of the posttreatment–pretreatment difference scores as the standardizer. Note that in the pretest–posttest design complications arise if one constructs a confidence interval for a $\Delta$ whose standardizer is based on $\sigma$ (based on a pretest or based on pooling) instead of $\sigma_D$. But if one uses $\sigma_D$ as the standardizer, then the methods that we previously discussed for independent groups can be used to construct an exact confidence interval (Cumming & Finch, 2001). Again, "exact" assumes that the usual assumptions are satisfied.

Consult Algina and Keselman (2003) for a method for constructing an approximate confidence interval in the case of dependent groups with equal or unequal variances. Their method appears to provide satisfactorily accurate confidence levels under the conditions they simulated for the true values of $\Delta$ and for the strengths of correlation between the two populations of scores. For a nominal .95 confidence level their slightly conservative method resulted in actual confidence levels that ranged from .951 to .972. The degree of correlation between the two populations of scores seemed to have little effect on the accuracy of the actual confidence levels; as the true value of $\Delta$ increased, the actual confidence levels became slightly more conservative. Specifically, as the true values of $\Delta$ ranged from 0 to 1.6, the actual confidence levels ranged from .951 to .971—values that are extremely close or satisfactorily close to the nominal confidence level of .95 in the simulations. The method can be undertaken using any software package that provides noncentrality parameters for noncentral $t$ distributions, such as SAS (the SAS function TNONCT), that Algina and Keselman (2003) recommended as being particularly useful for this purpose. Consult Wilcox (2003) for other approaches to effect sizes when comparing two dependent groups. In chapter 6 we discuss construction of confidence intervals for standardized-difference effect sizes when one is focusing on two of the multiple groups in a one-way between-groups or within-groups analysis of variance (ANOVA) design.

## QUESTIONS

1. In what circumstance might a standardized difference between means be more informative than a simple difference between means?
2. Define *latent variable*.
3. Assuming normality, interpret $d = +1.00$ when it is obtained by using Equation 3.1, and explain the interpretation.
4. If population variances are equal, what are two advantages of pooling sample variances to estimate the common population variance?

5. Distinguish among Glass' *d*, Cohen's *d*, and Hedges' *g*.
6. Why is it unlikely that Glass' *d* will equal Hedges' *g* even if population variances are equal?
7. What is the direction of bias of Hedges' *g* and Glass' *d*, what two factors influence this bias, and in what ways do these two factors influence the bias?
8. Why is Hedges' bias-adjusted version of *g* seldom used by researchers?
9. In what ways does heteroscedasticity cause problems for the use of standardized differences between means?
10. Which effect size is recommended when homoscedasticity is assumed, and why?
11. Discuss two approaches to estimating effect size that should be considered when homoscedasticity is not assumed.
12. Should all calculated estimates of effect size be reported by the researcher, and why?
13. What might be a solution to the problem of estimating effect size in the face of heteroscedasticity in areas of research that use a normed test for the measure of the dependent variable, and why is this so?
14. Why is nonnormality problematic for the usual interpretation of *d* or *g*?
15. In what way might a large effect size for a treatment for an addiction be too optimistically interpreted?
16. Describe two alternative standardized-difference estimators of effect size when there are outliers.
17. In what research context is the magnitude of the effect size of greatest interest?
18 Which part of expression 3.12 changes if one adopts a confidence level other than .95, and why?
19. Identify two ways in which a plan for data analysis can narrow the eventual confidence interval.
20. In a Results section, of what benefit is the presentation of a figure that contains current and past confidence intervals involving the same levels of an independent variable and the same dependent variable?
21. Contrast the central *t* distribution and a noncentral *t* distribution.
22. Which two factors influence the difference between the central and noncentral *t* distributions, and in what ways?
23. Define *counternull effect size* and *null–counternull interval*.
24. What is the rationale for a counternull effect size?
25. When might a researcher consider using a null–counternull interval?
26. Contrast a null–counternull interval and a confidence interval.
27. How can Equations 3.3, 3.4, 3.5, and 3.6 be applied to data from dependent groups?

# Chapter 4

# Correlational Effect Sizes for Comparing Two Groups

## THE POINT-BISERIAL CORRELATION

When $X$ and $Y$ are continuous variables the familiar Pearson correlation coefficient, $r$, provides an obvious estimator of effect size in terms of the size (magnitude of $r$) and direction (sign of $r$) of a linear relationship between $X$ and $Y$. However, thus far in this book, although the $Y$ variable has been continuous the independent variable ($X$) has been a dichotomous variable such as membership in Group a or Group b. Although computational formulas and software for $r$ obviously require both $X$ and $Y$ to be quantitative variables, calculating an $r$ between a truly dichotomous categorical $X$ variable and a quantitative $Y$ variable does not present a problem. By a *truly dichotomous* variable we mean a naturally dichotomous (or nearly so) variable, such as gender, or an independent variable that is created by assigning participants into two different treatment groups to conduct an experiment. We are not referring to the problematic procedure of creating a dichotomous variable by arbitrarily dichotomizing originally continuous scores into two groups, say, those above the median versus those below the median. When an originally continuous variable is dichotomized it will nearly always correlate lower with another variable than if it had not been dichotomized (Hunter & Schmidt, 2004). Similarly, as Hunter and Schmidt (2004) discussed, when a continuous variable has been dichotomized it cannot attain the usual maximum absolute value of correlation with a continuous variable, $|1|$.

The procedure for calculating an $r$ between a dichotomous variable and a quantitative variable is simply to code membership in Group a or Group b numerically. For example, membership in Group a can be coded as 1, and membership in Group b can be coded as 2. Thus, in a data file each member of Group a would be represented by entering a 1 in the $X$ column and each member of Group b would be represented by entering a 2 in the $X$ column. As usual, each participant's score on the dependent variable measure is entered in the $Y$ column of the data file. The magnitude of $r$ will remain the same regardless of which two numbers are chosen for the coding. The only aspect of the coding that the researcher must keep in mind when interpreting the obtained sample $r$ is which group was assigned the higher number. If $r$ is found to be positive, then the sample that had been assigned the higher number on $X$ (e.g., 2, instead of 1) tended to score higher than the other sample on the $Y$ variable. If $r$ is negative, then the sample that had been assigned the higher number on $X$ tended to score lower than the other sample on the $Y$ variable.

The correlation between a dichotomous variable and a continuous variable is called a *point-biserial correlation*, $r_{pb}$ in the sample, a commonly used estimator of effect size in the two-group case. When using $r_{pb}$ one does not have to look for statistical software that includes $r_{pb}$. One simply uses any software for the usual $r$ and enters the numerical codes in the $X$ column according to each participant's group membership. Refer to Levy (1967) for an alternative measure of effect size that is based on $r_{pb}$.

## EXAMPLE OF $r_{pb}$

To illustrate the use of $r_{pb}$ we again use the research that was discussed in chapter 3 in which the healthy parent–child relationship scores of mothers with normal children (Group b) were compared with those from mothers of disturbed children (Group a). In that example, $d = -.77$, indicating that, in the samples, mothers of normal children tended to outscore mothers of disturbed children by about .77 of a standard deviation unit. If we now code the mothers of the disturbed children with $X = 1$ and code the mothers of the normal children with $X = 2$, using any statistical software that calculates $r$ we now find that $r_{pb} = .40$. This result indicates that the sample that was coded 2 (normals) tended to outscore the sample that was coded 1 (disturbeds), a finding that $d$ already indicated in its own way. An $r$ of magnitude .4 would be considered to be moderately large in comparison to typical values of $r$ in behavioral research, as we discuss later in this chapter. Thus, finding that $d = -.77$ and $r_{pb} = .40$ suggest in their own ways that there is a moderately strong relationship between the independent and dependent variables in this example.

Software that calculates an $r$ ($r_{pb}$ in this case) will typically also test $H_0$: $r_{pop} = 0$ and provide a $p$ level for that test. There is an equation that relates $r_{pb}$ to $t$ (Equation 4.3), and the $p$ level attained by $r$ when conducting a two-tailed test of $H_0$: $r_{pop} = 0$ will be the same as the $p$ level attained by $t$ when conducting a two-tailed test of $H_0$: $\mu_a - \mu_b = 0$. Therefore, we already know $r_{pb} = .40$ is statistically significantly different from 0 because we found in chapter 3 that the sample means for the two kinds of mothers were significantly different in a $t$ test.

Values of $r$ and $r_{pb}$ are negatively biased (i.e., they tend to underestimate the correlation in the population, $r_{pop}$), usually slightly so. Bias is greater the closer $r_{pop}$ is to ± .5 and for small samples, but this is not of great concern if total sample size is, say, greater than 15 (Hedges & Olkin, 1985). When sample size is greater than 20 bias might be less than rounding error (Hunter & Schmidt, 2004). Exact values of an unbiased estimator as a function of $r$ (or $r_{pb}$) can be found in Table 1 in Hedges and Olkin (1985), who also provided the following equation for an approximately unbiased estimator,

$$r_{approx} = r + \frac{r\left(1 - r^2\right)}{2\left(N - 3\right)}.$$  (4.1)

Other versions of Equation 4.1 are available (e.g., Hunter & Schmidt, 2004), but a correction is rarely used because the bias is generally negligible.

## CONFIDENCE INTERVALS
## AND NULL–COUNTERNULL INTERVALS FOR $r_{pop}$

Construction of a confidence interval for $r_{pop}$ can be complex, and there may be no entirely satisfactory method. (When $r_{pop} \neq 0$, the sampling distribution of $r$ is not normal.) For details consult Hedges and Olkin (1985) and Wilcox (1996, 1997, 2003). Smithson (2003) presented a method for constructing an approximate confidence interval, noting that the approximation is less accurate the greater the absolute size of the correlation in the population and the smaller the sample size. Similarly, Wilcox (2003) presented an S-PLUS software function for a modified bootstrap method for a .95 CI that appears to have fairly accurate probability coverage (i.e., actual confidence level close to .95) provided that the absolute value of $r$ in the population is not extremely large, say, below .8 (but not 0). Such values for $r_{pop}$ would be the case in most correlational research in the behavioral sciences. (A basic bootstrap method was briefly introduced in chap. 2.) Wilcox's (2003) method seems to perform well when assumptions are violated, even with sample sizes as small as 20. These assumptions are discussed in the next section. [In the case of correcting correlation for attenuation attributable to unreliability (discussed later in this chapter in the section entitled "Unreliability") a confidence interval should first be constructed using the uncorrected $r$. Next, the limits of this confidence interval should be corrected by dividing by the square root of the reliability coefficient of the $X$ variable, or dividing by the product of the square roots of the reliability coefficients of the $X$ and $Y$ variables, as shown later in Equation 4.5 and immediately thereafter. Hunter and Schmidt (2004) provided extensive discussion of this topic.]

A null–counternull interval (discussed in chap. 3) can also be constructed for $r_{pop}$. If the null hypothesis is the usual $H_0$: $r_{pop} = 0$, the null value of such an interval is 0. Rosenthal et al. (2000) showed that the counternull value of an $r$, denoted $r_{cn}$ here, is given by

$$r_{cn} = \frac{2r}{\left(1 + 3r^2\right)^{\frac{1}{2}}}.$$ (4.2)

In the present example, $r_{pb} = .40$, so $r_{cn} = 2(.40) / [1 + 3(.40^2)]^{\frac{1}{2}} = .66$. Therefore, the interval runs from 0 to .66. Thus, the results would provide about as much support for the proposition that $r_{pop}$ is .66 as they would for the proposition that $r_{pop} = 0$. Perhaps a null–counternull interval for $r_{pop}$ would be most relevant for researchers who focus on the null-hypothesized value of 0 for $r_{pop}$. The counternull value brings attention also to an equally plausible value.

## ASSUMPTIONS OF $r$ AND $r_{pb}$

In the case of $r_{pb}$ there are three distributions of $Y$ to consider: the distribution of $Y$ for Group a, the distribution of $Y$ for Group b, and the overall distribution of $Y$ for the combined data for the two groups. The first two distributions are called the *conditional distributions* of $Y$ (conditional on whether one is considering the distribution of $Y$ values at $X = $ a or at $X = $ b) and the overall distribution of $Y$ is called the marginal distribution of $Y$. The three distributions are depicted in Fig. 4.1.

Recall that the ordinary t test assumes homoscedasticity. The Welch version of the $t$ test counters heteroscedasticity somewhat by using the $df_w$ of Equation 2.5 instead of $df = n_a + n_b - 2$ and by using $s_a^2$ and $s_b^2$ separately in the denominator of $t$ instead of pooling these two variances. Therefore, if software is using the ordinary $t$ test to test $H_0: r_{pop} = 0$, the software is assuming homoscedasticity; that is, it is assuming equal variances of the populations' conditional distributions of $Y$. If there is heteroscedasticity the denominator of $t$ (standard error of the difference between two means) will be incorrect, possibly resulting in lower statistical power and less accurate confidence intervals (Wilcox, 2003). Also, if the ordinary $t$ test is used and the printout $p$ and the actual (unknown) $p$ are below .05, this result might not in fact be signaling a nonzero correlation, but instead it merely might be signaling heteroscedasticity. Heteroscedasticity is actually another kind of dependency between $X$ and $Y$, a dependency between the variability of $Y$ and the value of $X$.

If the software's printout for $r$ does not indicate the statistical significance of $r$ and does not include the value of $t$ that corresponds to the obtained $r_{pb}$, convert $r_{pb}$ to $t$ using

$$t = r_{pb}\left[\frac{N-2}{1 - r_{pb}^2}\right]^{\frac{1}{2}},$$ (4.3)

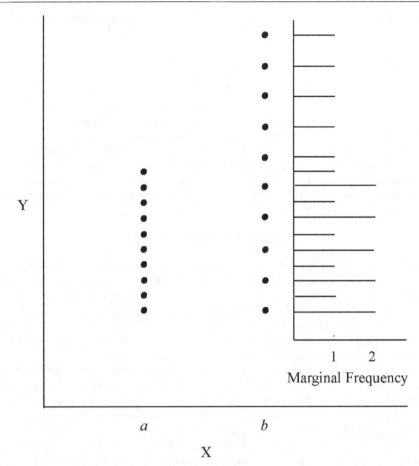

FIG. 4.1.   Unequal variabilities of the Y scores in Groups a and b results in skew in the marginal frequency distribution of Y.

where $N$ is the total number of participants. Then use a $t$ table, at the $df = N - 2$ row, to ascertain the statistical significance of this value of $t$, which, again, will also be the statistical significance of $r_{pb}$. If the table does not have a row for the $df$ required, interpolate for the significance level as was previously shown.

Bivariate normality is an assumption underlying $r$. However, although skew in the opposite direction for variables $X$ and $Y$ lowers the maximum value of $r$ (J. B. Carroll, 1961; Cohen, Cohen et al., 2003), nonnormality itself does not necessarily cause a problem for $r$, so we refer the interested reader to Glass and Hopkins (1996) for a brief discussion of the criteria for bivariate normality. Indeed, when using $r_{pb}$ the dichotomous $X$ variable cannot be normally distributed. The distribution of the $X$ variable in this case is merely a stack of, say, 1s and a stack of, say, 2s. However, outliers (even one outlier) and distributions with thicker tails (heavy-tailed distributions) than those of the normal curve can affect $r$, and $r_{pop}$ and a confidence interval for it (Wilcox, 2003). The use of large sample sizes might help in this situation somewhat but not under all conditions. Even slight changes in the shape of the overall distribution of $Y$ in the population can greatly alter the value of $r_{pop}$ (Wilcox, 1997, 2003).

Note that one should distinguish between a difference in the shapes of the conditional distributions for the underlying construct (e.g., true aptitude or a personality factor) in the two populations and a difference in the two conditional distributions for the measure of that construct (e.g., scores on a test of aptitude or on a test of a personality factor) in the two samples (Cohen, Cohen et al., 2003). In the case of different distributional shapes for the construct in the two populations, the resulting reduction in an upper limit below $|1|$ for $r_{pop}$ is not a problem; it is a natural phenomenon. However, there is a problem of $r_{pb}$ underestimating $r_{pop}$ if the two sample distributions differ in shape when the two populations do not or if the two sample distributions differ more in shape than the two population distributions do.

In reports of research that uses $r$ or $r_{pb}$ authors should include scatterplots and cautionary remarks about the possible effects of outliers, heavy tails, and heteroscedasticity. In the case of $r_{pb}$ a scatterplot may well suggest heteroscedasticity with respect to the two conditional distributions of $Y$ and skew of the marginal distribution of $Y$ or neither heteroscedasticity nor skew because such skew and heteroscedasticity are often associated (Cohen et al., 2003). Such is the case in the example in Fig. 4.1. In the case of $r$ a scatterplot that suggests skew in the marginal distribution of $X$ and/or $Y$ may well also suggest curvilinearity, heteroscedasticity, and nonnormal conditional distributions (McNemar, 1962). Recall that $r$ reflects only a linear component of a relationship between two variables in a sample. Curvilinearity reduces the absolute value of $r$. For detailed discussions of such matters in a broader context (regression diagnostics), consult Belsey, Kuh, and Welsch (1980), Cook and Weisberg (1982), and Fox (1999).

Refer to Wilcox (2001, 2003) for additional discussions of assumptions underlying the use of $r_{pop}$, shortcomings of nonparametric measures of correlation (Spearman's rho and Kendall's tau), and for alternatives to $r_{pop}$ for measuring the relationship between two variables. Wilcox (2003) also provided S-PLUS software functions for detecting outliers and for calculating robust alternative measures of correlation. Note that outliers are not always problematic. An $X_i$ and $Y_i$ pair of scores in which $X_i$ and $Y_i$ are equally outlying may not be importantly influencing the value of $r$. For example, a person who is 7 ft tall (outlier) and weighs 275 lb (outlier in the same direction) will not likely influence the sample value of the correlation between height and weight as much as person who is an outlier with respect to just one of the variables. The most influential case for an otherwise positive $r$ would be one in which a person is an outlier in the opposite direction with respect to $X$ and $Y$, influencing $r$ downward. Note finally that the use of $r$ and $r_{pb}$ do not assume equality of the variances of the $X$ and $Y$ variables.

## UNEQUAL SAMPLE SIZES

If $n_a \neq n_b$ in experimental research the value of $r_{pb}$ might be attenuated (reduced) causing an underestimation of $r_{pop}$. The degree of such attenuation of $r_{pb}$ increases the more disproportional $n_a$ and $n_b$ are and the larger the actual value of $r_{pop}$ is (McNemar, 1962). Note that when sample sizes are unequal, there is an increased chance that $X$ and $Y$ might be skewed in the opposite direction because unequal sample sizes in the case of the point-biserial $r$ amounts to skew in the $X$ variable. As noted in the previous section, skew of $X$ and $Y$ in the opposite direction lowers the absolute value of $r$. One can calculate an attenuation-corrected $r_{pb}$, that we denote as $r_c$, using

$$r_c = \frac{ar_{pb}}{\left[\left(a^2 - 1\right)r_{pb}^2 + 1\right]^{1/2}}, \tag{4.4}$$

where $a = [.25 / pq]^{1/2}$, and $p$ and $q$ are the proportions of total sample size in each group (Hunter & Schmidt, 2004). For example, if $N = 100$, $n_a = 60$, and $n_b = 40$, then $p = 60/100 = .6$ and $q = 40/100 = .4$. Of course, it does not matter which of $n_a$ or $n_b$ is associated with $p$ or $q$ because $pq = qp$. Note that in experimental research in which the sample sizes are unequal, different researchers who are studying the same $X$ variable and same $Y$ variable may obtain different values of uncorrected $r_{pb}$ partly due to different values of $n_a/n_b$ from study to study. Therefore, values of $r_{pb}$ should not be compared or meta-analyzed in such cases unless the values of $r_{pb}$ have been corrected using Equation 4.4. Refer to Hunter and Schmidt (2004) for further discussion.

## UNRELIABILITY

Unreliability is another factor that can attenuate $r_{pb}$ and standardized-difference estimators of effect sizes. Roughly, for our purpose here, *unreliability* means the extent to which a score is reflecting measurement error, something other than the true value of what is being measured. Measurement error causes scores from measurement instance to measurement instance to be inconsistent, unrepeatable, or unreliable in the sense that one cannot rely on getting consistent observed scores for an individual from the test or measure even when the magnitude of the underlying attribute that is being measured has not changed.

One common way to estimate the reliability of a test is to administer the test to a sample (the larger the better) and then readminister the same test to the same sample within a short enough period of time so that there is little opportunity for the sample's true scores to change. In this case measurement error would be reflected by inconsistency in the observed scores. If one calls the scores from the first administration of the test $Y_1$ values and calls the scores from the second administration of the test $Y_2$ values, and then one calculates the $r$ between these $Y_1$ values and $Y_2$ values, one will have an estimate of test reliability. Such a procedure is called *test–retest reliability* and the resulting $r$ is called a *reliability coefficient*, denoted $r_{yy}$. Because $r$ ranges from $-1$ to $+1$, ideally one would want $r_{yy}$ to be as close to $+1$ as possible, indicating perfect reliability. Unfortunately, some psychological and behavioral science tests (and perhaps some medical tests) have only modest values of $r_{yy}$. For example, the least reliable of the tests of personality may have $r_{yy}$ values that are approximately equal to .3 or .4. At the other extreme, we expect a modern digital scale to measure weight with $r_{yy}$ close to 1.

Because $r_{pb}$, as an $r$, is intended to estimate the covariation of $X$ and $Y$, that is, the extent to which true variation in $Y$ is related to true variation in $X$, unreliability results in an attenuation of $r$. The $r$ is attenuated because the measurement error that underlies the unreliability of $Y$ adds variability to $Y$ (increases $s_y$), but this additional variability is an unsystematic variability that is not related to variation in the $X$ variable. (Recall from introductory statistics that $r$ is a mean of products of $z$ scores, $r = \Sigma[z_x z_y] / N$, and that a $z$ score has $s$ in its denominator.) Because the $t$ statistic and standardized-difference estimators of effect sizes have $s$ values in their denominators and unreliability increases $s$, unreliability reduces the value of $t$ and a standardized-difference estimator of effect size.

Although simple physical measurements can be made very reliably, when using measures of more abstract dependent variables, such as personality variables, unreliability should be of some concern to the researcher. In such cases the researcher should conduct a search of the literature to choose the most reliable alternative measure that may be available for the dependent variable and for the type of participants at hand. If the researcher conducts in-house test–retest reliability research to estimate $r_{yy}$ prior to using a particular measure of the dependent variable in the main research, or learns of the measure's $r_{yy}$ from a search of the literature, the value of $r_{yy}$ should be included in the research report. The value of $r_{yy}$ is not only relevant to the magnitude of the reported effect size, but it is also relevant to the statistical power of the test of significance that was used to make an inference about the effect size, especially if the result was statistically insignificant. Unreliability can reduce the power of a statistical test sufficiently to cause a Type II error.

Information about the reliability (and validity) of many published tests can be found in the regularly updated book called the *Mental Mea-*

*surements Yearbook* (as of the time of this writing, *The Fifteenth Mental Measurements Yearbook*; Plake, Impara, & Spies, 2003). An index of the tests and measurements that have been reviewed there can currently be found at http://www.unl.edu/buros/indexbimm.html. Wilkinson and the American Psychological Association's Task Force on Statistical Inference (1999) noted that an assessment of reliability is required to interpret estimates of effect size. A confidence interval for $r_{yy}$ in the population can be constructed as was discussed in this chapter for any $r_{pop}$.

Note that it may be the case that reliability is greater when using as participants a group of people with certain demographics than when using another group of people with different demographics. For examples, $r_{yy}$ may be different when using men or women, young or old, or college students or nonstudents. The most relevant $r_{yy}$ that a researcher should seek in the literature is an $r_{yy}$ that has been obtained when using participants who are as similar as possible to the participants in the pending research. If a relevant $r_{yy}$ cannot be found in a search of the literature, a researcher who is using a measure of questionable reliability should consider conducting a reliability study on an appropriate sample prior to the main research.

The reliabilities of the scores across studies of the same underlying outcome variable may vary either because of relevant differences between the participants across studies or because of the use of different measures of the outcome variable. Therefore, one should not compare effect sizes without considering the possible influence of such differential reliability.

Researchers should also be interested in the reliability with which the *X* variable is being measured or administered because the previous discussion about the reliability of the *Y* variable also applies to the *X* variable. Even in the case of $r_{pb}$, in which *X* has only two values, membership in Group a or Group b, unreliability of the *X* variable can occur, along with its attenuating effects. For example, consider the case of research with preexisting groups, such as the comparison of the mothers of schizophrenic children and normal children that we undertook in chapter 3 and earlier in this chapter. In such cases $r_{pb}$ and *d* would be attenuated to the extent that the diagnosis of schizophrenia was made unreliably. In experimental research the reliability of administration of the dichotomous *X* variable is maintained to the extent that all members of Group a are in fact treated in the same way (the "a" way) and all members of Group b are treated in the same way (the "b" way) as planned and that all members of a group understand and follow their instructions in the same way.

In some areas of research it may be more difficult to administer treatment reliably than in other areas of research. For example, in experiments that compare Psychotherapy a to Psychotherapy b, although with any degree of care on the part of the clinical researcher all members of a particular therapy group will very likely receive at least the same general kind of therapy, for a variety of reasons it may not be possible to treat all members of a particular therapy group in exactly the same way in all details for every moment of the course of therapy. Psychotherapy can be a complex and dynamic process involving two interacting people, the therapist and the patient, not a static exactly repeatable procedure in which each patient in a group is readily spoon-fed the therapy in exactly the same way. The same kind of problem may arise in research that compares two methods of teaching. The extent to which a treatment is administered according to the research plan, and therefore administered consistently across all of the members of a particular treatment group, is called *treatment integrity*. To maintain treatment integrity, for some behavior therapies there are detailed manuals for the consistent administration of those particular therapies.

When treatment integrity has not been at the highest level, the values of the estimator of effect size, the value of $t$, and the power of the $t$ test may have been seriously reduced by such unreliability. In such cases a researcher should comment about the level of treatment integrity in the research report. A more general name for treatment integrity in experimental research is *experimental control*. Of course, researchers should control all extraneous variables to maximize the extent to which variation of the independent variable itself is responsible for variation of the values of the dependent variable from Group a to Group b. To the extent that extraneous variables are not controlled, they will inflate $s$ values with unsystematic variability, resulting in the previously discussed consequences for $t$ testing and estimation of effect sizes.

There is an equation for correcting for the attenuation in $r$, $r_{pb}$, or other estimator of effect size that has been caused by unreliable measurement of the dependent variable (Hunter & Schmidt, 2004; Schmidt & Hunter, 1996). The equation for correcting for attenuation results in an estimate of an adjusted effect size that would be expected to occur if $Y$ could be measured perfectly reliably. In general an estimator of effect size that is adjusted for unreliability of the scores on the dependent variable, denoted here $ES_{adj}$, is given by

$$ES_{adj} = \frac{ES}{r_{yy}^{1/2}}. \qquad (4.5)$$

In the case of nonexperimental studies, an adjustment for unreliability of the $X$ variable can be made by substituting $r_{xx}$ for $r_{yy}$ in Equation 4.5, or $(r_{xx} r_{yy})^{1/2}$ can be used instead for the denominator to adjust for both kinds of reliability at once. For the more complicated case of adjusting estimators of effect size for unreliability of the $X$ variable in experimental studies and for other discussion, refer to Hunter and Schmidt (1994, 2004). For additional discussion of correction of effect sizes for unreliability, consult Baugh (2002a, 2002b). If a confidence interval is to be constructed for the population value of a reliability coefficient, then Equation 4.5 can be applied separately to the lower and to the upper limit of the effect size that is to be adjusted. In this case the adjusted and the original lower and upper limits should be reported.

The adjustment for unreliability is rarely used, apparently for one or more reasons other than the fact that, unfortunately, interest in psychometrics as part of undergraduate and graduate curricula is decreasing. (Psychometrics is, defined minimally here, the study of methods for constructing tests, scales, and measurements in general and assessing their reliability and validity.) The first possible reason for not making the adjustment is simply that $r_{yy}$ may not be known in the literature and the researcher does not want to delay the research by preceding it by one's own in-house reliability check. Second, some researchers use variables whose scores are known to be, or are believed to be, generally very reliable. Third, some researchers may be satisfied merely to have their results attain statistical significance, believing that unreliability was not a problem if it was not extreme enough to have caused a statistically insignificant result. Note, however, that even if results do attain statistical significance, reliability may still have been low enough to result in a substantial underestimation of effect size for the underlying dependent variable in the population. Fourth, some researchers might be concerned that their estimates of effect size will be less accurate to the extent that their estimation of reliability is inaccurate. We have not included the possibility that some researchers might be forgoing the correction for unreliability because they believe that underestimation of effect size is acceptable and only overestimation is unacceptable. Refer to Hunter and Schmidt (2004) for a contrary opinion. The reader is encouraged to reflect on the merits of all of these reasons for not calculating and reporting a corrected estimate of effect size.

Finally, there is a philosophical objection to the adjustment on the part of some researchers who believe that it is not worthwhile to calculate an estimate of an effect size that is only theoretically possible in an ideal world in which the actually unreliable measure of the dependent variable could be measured perfectly reliably, an ideal that is not currently realized for the measures of their dependent variables. Hunter and Schmidt (2004) represent the opposing view with regard to correcting for unreliability and other artifacts. To accommodate both sides in this controversy we recommend that researchers consider reporting adjusted estimates of effect size and the original unadjusted estimates. In this regard researchers should recognize that some readers of their reports might be more, or less, interested in the reporting of corrected estimates of effect sizes than the researchers are.

In the preceding discussion we did not mention the fact that correcting for unreliability increases sampling variability of an effect size. However, the greater the reliability of a measure, the less the increase in sampling variability that will result from the correction for unreliability. Therefore, one should still strive to use the most reliable measures even when planning to use the correction for unreliability. Consult Hunter and Schmidt (2004) for an elaboration of this issue and a discussion of correcting estimates of effect size for unreliability when the estimates are to be combined in a meta-analysis. Hunter and Schmidt (2004) provided a very extensive and authoritative treatment of the attenuating effects of artifacts such as unreliability, and correcting for them. Additional artifacts include sampling error, imperfect construct validity of the independent and dependent variables, computational and other errors, extraneous factors introduced by aspects of a study's procedures, and restricted range. It would be far beyond the scope of this book to discuss this list of topics. It will have to suffice for us to discuss only the artifact of restricted range, to which we turn in the next section. Refer to Schmidt, Le, and Ilies (2003) for discussion of a broader type of reliability coefficient (the coefficient of equivalence and stability) that estimates measurement error from an additional source beyond those that the test–retest reliability coefficient reflects. For further discussions of unreliability refer to Onwuegbuzie and Levin (2003) and the references therein. At the time of this writing, Windows-based commercial software is available, called "Hunter-Schmidt Meta-Analysis Programs Package" for calculating artifact-adjusted estimates of correlations and standardized differences between means. These programs were written to accompany the book on meta-analysis by Hunter and Schmidt (2004), but they also include programs for correcting individual correlations and standardized differences between means for primary researchers. Currently the package can be ordered from frank-schmidt@uiowa.edu, flschmidt@mchsi.com, or huy-le@uiowa.edu. Hunter and Schmidt (2004) discussed other software for similar purposes.

## RESTRICTED RANGE

Another possible attenuator of $r_{pb}$ is called *restricted* (or *truncated*) *range*, that usually means using samples whose extent of variation on the independent variable is less than the extent of variation of that variable in the population to which the results are to be generalized. An example of restricted range would be research in which patients generally receive up to, say, 26 weeks of a certain therapy in the "real world" of clinical practice, but a researcher studying the effect of duration of therapy compares a control group (0 weeks) to a treated group that is intentionally given, say, 16 weeks of that therapy. Another example would be drug research involving a drug for which the usual prescribed doses in clinical practice ranges from, say, 250 mg to 600 mg, but a researcher compares groups that are intentionally prescribed, say, either 300 mg or 500 mg. An example of the effect of restricted range is the lower $r$ between SAT scores and GPAs at universities with the most demanding admissions standards (restricting most admissions to those ranging from high to very high SATs), compared to the $r$ between SATs and GPAs at less restrictive universities (accepting students across a wider range of SAT scores).

The examples thus far are examples of *direct range restriction* because the researcher knows in advance that the range of the independent variable is restricted. Instances in which this range is restricted because the available participants merely happen to be, instead of being selected to be, less variable than the population are examples of *indirect range restriction*. Hunter and Schmidt (2004) discussed methods for correcting for direct and indirect range restriction. However, as should be the case under a fixed-effect approach, when generalizations of results are confined to populations of whom the samples are representative in their range of the independent variable, instead of more general populations, no such correction need be made.

Consult Chen and Popovich (2002), Cohen, Cohen et al. (2003), and Hunter and Schmidt (2004) for further discussion of restricted range and how to correct for it, and consult Auguinis and Whitehead (1997) and Callender and Osburn (1980) for related discussions. Many additional references can be found in Chan and Chan (2004). Note that restricted range in the measure of the dependent variable can occur if would-be high scoring or would-be low scoring participants drop out of the research before their data are obtained. Figure 4.2 depicts the great lowering of the value of $r$ (compared to $r_{pop}$) in samples in which $X$ varies much less than it does in the population. Hunter and Schmidt (2004) provided a statistical correction for the case in which restriction of the range of the dependent variable is not accompanied by restriction of the range of the independent variable.

Although typically not the case, sometimes restricted range can cause an increase in r. Refer to Wilcox (2001) for an example involving a curvilinear relationship in which restricted range causes an increase in the magnitude of $r$ and a change in its sign when the restricted range results from the removal of outliers. Suppose also, for example, that a relationship between two variables is curvilinear in the population and the sample is one in which the range of $X$ is restricted. In this case the magnitude and sign of r in the sample can depend on whether the range is restricted to low, moderate, or high values of $X$. This case is depicted in Fig. 4.3. Recall again that $r$ reflects only a linear component of a relationship between two variables.

In the case of standardized-difference estimators of effect size, not letting Treatment a and Treatment b differ as much in the research as they do or might do in real-world application of these two treatments is also a restriction of range that lowers the value of the estimator. In experimental research the extent of difference between or among the treatments is called the *strength of manipulation*. A weaker manipulation of the independent variable in the research setting than occurs in the world of practice would be a case of restricted range.

Restricted range is not only likely to lower the value of any kind of estimator of effect size, it can also lower the value of test statistics, such as $t$, thereby lowering statistical power. Therefore, in applied areas researchers should use ranges of the independent variable that are as similar as possible to those that would be found in the population to which the results are to be generalized. Note in this regard that it is also possi-

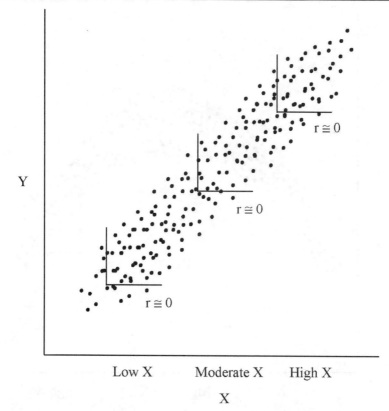

Y

Low X          Moderate X     High X

X

FIG. 4.2.　A case in which the overall correlation between $X$ and $Y$ ($r_{pop}$) is much higher than it would be estimated to be if the range of $X$ in the sample were restricted to only low values, only moderate values, or only high values.

ble, but we warn against it, for an applied researcher to use an excessive range of the independent variable, a range that increases the value of the estimate of effect size and increases statistical power, but at a price of being unrealistic (externally invalid) in comparison to the range of the independent variable that would be used in practice.

Consider clinical research involving a disease for which there is at least one somewhat effective treatment and for which it is known that without treatment there is not a spontaneous remission of the disease. Because using no treatment is already known in this case to be worse than using the current treatment, conducting research on this disease by comparing a control group (no treatment) with a group that is given a new proposed treatment results in a wide range of the independent variable and might yield a relatively large estimate of effect size and high statistical power but at a price of being unrealistic as well as unethical. The more realistic and ethical research on treating this disease

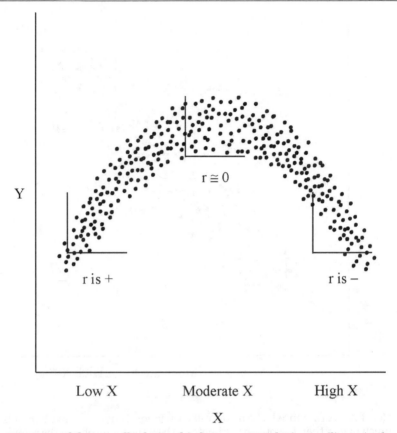

FIG. 4.3.   If the overall relationship between X and Y is curvilinear in the population, restricting the range of X in the sample to only low, only moderate, or only high values can influence the size and sign of r in the sample.

would compare a group of patients that is given the current best treatment and a group that is given the new proposed treatment. Similarly, obviously in educational research one would not conduct research that compares the performance of children who are taught a basic subject in a new way to the performance of a control group of children who are not taught the subject at all. Consult Abelson (1995) for a discussion of the *causal efficacy ratio* as an effect size that is relative to the *cause size* (i.e., an effect size that is relative to the strength of the manipulation). Also refer to Tryon's (2001) discussion of such an effect size. Chan and Chan (2004) discussed the results of Monte Carlo simulations of a bootstrap method for estimating the standard error and constructing a confidence interval for a correlation coefficient that has been corrected for range restriction.

## SMALL, MEDIUM, AND LARGE EFFECT SIZE VALUES

Because it is a type of $z$ score, there is no theoretical limit to the magnitude of a standardized-difference effect size, and theoretically $r_{pop}$ can range from $-1$ to $+1$. However, some readers of this book may want to have a better sense of the different magnitudes of estimates of effect sizes that have been reported so that they can be better able to place newly encountered estimates in context. In behavioral, psychological, and educational research, standardized-difference estimates are rarely more extreme than (ignoring sign) 2.00, and $r_{pb}$ estimates are rarely beyond .70, with both kinds of estimates typically being very much less extreme than these values.

Categorizing values of estimates of effect size as small, medium, or large is necessarily somewhat arbitrary. Such categories are, as Cohen (1988) pointed out, very relative terms—relative, for example, to such factors as the particular area of research and to its degree of experimental control of extraneous variables and the reliabilities of the scores on its measures of dependent variables. For example, an effect size of a certain magnitude may be relatively large if it occurs in some area of research in social psychology, whereas that same value may not be relatively large if it occurs in some possibly more controlled area of research such as neuropsychology. Also, even in the same field of study two observers of a given value of effect size may rate that value differently.

With appropriate tentativeness and a disclaimer Cohen (1988) offered admittedly rough criteria for small, medium, and large effect sizes, and examples within each category. (We ignore the sign of the effect sizes, which is not relevant here.) We also relate Cohen's criteria to the distribution of standardized-difference estimates of effect sizes that were found by Lipsey and Wilson (1993) in psychological, behavioral, and educational research and to the findings reported by Grissom (1996) on psychotherapy research and cited previously in chapter 3.

Cohen (1988) categorized as small $\Delta \leq .20$ and $r_{pop} \leq .10$, with regard to the point-biserial correlation. Cohen's examples of sample values of effect size that fall into this category include (a) the slight superiority of mean IQ in nontwins compared to twins, (b) the slightly greater mean height of 16-year-old girls compared to 15-year-old girls, and (c) some differences between women and men on some scales of the Wechsler Adult Intelligence Test. Lipsey and Wilson (1993) found that the lowest 25% of the distribution of psychological, behavioral, and educational examples of standardized-difference estimators of effect size were on the order of $d \leq .30$, which is equivalent to $r_{pb} \leq .15$ and somewhat supports Cohen's criteria.

Cohen (1988) categorized as medium, $\Delta = .5$ and $r_{pop} = .243$. Consistent with these criteria for a medium effect size, Lipsey and Wilson (1993) found that the median $d = .5$. This criterion is also consistent with typical effect sizes in counseling psychology (Haase, Waechter, &

Solomon, 1982) and in social psychology (Cooper & Findley, 1982). Cohen's approximate examples include the greater mean height of 18-year-old women compared to 14-year-old girls and the greater mean IQ of clerical compared to semi-skilled workers and professional compared to managerial workers. Recall from chapter 3 that Grissom (1996) found a median $d = .44$ when comparing placebo groups to control groups in psychotherapy research and a median $d = .58$ when comparing treated groups to placebo groups, which are roughly equivalent to $r_{pb} = .22$ and $.27$, respectively.

Cohen (1988) categorized as large $\Delta \geq .8$ and $r_{pop} \geq .371$. His examples include the greater mean height of 18-year-old women compared to 13-year-old girls and a higher mean IQ of holders of PhD degrees compared to first-year college students. Somewhat consistent with Cohen's criteria, Lipsey and Wilson (1993) found that the top 25% of values of $d$ were $d \geq .67$, roughly corresponding to $r_{pb} \geq .32$. Recall again from chapter 3 that Grissom (1996) found that the most efficacious therapy produced a (very rare) median $d = 2.47$, roughly corresponding to $r_{pb} = .78$. Note that Cohen's (1988) lower bound for a medium $\Delta$ (i.e., .5) is equidistant from his upper bound for a small effect size ($\Delta = .2$) and his lower bound for a large effect size ($\Delta = .8$). Consult Cohen (1988) and Lipsey and Wilson (1993) for further discussion. Rosenthal et al. (2000), Wilson and Lipsey (2001), and chapter 5 of this book have tables that show the corresponding values of various kinds of measures of effect size ($\Delta$, $r_{pop}$, and others that are discussed in chap. 5).

Note that the designations of small, medium, and large effect sizes do not necessarily correspond to the degree of practical significance of an effect. As we previously noted, judgment about the practical significance of an effect depends on the context of the research, and the expertise and values of the person who is judging the practical significance. For example, finding a small lowering of death rate from a new therapy for a widespread and likely fatal disease would be of greater practical significance than finding a large improvement in cure rate for a new drug for athlete's foot. The practical significance of an effect is considered further in the next section. Refer to Glass et al. (1981) for opposition to the designations small, medium, and large.

Sometimes the practical significance of an effect can be measured tangibly. For example, Breaugh (2003) reviewed cases of utility analyses in which estimates were made of the amount of money that employers could save by subjecting job applicants to realistic job previews (RJPs). Although the correlation between the independent variable of RJP versus no RJP and the dependent variable of employee turnover was very small, $r = .09$, employers could judge the practical significance of the results by evaluating the amount of money that utility analysis estimated would be saved by the small reduction of employee turnover that was associated with the RJP program. Also, Breaugh (2003) cited an example from Martell, Lane, and Emrich (1996) in which small but consistent bias effects in ratings of the performance of female employees can result over the years in a large number of women unfairly denied promotion. Consult Prentice and Miller (1992) for additional examples of apparently small effect sizes that can be of practical importance.

When interpreting an estimate of effect size one should also consider the factors, discussed earlier in this chapter, that can affect the magnitude and statistical significance of such an estimate. Also, one should not be prematurely impressed with a reported nonzero $r$ or $d$ when there is no rational explanation for the supposed relationship and the result has not been replicated by other studies. Of course, such findings, especially when based on small samples, may be just chance findings. For examples, nonzero correlations have been reported over a certain period of time between stock market values and which football conference wins the Superbowl of United States football and the amount of butter produced in Bangladesh (both nonsense correlations?). There are likely many thousands of values of $r$ calculated annually throughout the world. Even if it were literally true that all $r_{pop} = 0$, at the $p < .05$ significance level approximately 5% of these thousands of $r$ values will falsely lead to a conclusion that $r_{pop} \neq 0$.

## BINOMIAL EFFECT SIZE DISPLAY

Rosenthal and Rubin (1982) presented a table to aid in the interpretation of any kind of $r$, including the point-biserial $r$. The table is called the *binomial effect size display, BESD*, and was intended especially to illustrate the possibly great practical importance of a supposedly small value for any type of $r$. The BESD, as we soon discuss, is not itself an estimator of effect size but is intended instead to be a hypothetical illustration of what can be inferred about effect size from the size of any $r$. The BESD has become a popular tool among researchers. We discuss its limitations in the next section.

The BESD develops from the fact that $r$ can also be applied to data in which both the $X$ and $Y$ variables are dichotomies. In the case of dichotomous $X$ and $Y$ variables the name for $r$ in a sample is the *phi coefficient*, $\phi$. For example, $X$ could be Treatment a versus Treatment b, and $Y$ could be the categories: participant better after treatment and participant not better after treatment. One codes $X$ values, say, 1 for Treatment a and, say, 2 for Treatment b, as one would if one were calculating $r_{pb}$, but now for calculating phi $Y$ is also coded numerically, say, 1 for better and, say, 2 for not better. Phi is simply the $r$ between the $X$ variable's set of 1s and 2s and the $Y$ variable's set of 1s and 2s. Although software may not seem to indicate that it can calculate phi, when calculating the usual $r$ for the data in a file with two values, such as 1 and 2, in the $X$ column and two values, such as 1 and 2, in the $Y$ column, the software is in fact calculating phi. (In chap. 8 we discuss another context for phi as an estimator of effect size and another way to calculate it.)

By supposing that $n_a = n_b$ and by treating a value of an $r$ for the moment as if it had been a value of phi, we now observe that one can construct a hypothetical table (the BESD) that illustrates another kind of interpretation or implication of the value of an $r$. For example, suppose that an obtained value of an $r$ is a modest .20. Although the $r$ is based on a continuous $Y$ variable, to obtain a different perspective on this result the BESD pretends for the moment that $X$ and $Y$ had both been dichotomous variables and that the $r = .20$ had, therefore, instead been a $\phi = .20$. Table 4.1 depicts what results would look like if $\phi = .20$ and, for example, $n_a = n_b = 100$. An $r$ equal to .20 might not seem to some to represent an effect size that might be of great practical importance. However, observe in Table 4.1 that if the $r$ of .20 had instead been a $\phi = .20$ (the basis of Table 4.1), such results would have indicated that 20% more participants improve under Treatment a than improve under Treatment b (i.e., 60% − 40% = 20%).

We observe in Table 4.1 that 60 out of a total of 100 participants (60%) in Treatment a are classified as being better after treatment than they had been before treatment, and 40 out of a total of 100 participants in Treatment b are classified as being better after treatment than they had been before treatment. These percentages are called the *success percentages* for the two treatments. The result appears now, in terms of the BESD-produced success percentages, to be more impressive. For example, if many thousands or millions of patients in actual clinical practice were going to be given Treatment a instead of the old Treatment b because of the results in Table 4.1 (assuming for the moment that the sample phi of .20 is reflecting a population phi of .20; Hsu, 2004), then we would be improving the health of an additional 20% of many thousands or millions of people beyond the number that would have been improved by the use of Treatment b.

The more serious the type of illness, the greater would be the medical and social significance of the present numerical result (assuming also that Treatment a were not prohibitively expensive or risky). The most extreme example would be the case of any fairly common and possibly fatal disease of which 20% more of hundreds of thousands or millions of patients worldwide would be cured by using Treatment a

TABLE 4.1

A BESD

| | Participant Better (Y = 1) | Participant Not Better (Y = 2) | Totals |
|---|---|---|---|
| Treatment a  (X = 1) | 60 | 40 | 100 |
| Treatment b  (X = 2) | 40 | 60 | 100 |

instead of Treatment b. Again, such results are more impressive than an $r = .20$ would seem to indicate at first glance. However, as Rosenthal et al. (2000) pointed out, the 20% increase in success percentage for Treatment a versus Treatment b does not apply directly to the original raw data because the BESD table is hypothetical. (This disclaimer leads to a criticism of the BESD that is discussed in the next section.) The BESD is simply a hypothetical way to interpret an $r$ (or $r_{pb}$) by addressing the following question: What if both $X$ and $Y$ had been dichotomous variables, and, therefore, the $r$ had been a phi coefficient, and the resulting $2 \times 2$ table had uniform margin totals (explained later), what would the increase in success percentage have been by using Treatment a instead of Treatment b? Note that in many instances of research the original data will already have arisen from a $2 \times 2$ table but not always one that satisfies the specific criteria for a BESD table, which is discussed in the next section.

In general for any $r$, to find the success percentage (better) for the treatment coded $X = 1$, use $100[.50 + (r/2)]\%$. Because the two percentages in a row of a BESD must add to 100%, the failure percentage for the row $X = 1$ is, of course, 100% minus the row's success percentage. The success percentage for the row $X = 2$ is given by $100[.50 - (r/2)]\%$, and its failure percentage is 100% minus the success percentage for that row. In Table 4.1, $r = \phi = .20$, so the success percentage for Treatment a is $100[.50 + (.20/2)]\% = 60\%$, and its failure percentage is $100\% - 60\% = 40\%$. The greater the value of $r$, the greater the difference will be between the success percentages of the two treatments. Specifically, the difference between these two success percentages will be given by $(100 r)\%$. Therefore, even before constructing the BESD one knows that when $r = .20$ the difference in success percentages will be $[100(.20)]\% = 20\%$ if the original data are recast into an appropriate BESD. Note that one can also construct a BESD, and estimate the difference in success percentages for the counternull value of $r$ by starting with Equation 4.2 and then proceeding as has just described in this section. We discuss other approaches to effect sizes for a $2 \times 2$ table in chapter 8.

## LIMITATIONS OF THE BESD

There are limitations of the BESD and its resulting estimation of the difference between the success percentages of two treatments. First, the difference in the success percentages from the BESD is only equal to $\phi$ if the overall success percentage = overall failure percentage = 50% and if the two groups are of the same size (Strahan, 1991). The result is a table that is said to have uniform margins. Observe that Table 4.1 satisfies these criteria because the two samples are of the same size, the overall (marginal) success percentage equals $(60 + 40)/200 = 50\%$, and the overall (marginal) failure percentage equals $(40 + 60)/200 = 50\%$. Note, however, that we are aware of an opinion that this first criticism is actually not a limitation but merely part of the definition of a BESD. Refer to Hsu (2004) for an argument that such an opinion is problematic in many cases.

When the criteria for a BESD are satisfied the resulting difference in success percentages is relevant to the hypothetical population whose data are represented by the BESD. However, are the results relevant to the population that gave rise to the original real data that were recast into the BESD table or relevant to any real population (Crow, 1991; Hsu 2004; McGraw, 1991)? The population for which the BESD-generated difference in success percentages in a table such as Table 4.1 is most relevant is a population in which each half received either Treatment a or Treatment b and half improved and half did not. Again, this limitation may be considered by some to be merely an inherent aspect of the definition of the BESD.

Cases in which the original data are available are the cases that are most relevant to this book because this book is addressed to those who produce data (primary researchers). It makes more sense in such cases of original 2 × 2 tables to compare the success rates for the two treatments based on the actual data instead of the hypothetical BESD. For example, in such cases one may use the relative risk or other effect sizes for data in a 2 × 2 table that are discussed in chapter 8. The measure that we call *the probability of superiority* in chapters 5 and 9 is also applicable. Also, suppose that the success percentage and failure percentage in the real population to which the sample results are to be generalized are not each equal to 50%. In this case a BESD-based difference between success percentages in the sample will be biased toward overestimating the difference between success percentages for the two treatments in that population (Hsu, 2004; Preece, 1983; Thompson & Schumacker, 1997).

Additional problems can arise when the original measure of the dependent variable is continuous instead of dichotomous. In this case researchers often split scores of each of the two samples at the overall median of the scores to form equal-sized overall successful and failing categories, thereby satisfying the criteria for the hypothetical BESD table. However, defining success or failure in terms of scoring below or above the overall median score often may not be realistic (Preece, 1983; Thompson & Schumacker, 1997). For example, not every treated depressive who scores below the median on a test of depression can be considered to be cured or a success. Similarly, it has been reported that a school district had such great difficulty in filling its quota of teachers that it even hired teachers who had scored very much below the median on a hiring test. In that case, scoring well below the median on a hiring test actually resulted in a "success" for some applicants (getting hired). Furthermore, recall that dichotomizing a continuous variable is also unwise because it can decrease statistical power. Hunter and Schmidt (2004) discussed correcting for the attenuation of a correlation coefficient that occurs when a continuous variable is dichotomized.

For a response to some of the criticisms of the BESD method refer to Rosenthal (1991a). Refer to Hsu (2004) for an extensive critique of the

BESD. Common measures of effect size for data that naturally, not hypothetically, fall into 2 × 2 tables (relative risk, odds ratio, and the difference between two proportions) are discussed in chapter 8 of this book. Consult Rosenthal (2000) for further discussion of the BESD and the three measures of effect size that were just mentioned. Refer to Levy (1967) for another interpretation of phi.

## THE COEFFICIENT OF DETERMINATION

The square of the sample correlation coefficient, $r^2$ (or $r_{pb}^2$), which is called the *sample coefficient of determination*, has been widely used as an estimator of $r_{pop}^2$, which is called the *population coefficient of determination*. There are several phrases that are typically used (accurately or inaccurately, depending on the context) to define or interpret a coefficient of determination. The usual interpretation is that $r_{pop}^2$ indicates the proportion of the variance of the dependent variable (i.e., the proportion of $\sigma_y^2$) that is predictable from, explained by, shared by, related to, associated with, or determined by variation of the independent variable. (However, the applicability of one or more of these descriptions depends on which of its variety of uses $r$ is being applied to, e.g., measuring reliability or estimating the size of an experimental effect, and on models of the $X$ and $Y$ variables; Beatty, 2002; Ozer, 1985.)

It can be shown mathematically that, under certain conditions and assumptions (Ozer, 1985) but not others, $r_{pop}^2$ is the ratio of (a) the part of the variance of the scores on the dependent variable that is related to variation of the independent variable (explained variance) and (b) the total variance of the scores (related and not related to the independent variable). For the first of the two most extreme examples, if $r_{pop} = 0$, $r_{pop}^2 = 0$ and none of the variation of the scores is explained by variation of the independent variable. On the other hand, if $r_{pop} = 1$, $r_{pop}^2 = 1$ and all of the variation of the scores is related to the variation of the independent variable. In other words, when the coefficient of determination is 0, by knowing the values of the independent variable one knows 0% of what one needs to know to predict the scores on the measure of the dependent variable, but when this coefficient is 1, one knows 100% of what one needs to know to predict the scores. In this latter case all of the points in the scatterplot that relates variables $X$ and $Y$ fall on the straight line of best fit through the points (a regression line or prediction line of perfect fit in this case) so that there is no variation of $Y$ at a given value of $X$, rendering $Y$ values perfectly predictable from knowledge of $X$.

For the approximate median $r_{pb}$ found in behavioral and educational research, $r_{pb} = .24$, $r_{pb}^2 = .24^2 = .06$; therefore, typically independent variables in these areas of research on average are estimated to explain about 6% of the variance of scores on the measures of dependent variables. (Note that in this chapter wherever we restrict our use of the coefficient of determination to the case of the squared point-biserial correlation, $r^2_{pb}$, we do not have to distinguish between a linear and a curvilinear relationship between the two-valued $X$ variable and the continuous $Y$ variable. In the case of the relationship between two continuous variables $r^2$ only estimates the proportion of variance in $Y$ that is explained by its linear relationship with $X$.) Consult Smithson (2001) for a discussion of a method for constructing a confidence interval for $r^2_{pop}$. Refer to Ozer (1985) and Beatty (2002) for discussions of the circumstances in which the absolute value of $r$ itself (not $r^2$) may be an appropriate estimator of a kind of coefficient of determination. For more discussion and references on this topic see the section on epsilon squared and omega squared in chapter 6.

Note that the words *determined* and *explained* can be misleading to some when used in the context of nonexperimental research. To speak of the independent variable determining variation of the dependent variable in the context of nonexperimental research might imply to some a causal connection between variation of the independent variable and the magnitudes of the scores. In this nonexperimental case a correlation coefficient is reflecting covariation between $X$ and $Y$, not causality of the magnitudes of the scores. In this case if, for example, the coefficient of determination in the sample is equal to .49, it is estimated that 49% of the variance of the scores (not their magnitudes) is explained by variation in the $X$ variable. Accounting for the degree of variation of scores is not the same as accounting for the magnitudes of the scores.

Only in research in which participants have been randomly assigned to treatments (experiments) and, therefore, there has been control of extraneous variables can we reasonably speak of variation (manipulation) of the independent variable causing or determining the scores. Therefore, in nonexperimental research perhaps one should consider foregoing the use of the word *determination* and instead speak of $r^2$ as the proportion of variance of the scores that is associated with or related to variation of the independent variable. However, it has been argued that squaring $r$ to obtain a coefficient of determination is not appropriate in the case of experimental research and that $r$ itself is the appropriate estimator of an effect size in the experimental case. Again consult Ozer (1985) and Beatty (2002) for this argument. Of course, a reader of a research report can readily calculate $r^2$ if only $r$ is reported or calculate $r$ (at least its magnitude if not its sign in all cases) if only $r^2$ is reported.

We will consider three reasons why the use of $r^2$ has fallen out of favor recently in some quarters. First, squaring the typically small or moderate values of $r$ (i.e., $r$ typically closer to 0 than to 1) that are found in psychological, behavioral, and educational research results in yet smaller numerical values of $r^2$, such as the typical $r^2 = .06$ compared to the underlying $r_{pb} = .24$ itself. Some have argued that such small values for an estimator can lead to the underestimation of the practical importance of the effect size. However, this is a less compelling reason for discarding $r^2$ when the readership of a report of research has sufficient familiarity with statistics and when the author of the report has provided the readers with discussion of the implications and limitations of the $r^2$ and also provided them with other perspectives on the data. In addition, the typically low or moderate values of $r^2$ can often be very informative in some contexts. For example, some reports of research make very much of, say, an obtained $r = .7$. In model-testing research the accompanying $r^2 = .49$ informs us that the $X$ variable is estimated to explain less than half (49%) of the variance in the $Y$ variable. Such a result alerts us to the need to search for additional $X$ variables (multiple correlation) to explain a greater percentage of the variance of $Y$.

Breaugh (2003) reviewed an example from a newspaper article in which the independent variable was which of two hospitals conducted coronary bypass surgery and the dependent variable was surviving versus not surviving the surgery. In this example it was found that $r = .07$, so the coefficient of determination was .0049. Therefore, because choice of hospital only related to less than one half of 1% of the variance (.0049) in the survivability variable, one might conclude that choosing between the two hospitals would be of little effect and of little practical importance. However, looking at the data from another perspective, one learns that the mortality rate for the surgery at one of the hospitals was 1.40%, whereas the mortality rate at the other hospital was 3.60%— a mortality rate that is 2.57 times greater. Again we observe that it can be very instructive to analyze a set of data from different perspectives. (In chap. 8 we discuss other effect sizes for such data.)

Recall that Rosenthal and Rubin (1982) intended the previously discussed BESD to rectify the perceived problem of undervaluation of a correlational effect size. In the BESD example we discussed a way (however problematic) to look at an $r_{pb}$ of .20 that increased the apparent practical importance of the finding (Table 4.1). On the other hand, $r^2$ in that example is $(.20)^2 = .04$, indicating that only 4% of the variance of the dependent variable is related to varying treatment from Treatment a to Treatment b. If 4% of the variability in the dependent variable is determined by variation of the independent variable, then $100\% - 4\% = 96\%$ of the variability of the dependent variable is not determined by variation of the independent variable. (Thus, $1 - r^2$ is called the *coefficient of nondetermination*.) Even Cohen's (1988) so-called large effect size of $r_{pop} \geq .371$ results in $r^2 = .138$, less than 14% of the variance of the dependent variable being associated with variation of the independent variable when the effect size has attained Cohen's minimum standard for large.

Breaugh (2003) provided additional examples of the underestimation of the practical importance of an effect size that can be caused by incautious or incomplete interpretation of the coefficient of determination. In the 1960s the use of personality variables to predict employee performance began to fall out of favor because the resulting coefficients of determination were generally only about .05. Breaugh (2003) also noted that in early court cases, which involved challenged hiring practices, judges and expert witnesses may have underestimated the relationship between various hiring criteria and job performance based on low values of the coefficient of determination. (In a special issue on sexual harassment the journal *Psychology, Public Policy, and Law*, Wiener & Gutek, 1997, cited many examples of the use of effect sizes in courts.)

More recently it has been recognized that modest values of the coefficient of determination can be of practical significance. In this regard, Breaugh (2003) cited a 1997 health campaign urging pregnant women not to smoke. This campaign was based on a coefficient of determination equal to about .01 when correlating smoking versus not smoking with newborns' birth weights. Also, consider the correlation between scores on a personnel-selection test and performance on the job (a validity coefficient). A typical validity coefficient of $r = .4$ results in a coefficient of determination of only .16. However, a validity coefficient of .4 means that for each 1-standard-deviation-unit increase in mean test score that an employer sets as a minimum criterion for hiring, there is an estimated .40 standard deviation unit increase in job performance. Hunter and Schmidt (2004) noted that such an increase can be of substantial economic value to an employer.

The fact that each 1-standard-deviation-unit increase in the mean value of $X$ results in an estimated $r$ standard-deviation-unit increase in $Y$ (e.g., increase by .4s units when $r = .4$) can be explained by recourse to the $z$ score form of the equation for a prediction line: $z_y' = rz_x$, where $z_y'$ is the predicted $z$ score on the $Y$ variable. Recall that $z$ scores are deviation scores in standard deviation units. Therefore, one observes in the equation that the value of $r$ determines the number of standard deviation units of $Y$ the value of $Y$ is predicted to increase for individuals for each standard deviation unit increase in their scores on $X$ (i.e., $r$ is the multiplier).

A second reason for the decreasing use of $r^2$ as an estimator of an effect size in some quarters is that, unlike $r$ or $r_{pb}$, it is directionless; it cannot be negative. For example, if in gender research men had been assigned the lower of the two numerical codes (e.g., $X = 1$), when $r_{pb}$ is positive one knows that men produced the lower mean score on the dependent variable, and when $r_{pb}$ is negative one knows that men produced the higher mean. However, of course, the square of a positive $r$ and the square of a negative $r$ of the same magnitude are the same value. Therefore, meta-analysts cannot meaningfully average the values of $r^2_{pb}$ from a set of studies in which some yielded negative and some yielded positive values of $r_{pb}$. Primary researchers who report $r^2$ should always report it together with $r$ or $r_{pb}$, both of which can be averaged by meta-analysts. Refer to Hunter and Schmidt (2004) for further discussion.

A third reason for the current disfavor of $r^2$ among some researchers is the availability of alternative kinds of measures of effect size that did not exist or were not widely known when $r^2$ became popular many decades ago. Those who advocate the use of more robust methods than Pearson's correlation coefficient to measure the relationship between variables (e.g., Wilcox, 2003) would also argue that another reason to avoid the use of the coefficient of determination is that its magnitude can be affected by the previously discussed conditions that can influence the correlation coefficient, such as curvilinearity (not relevant to $r_{pb}$) and skew.

Finally, regarding the typically small values of $r^2$ outside of the physical sciences, human behavior is multiply determined; that is, there are many genetic and experiential differences among people. Therefore, pre-existing genetic and experiential differences among individuals likely often determine much of the variability in the dependent variables that are used in behavioral science and in other "people sciences," often leaving little opportunity for a researcher's single independent variable to contribute a relatively large proportion of the total variability. Consult O'Grady (1982) and Ahadi and Diener (1989) for further discussion. Of course, in more informative factorial designs (see chap. 7) one can vary multiple independent variables to estimate their combined and individual relationships with the scores on the dependent variable. Also, unless one is very unwise in one's choice of independent variables, the multiple correlation, $R$, between a set of independent variables and a dependent variable will be greater than any of the separate values of $r$, and the resulting multiple coefficient of determination, $R^2$, will be greater than any of the separate values of $r^2$. The current edition of a widely used classic book on multiple correlation, a topic which is not discussed further in this book, is by Cohen, Cohen, West, and Aiken (2002). In this book we discuss other measures of the proportion of explained variance in chapters 6 and 7. Consult Hunter and Schmidt (2004) for an unfavorable view of the coefficient of determination.

## QUESTIONS

1. Define a *truly dichotomous* variable.
2. State two possible consequences of dichotomizing a continuous variable.
3. Describe the procedure for setting up a calculation of the $r$ between a qualitative dichotomous variable and a continuous variable.
4. Define point-biserial $r$, and what is its interpretation in the sample when it is negative and when it is positive?
5. What is the relationship between a two-tailed test of the null hypothesis that states that the point-biserial $r$ in the population is 0 and a two-tailed test of the null hypothesis that states that the two population means are equal?
6. What is the direction of bias of the sample $r$ and point-biserial $r$, and which two factors influence the magnitude of this bias and in what way does each exert its influence?
7. What would be the focus of researchers who would be interested in a null–counternull interval for $r$ in the population?
8. To which possible value of a parameter such as a population $r$ does a counternull value brings one's attention?
9. Name and describe three distributions that are relevant in the case of a point-biserial $r$.

10. State three possible consequences, if there is heteroscedasticity, of using software that assumes homoscedasticity when testing the null hypothesis that the population $r$ equals 0.
11. In what circumstance might skew be especially problematic for $r$, and in what way?
12. Considering the possibility of a difference in the direction of skew in the distributions of the $Y$ variable in Samples a and b, what difference in one's response to Question 11 would there be if the difference in skew also occurs in the two populations?
13. What is the effect of curvilinearity on $r$?
14. Describe a circumstance (other than sample size) in which an outlier of a given degree of extremeness would have greater influence on the value of $r$ than that same outlier would have in another circumstance.
15. How does the possible reduction of the value of a point-biserial $r$ by an unequal sample size relate to Question 11?
16. Why might it be problematic to compare point-biserial correlations from different experiments that used unequal sample sizes, and what can resolve this problem?
17. Define *test–retest unreliability*, and what is its effect on a correlation coefficient and on statistical power?
18. What is the relevance of possible differences in the reliabilities of different measures of the dependent variable for comparisons of effect sizes across studies?
19. How can unreliability of the independent variable come about?
20. Define and discuss *treatment integrity*.
21. List six reasons why the adjustment for unreliability is rarely used.
22. Discuss what the text calls a "philosophical objection" that some researchers have regarding the use of an adjustment for unreliability.
23. Define *restricted range*, and state how it typically (not always) influences $r$.
24. How can restricted range occur in a dependent variable?
25. Describe how restricted range might result in an increase in $r$.
26. What is the usual effect of restricted range on statistical power?
27. What is meant by *strength of manipulation*, and what is its effect on effect size?
28. What is the justification for and the possible problem with distinguishing between small, medium, and large effect sizes?
29. Provide a possible example, not from the text, of a large effect size that would not be of great practical significance.
30. Why should one not be overly impressed with a reported large effect size of which there has not yet been an attempt at replication?
31. Define a *binomial effect size display*.
32. How does one find the difference between the two success percentages in a BESD?
33. Discuss three possible limitations of the BESD.
34. Define *coefficient of determination*.

35. How might the word *determination* be misinterpreted in the label *coefficient of determination*?
36. Describe and discuss three reasons for the reduced use of the coefficient of determination in recent years.
37. Discuss why it should not be surprising that coefficients of determination are typically not very large in research involving human behavior (ignoring the issue of squaring for the purpose of this question).

# Chapter 5

# Effect Size Measures That Go Beyond Comparing Two Centers

## THE PROBABILITY OF SUPERIORITY: INDEPENDENT GROUPS

Consider estimating an effect size that would reflect what would happen if one were able to take each score from Population a and compare it to each score from Population b, one at a time, to see which of the two scores is larger, repeating such comparisons until every score from Population a had been compared to every score from Population b. If most of the time in these pairings of a score from Population a and a score from Population b the score from Population a is the higher of the two, this would indicate a tendency for superior performance in Population a, and vice versa, if most of the time the higher score in the pair is the one from Population b. The result of such a method for comparing two populations is a measure of effect size that does not involve comparing the centers of the two distributions, such as means or medians. This effect size is defined as the probability that a randomly sampled member of Population a will have a score ($Y_a$) that is higher than the score ($Y_b$) attained by a randomly sampled member of Population b. This definition will become much clearer in the examples that follow.

The expression for the current effect size is $Pr(Y_a > Y_b)$, where $Pr$ stands for probability. This $Pr(Y_a > Y_b)$ measure has no widely used name, although names have been given to its estimators (Grissom, 1994a, 1994b, 1996, Grissom & Kim, 2001; McGraw & Wong, 1992). In the just-cited references Grissom named an estimator of $Pr(Y_a > Y_b)$ the *probability of superiority* (PS). In this book we will instead use *probability of superiority* to label $Pr(Y_a > Y_b)$ itself (not an estimator of it), so that we now define it as follows:

$$PS = Pr(Y_a > Y_b). \qquad (5.1)$$

The *PS* measures the stochastic (i.e., probabilistic) superiority of one group's scores over another group's scores. Because the *PS* is a probabil-

**98**

ity and probabilities range from 0 to 1, the *PS* ranges from 0 to 1. Therefore, the two most extreme results when comparing Populations a and b would be (a) *PS* = 0, in which every member of Population a is outscored by every member of Population b; and (b) *PS* = 1, in which every member of Population a outscores every member of Population b. The least extreme result (no effect of group membership one way or the other) would result in *PS* = .5, in which members of Populations a and b outscore each other equally often.

A proportion in a sample estimates a probability in a population. For example, if one counts, say, 52 heads results in a sample of 100 (random) tosses of a coin, the proportion of heads in that sample's results is $52/100 = .52$, and the estimate of the probability of heads for a population of random tosses of that specific coin would be .52. Similarly, the *PS* can be estimated from the proportion of times that the $n_a$ participants in Sample a outscore the $n_b$ participants in Sample b in head-to-head comparisons of scores within all possible pairings of the score of a member of one sample with the score of a member of the other sample. The total number of possible such comparisons is given by the product of the two sample sizes, $n_a n_b$. Therefore, if, say, $n_a = n_b = 10$ (but sample sizes do not have to be equal), and in 70 of the $n_a n_b = 100$ comparisons the score from the member of Sample a is greater than the score from the member of Sample b, then the estimate of *PS* is $70/100 = .70$.

For a more detailed but simple example, suppose that Sample a has three members, Persons A, B, and C; and Sample b has three members, Persons D, E, and F. The $n_a n_b = 3 \times 3 = 9$ pairings to observe who has the higher score would be A versus D, A versus E, A versus F, B versus D, B versus E, B versus F, C versus D, C versus E, and C versus F. Suppose that in five of these nine pairings of scores the scores of Persons A, B, and C (Sample a) are greater than the scores of Persons D, E, and F (Sample b), and in the other four pairings Sample b wins. In this example the estimate of *PS* is $5/9 = .56$. Of course, in actual research one would not want to base the estimate on such small samples.

The estimate of *PS* will be greater than .5 when members of Sample a outscore members of Sample b in more than one half of the pairings, and the estimate will be less than .5 when members of Sample a are outscored by members of Sample b in more than one half of the pairings. When there are ties the simplest solution is to allocate one half of the ties to each group. (There are other methods for handling ties; see Brunner & Munzel, 2000; Fay, 2003; Pratt & Gibbons, 1981; Randles, 2001; Rayner & Best, 2001; Sparks, 1967.) Thus, in this example if members of Sample a had outscored members of Sample b not five but four times in the nine pairings, with one tie, one half of the tie would be awarded as a superior outcome to each sample. Therefore, there would be 4.5 superior outcomes for each sample in the nine pairings of its members with the members of the other sample, and the estimate of *PS* would, therefore, be $4.5/9 = .5$. A measure that is related to the *PS* but ignores ties (Cliff, 1993) is considered later in this chapter (in Equation 5.5).

The number of times that the scores from one specified sample are higher than the scores from the other sample with which they are paired (i.e., the numerator of the sample proportion that is used to estimate the *PS*) is called the *U statistic* (Mann & Whitney, 1947). Recalling that the total number of possible comparisons (pairings) is $n_a n_b$ and using $\hat{p}_{a>b}$ to denote the sample proportion that estimates the *PS*, we can now define:

$$\hat{p}_{a>b} = \frac{U}{n_a n_b}. \tag{5.2}$$

In other words, in Equation 5.2 the numerator is the number of wins for a specified sample and the denominator is the number of opportunities to win in head-to-head comparisons of each of its member's scores with each of the scores of the other sample's members. The value of $U$ can be calculated manually, but it can be laborious to do so except for very small samples. Although currently major statistical software packages do not calculate $\hat{p}_{a>b}$, many do calculate the Mann–Whitney $U$ statistic or the equivalent $W_m$ statistic. If the value of $U$ is obtained through the use of software, one then divides this outputted $U$ by $n_a n_b$ to find the estimator, $\hat{p}_{a>b}$. If software provides the equivalent Wilcoxon (1945) $W_m$ rank-sum statistic instead of the $U$ statistic, if there are no ties, find $U$ by calculating $U = W_m - [n_s(n_s + 1)] / 2$, where $n_s$ is the smaller sample size or, if sample sizes are equal, the size of one sample. Note that Equation 5.2 satisfies the general formula, which was presented in chapter 1, for the relationship between an estimate of effect size ($ES_{EST}$) and a test statistic ($TS$); $ES_{EST} = TS / [f(N)]$. In the case of Equation 5.2, $ES_{EST} = \hat{p}$, $TS = U$, and $f(N) = n_a n_b$.

Researchers who focus on means and assume normality and homoscedasticity might prefer to use the $t$ test to compare the means and use a standardized-difference effect size. Researchers who do not assume normality and who are interested in a measure of the extent to which the scores in one group are stochastically superior to those in another group will prefer to use the *PS* or a similar measure. Under homoscedasticity (in this case, equal variability of the overall ranks of the scores in each group) one may use the original Mann–Whitney $U$ test to test $H_0$: *PS* = .5 against $H_{alt}$: *PS* ≠ .5. However, the ordinary $U$ test that is usually provided by software is not robust against heteroscedasticity (Delaney & Vargha, 2002; B. P. Murphy, 1976; Pratt, 1964; Zimmerman & Zumbo, 1993). Further discussion of homoscedasticity and discussion of a researcher's choice between comparing means and using the *PS* is found in the forthcoming section on assumptions.

Consult Wilcox (1996, 1997), Vargha and Delaney (2000), and Delaney and Vargha (2002) for extensive discussions of robust methods for testing $H_0$: *PS* = .5. Wilcox (1996) presented a Minitab macro and S-PLUS software functions (Wilcox, 1997) for constructing a confidence interval for the *PS* based on Fligner and Policello's (1981) heteroscedasticity-adjusted *U* statistic, *U'*, and on a method for constructing a confidence interval by Mee (1990) that appears to be fairly accurate. The Fligner–Policello *U'* test can be further improved by making a Welch-like adjustment to the degrees of freedom (cf. Delaney & Vargha, 2002). Refer to Vargha and Delaney (2000) for critiques of alternative methods for constructing a confidence interval for the *PS*, equations for manual calculation, and extension of the *PS* to comparisons of multiple groups.

Also refer to Brunner and Puri (2001) for extensions of the *PS* to multiple groups and to factorial designs. (Factorial designs are discussed in chap. 7 of this book.) Brunner and Munzel (2000) presented a further robust method that can be used to test the null hypothesis that *PS* = .5 and to provide an estimate of the *PS* and construct a confidence interval for it. This method is applicable when there are ties, heteroscedasticity, or both. Wilcox (2003) provided an accessible discussion of the Brunner–Munzel method and S-PLUS software functions for the calculations in the current case of only two groups and for extension to the case in which groups are taken two at a time from multiple groups. (Wilcox called the *PS* *p* or *P*, and Vargha and Delaney called it *A*.)

## EXAMPLE OF THE *PS*

Recall from chapters 3 and 4 the example in which the scores of the mothers of schizophrenic children (Sample a) were compared to those of the mothers of normal children (Sample b). We observed from two different perspectives in those chapters that there is a moderately strong relationship between type of mother and the score on a measure of healthy parent–child relationship, as was indicated by the results $d = -.77$ and $r_{pb} = .40$. We now estimate the *PS* for the data of this example. Because $n_a = n_b = 20$ in this example, $n_a n_b = 20 \times 20 = 400$. Four hundred is too many pairings for manually calculating *U* conveniently and with confidence that the calculation will be error free. Therefore, we used software (many kinds of statistical software can do this) to find that $U = 103$. We can then calculate $\hat{p}_{a>b} = U/n_a n_b = 103/400 = .26$. We thus estimate that in the populations there is only a .26 probability that a randomly sampled mother of a schizophrenic child will outscore a randomly sampled mother of a normal child.

Under the assumption of homoscedasticity one can test $H_0$: *PS* = .5 using the ordinary *U* test or equivalent $W_m$ test, one of which is often provided by statistical software packages. Because software reveals a statistically significant *U* at $p < .05$ for these data, one can conclude in this case that *PS* ≠ .5. Specifically, assuming homoscedasticity for the current example, we conclude that the population of schizophrenics' mothers is inferior (as defined by the *PS*) in its scoring when compared to the population of the normals' mothers (i.e., *PS* < .5). A researcher who does not assume homoscedasticity should choose to use one of the alternative methods that can be found in the sources that were cited in the previous section.

Note that we reported $p < .05$ for our result instead of reporting a specific value for $p$. There are two reasons why we did this. First, different statistics packages might output different results for the $U$ test (Bergmann, Ludbrook, & Spooren, 2000). Second, we are not confident in specific outputted $p$ values beyond the .05 level for the sample sizes in this example. We provide further discussion of these two issues in the remainder of this section.

As sample sizes increase, the sampling distributions of values of $U$ or $W_m$ approach the normal curve. Therefore, some software that includes the Mann–Whitney $U$ test or the equivalent Wilcoxon $W_m$ test or some researchers who do the calculations for the test manually may be basing the critical values needed for statistical significance on what is called a *large-sample approximation* of these critical values. Because some textbooks do not have tables of critical values for these two statistics or may have tables that lack critical values for the particular sample sizes or for the alpha levels of interest in a particular instance of research, recourse to the widely available table of the normal curve would be very convenient. Unfortunately, the literature is inconsistent in its recommendations about how large samples should be before the convenient normal curve provides a satisfactory approximation to the sampling distributions of these statistics. However, computer simulations by Fahoome (2002) indicated that, if sample sizes are equal, each $n = 15$ is a satisfactory minimum when testing at the .05 alpha level and each $n = 29$ is a satisfactory minimum when testing at the .01 level. Also, Fay (2002) provided Fortran 90 programs for use by researchers who need exact critical values for $W_m$ for a wide range of sample sizes and for a wide range of alpha levels.

If sample sizes are sufficient for use of the normal curve for an approximate test and, assuming homoscedasticity, if there are no ties, then one may test the null hypothesis that $PS = .5$ by using Equation 5.3 to convert $U$ to $z$:

$$|z| = \frac{\left| U - \frac{n_a n_b}{2} \right|}{\left[ \dfrac{n_a n_b (n_a + n_b + 1)}{12} \right]^{1/2}} . \tag{5.3}$$

Reject the null hypothesis at two-tailed level $\alpha$ if the value of $|z|$ exceeds $z_{\alpha/2}$ in a table of the normal curve. Applying the values from the example of the two groups of mothers, we find that $|z| = |103 - (20 \times 20)/2| / [(20(20)(20 + 20 + 1)) / 12]^{1/2} = 2.624$. Inspecting a table of the normal curve we find that $|z| = 2.624$ is a statistically significant result at the $p < .05$ level, two-tailed. If there are ties, replace the denominator in Equation 5.3 with $S_{adj}$, which can be obtained from Equation 9.5 in chapter 9.

## A RELATED MEASURE OF EFFECT SIZE

Because the maximum probability or proportion equals 1, the sum of the probabilities or proportions of occurrences of all of the possible outcomes of an event must sum to 1. For example, the probability that a toss of a coin will produce either a head or a tail equals $\frac{1}{2} + \frac{1}{2} = 1$. Therefore, if there are no ties or ties are allocated equally, then $\hat{p}_{a>b} + \hat{p}_{a<b} = 1$, and $\hat{p}_{a<b} = 1 - \hat{p}_{a>b}$. Thus, an estimator of another kind of effect size arises when there are no ties or ties are allocated equally by calculating the ratio $\hat{p}_{a<b}/\hat{p}_{a>b}$, or the inverse of this ratio. When there is no relationship between the independent variable of membership in either Sample a or Sample b and the overall ranking of the scores on the measure of the dependent variable, $\hat{p}_{a<b} = \hat{p}_{a>b} = .5$ and $\hat{p}_{a<b}/\hat{p}_{a>b} = .5/.5 = 1$. The greater the relationship between the independent variable and the overall ranking of the scores in the samples, the more this ratio moves above 1 when Sample b generally has the higher scoring member (more wins in the head-to-head comparisons) or away from 1 toward 0 when Sample a generally has the higher scoring member. This ratio estimates an answer to the following question about the two populations. For all pairings of a member of Population a with a member of Population b, how many times more pairings would there be in which a member of Population a scores lower than in which a member of Population b scores lower? When using instead the ratio $\hat{p}_{a>b}/\hat{p}_{a<b}$ as an estimator (the inverse of the previous ratio), replace the word *lower* with the word *higher* in the preceding question. The two versions of the ratio are related to estimators of a generalized odds ratio, about which there is more discussion in chapter 9.

For an example consider again the data involving the two samples of mothers. Recall that in this example $\hat{p}_{a>b} = .26$, so now we find that $\hat{p}_{a<b} = 1 - \hat{p}_{a>b} = 1 - .26 = .74$, and $\hat{p}_{a<b}/\hat{p}_{a>b} = .74/.26 = 2.8$. We are thus estimating that in the populations there would be 2.8 times more pairings in which the schizophrenics' mothers are outscored by the normals' mothers than in which the schizophrenics' mothers outscore the normals' mothers.

## ASSUMPTIONS

The original purpose of the U test was to test if scores in one population are stochastically larger (i.e., likely to be larger) than scores in another population, assuming that both populations have the same, but not necessarily normal, shape (Mann & Whitney, 1947). (This test was later observed to be equivalent to an earlier test by Wilcoxon, 1945, the $W_m$ rank-sum test.) In other words, the purpose of the U test was to test if the score at the $i$th percentile of Population a is larger than the score at that same $i$th percentile in Population b. A percentile that is frequently of interest is the 50th percentile, which is the median ($Mdn$) in general and also the mean in the case of symmetrical distributions.

When using the $U$ test to test $H_0$: $Mdn_a = Mdn_b$ against the alternative $H_{alt}$: $Mdn_a \neq Mdn_b$, one is in effect assuming that if treatment or group membership has an effect it will be to add (or subtract) a certain constant number of points, say, $k$ points, to each score in a group's distribution. Adding a constant $k$ to each score in a group shifts its distribution to the right by $k$ points without changing its shape. This concept of an additive effect of treatment is called a *shift model*, in which a treatment merely always adds (or always subtracts) a constant number of points to what the score of each participant in a group would have been if each of those participants had been in the other group. The independent-groups $t$ test for the difference between two means also assumes a shift model.

The shift model may often not be the most realistic model of the effect of treatments (or group membership) in behavioral, psychological, educational, or medical research. It seems reasonable to assume instead that treatment may often have a varying effect on the individuals in a treated group. In this case a treatment may perhaps increase the scores of all participants by varying amounts, decrease scores of all participants by varying amounts, or increase the scores of some while decreasing the scores of others by varying amounts. In such cases scores are "pulled" to the right and/or to the left by varying amounts. The well-known name for the varying effect of treatment on different individuals is *Treatment × Subject interaction*. Hunter and Schmidt (2004) provided an extensive discussion of the implications of Treatment × Subject interaction in the context of independent-and dependent-groups designs.

As Delaney and Vargha (2002) pointed out with examples, the shift model, with its usual resulting comparison of means (or medians), is appropriate when one is interested in information about which treatment produces the lower or higher average score, but the *PS* is appropriate when one is interested in information about which treatment is likely to help the greater number of people. For example, a therapist may be more interested in the latter, whereas a medical insurance company may well be more interested in information about which treatment on average results in the lower cost. Delaney and Vargha (2002) also provided an example, necessarily involving skewed data, in which a sample that has superiority over another sample in terms of the *PS* actually has a mean that is lower than the mean of the inferior group.

In the case of the $U$ test that uses the actual probability distribution of $U$ instead of the normal approximation, heteroscedasticity can influence the result because the critical values of the test were derived assuming equal shapes of the two populations, an assumption that might be violated by heteroscedasticity. When using the standard normal approximation for the $U$ test, heteroscedasticity might result in an incorrect estimation of the standard error of $U$ (the denominator of Equation 5.3). This problem for the normal approximation can cause an increase in rate of Type I error if there is a negative relationship between the variances of the populations and the sample sizes. If instead there is a positive relationship between the variances and the sample sizes, heteroscedasticity might cause a decrease in the power of the test. For further discussion consult Delaney and Vargha (2002), Vargha and Delaney (2000), and Wilcox (1996, 2001, 2003).

Finally, regarding precedence for the underlying ideas that have been presented thus far in this chapter, because the Wilcoxon (1945) $W_m$ test and the Mann–Whitney $U$ test (Mann & Whitney, 1947) are known to be equivalent, the $U$ test is often called the Wilcoxon–Mann–Whitney $U$ test. Nonetheless, the basic ideas can perhaps be traced back to at least 1914 (Kruskal, 1957). Note also that there are other versions of this test (Bergmann, Ludbrook, & Spooren, 2000).

## THE COMMON LANGUAGE EFFECT SIZE STATISTIC

The estimates of $PS$ from various studies can be combined in a meta-analysis (Colditz, Miller, & Mosteller, 1988; Mosteller & Chalmers, 1992). However, because raw scores are not typically available to meta-analysts, they cannot calculate values of the estimator $\hat{p}_{a>b}$ using Equation 5.2. Fortunately, the $PS$ can also be estimated from sample means and variances, assuming normality and homoscedasticity, using a statistic that McGraw and Wong (1992) called the *common language effect size statistic*, symbolized $CL$. The $CL$ is based on a z score, $Z_{CL}$, where

$$Z_{CL} = \frac{\overline{Y}_a - \overline{Y}_b}{\left(s_a^2 + s_b^2\right)^{1/2}}. \qquad (5.4)$$

The proportion of the area under the normal curve that is below $Z_{CL}$ is the $CL$ statistic that estimates the $PS$ from a study. For examples, if a study's $Z_{CL} = +1.00$ or $-1.00$, inspection of a table of the normal curve reveals that the $PS$ would be estimated to be .84 or .16, respectively. For the example that compares the two groups of mothers, using Equation 5.4 and the means and variances that were presented for this study in chapter 3, $Z_{CL} = (2.10 - 3.55) / (2.41 + 3.52)^{1/2} = -.60$. Inspecting a table of the normal curve we find that approximately .27 of the area of the normal curve is below $z = -.60$, so our estimate of $PS$ when the schizophrenics' mothers are Group a is .27. Note that this estimate of .27 for the $PS$ using the $CL$ is close to the estimate .26 that we previously obtained when using $\hat{p}_{a>b}$. Refer to Grissom and Kim (2001) for comparisons of the values of the $\hat{p}_{a>b}$ estimates and the $CL$ estimates applied to sets of real data and for the results of some computer simulations on the effect of heteroscedasticity on the two estimators. For further results of computer simulations of the robustness of various methods for testing $H_0$: $PS = .5$, consult Vargha and Delaney (2000) and Delaney and Vargha (2002). Refer to Dunlap (1999) for software to calculate the $CL$.

## TECHNICAL NOTE 5.1: THE $PS$ AND ITS ESTIMATORS

The $PS$ measures the tendency of scores from Group a to outrank the scores from Group b across all pairings of the scores of the members of each group. Therefore, the $PS$ is an ordinal measure of effect size, reflecting not the absolute magnitudes of the paired scores but the rank order of these paired scores. Although, outside of the physical sciences, one often treats scores as if they were on an interval scale, many of the measures of dependent variables are likely monotonically, but not necessarily linearly, related to the latent variables that they are measuring. In other words, the scores presumably increase and decrease along with the latent variables (i.e., they have the same rank order as the latent variables) but not necessarily to the same degree. Monotonic transformations of the data leave the ordinally oriented $PS$ invariant. Therefore, different measures of the same dependent variable should leave the $PS$ invariant. If a researcher is interested in the tendency of the scores in one group to outrank the scores in another group over all pairings of the two, then use of the $PS$ is reasonable.

Theoretically, $\hat{p}_{a>b}$ is a consistent and unbiased estimator of the $PS$, and it has the smallest sampling variance of any unbiased estimator of the $PS$. (A *consistent estimator* is one that converges randomly toward the parameter that it is estimating as sample sizes approach infinity.) Also, using $\hat{p}_{a>b}$ to test $H_0$: $PS = .5$ against $H_{alt}$: $PS \neq .5$, or against a one-tailed alternative, is a consistent test in the sense that the power of such a test approaches 1 as sample sizes approach infinity.

Some readers may question the statement that the $CL$ assumes homoscedasticity because the variance of $(Y_a - Y_b)$ is $\sigma_a^2 + \sigma_b^2$ regardless of the values of $\sigma_a^2$ and $\sigma_b^2$. However, it can be shown that the $CL$ strictly only estimates the $PS$ under normality and homoscedasticity and that it is not quite an unbiased estimator of the $PS$ unless it is adjusted (Pratt & Gibbons, 1981). McGraw and Wong (1992), who named the $CL$, were correct in assuming homoscedasticity. For more discussions of the $PS$ and its estimators consult Lehmann (1975), Laird and Mosteller (1990), Pratt and Gibbons (1981), and Vargha and Delaney (2000). Note that in these sources you will typically find the parameter symbolized in a manner similar to $Pr(Y_a > Y_b)$ with no name attached to it.

## INTRODUCTION TO OVERLAP

Measures of effect size can be related to the relative positions of the distributions of Populations a and b. When there is no effect, $\Delta = 0$, $r_{pop} = 0$, and $PS = .5$. In this case, if assumptions are satisfied, Distributions a and b completely overlap. When there is a maximum effect, $\Delta$ is at its maximum negative or positive value for the data, $r_{pop} = +1$ or $-1$, and $PS = 0$ or 1 depending on whether it is Population b or Population a, respectively, that is superior in all of the comparisons within the paired scores. In this case of maximum effect there is no overlap of the two distributions; even the lowest score in the higher scoring group is higher than the highest score in the lower scoring group. Intermediate values of effect size result in less extreme amounts of overlap than in the two previous cases. Recall the example in chapter 3 in which Fig. 3.1 depicted the mean of the treated population's distribution shifting 1 $\sigma_y$ unit to the right of the mean of the control population's distribution when $\Delta = +1$.

## THE DOMINANCE MEASURE

Cliff (1993) discussed a variation on the *PS* concept that avoids dealing with ties by considering only those pairings in which $Y_a > Y_b$ or $Y_b > Y_a$. We call this measure the *dominance measure of effect size* (*DM*) here because Cliff (1993) called its estimator the *dominance statistic*, which we denote by *ds*. This measure is defined as

$$DM = Pr(Y_a > Y_b) - Pr(Y_b > Y_a), \qquad (5.5)$$

and its estimator, *ds*, is given by

$$ds = \hat{p}_{a>b} - \hat{p}_{b>a}. \qquad (5.6)$$

Here the $\hat{p}$ values are, as before, given by $U/n_a n_b$ for each group, except for including in each group's $U$ only the number of wins in the $n_a n_b$ pairings of scores from Groups a and b, with no allocation of any ties. For example, suppose that $n_a = n_b = 10$, and of the $10 \times 10 = 100$ pairings Group a has the higher of the two paired scores 50 times, Group b has the higher score 40 times, and there are 10 ties within the paired scores. In this case, $\hat{p}_{a>b} = 50/100 = .5$, $\hat{p}_{b>a} = 40/100 = .4$; therefore, the estimate of the *DM* is $.5 - .4 = +.1$, suggesting a slight superiority of Group a. Because, as probabilities, both *Pr* values can range from 0 to 1, *DM* ranges from $0 - 1 = -1$ to $1 - 0 = +1$. When $DM = -1$ the population's distributions do not overlap, with all of the scores from Group a being below all of the scores from Group b, and vice versa when $DM = +1$. For values of the *DM* between the two extremes of $-1$ and $+1$, there is intermediate overlap. When there is an equal number of wins for Groups a and b in their pairings, $\hat{p}_{a>b} = \hat{p}_{b>a} = .5$ and the estimate of the *DM* is $.5 - .5 = 0$. In this case there is no effect and complete overlap.

Refer to Cliff (1993) for discussions of significance testing and construction of confidence intervals for the *DM* for the independent-groups and the dependent-groups cases, and for software to undertake the calculations. Also refer to Vargha and Delaney (2000) for further discussion. Wilcox (2003) provided S-PLUS software functions for Cliff's (1996) robust method for constructing a confidence interval for the *DM* for the case of only two groups and for the case of groups taken two at a time from multiple groups. Preliminary findings by Wilcox (2003) indicated that Cliff's (1993) method provides good control of Type I error even when there are many tied values, a situation that may be problematic for competing methods. Many ties are likely when there are relatively few possible values for the dependent variable, such as is the case for rating-scale data as discussed in chapter 9. An example of the *DM* is presented in chapter 9 along with more discussion.

## COHEN'S $U_3$

If assumptions of normality and homoscedasticity are satisfied and if populations are of equal size (as they always are in experimental research), one can estimate the percentage of nonoverlap of the distributions of Populations a and b. One of the methods uses as an estimate of nonoverlap the percentage of the members of the higher scoring sample who score above the median (which is same as the mean when normality is satisfied) of the lower scoring sample. We observed with regard to Fig. 3.1 of chapter 3 that when $\Delta = +1$, the mean of the higher scoring population lies 1 $\sigma_y$ unit above the mean of the lower scoring population. Because, under normality, 50% of the scores are at or below the mean and approximately 34% of the scores lie between the mean and 1 $\sigma_y$ unit above the mean (i.e., $z = +1$), when $\Delta = +1$ we infer that approximately 50% + 34% = 84% of the scores of the superior group exceed the median of the comparison group. Cohen (1988) denoted this percentage as a measure of effect size, $U_3$, to contrast it with his related measures, $U_1$ and $U_2$, which we do not discuss here.

When there is no effect we have observed that $\Delta = 0$, $r_{pop} = 0$, and the *PS* = .5, and now we note that $U_3 = 50\%$. In this case 50% of the scores from Population a are at or above the median of the scores from Population b, but, of course, so too are 50% of the scores from Population b at or above its median; there is complete overlap (0% nonoverlap). As $\Delta$ increases above 0, $U_3$ approaches 100%. For example, if $\Delta = +3.4$, then $U_3 > 99.95\%$, with nearly all of the scores from Population a being above the median of Population b.

In research that is intended to improve scores compared to a control, placebo, or standard-treatment group, a case of *successful treatment* is sometimes defined (but not always justifiably so) as any score that exceeds the median of the comparison group. Then, the percentage of the scores from the treated group that exceed the median score of the comparison group is called the *success percentage* of the treatment. When assumptions are satisfied the success percentage is, by definition, $U_3$. For further discussions consult Lipsey (2000) and Lipsey and Wilson

(2001). For a more complex but robust approach to an overlap measure of effect size that does not assume normality or homoscedasticity, refer to Hess, Olejnik, and Huberty (2001).

## RELATIONSHIPS AMONG MEASURES OF EFFECT SIZE

Although Cohen's (1988) use of the letter $U$ is apparently merely coincidental to the Mann–Whitney $U$ statistic, when assumptions are met, there is a relationship between $U_3$ and the $PS$. Indeed, many of the measures of effect size that are discussed in this book are related when assumptions are met. Numerous approximately equivalent values among many measures can be found by combining the information that is in tables presented by Rosenthal et al. (2000, pp. 16–21), Lipsey and Wilson (2001, p. 153), Cohen (1988, p. 22), and Grissom (1994a, p. 315). Table 5.1 presents an abbreviated set of approximate relationships among measures of effect size. The values in Table 5.1 are more accurate the more nearly normality, homoscedasticity, and equality of sample sizes are satisfied, and the larger the sample sizes.

In chapter 4 we discussed Cohen's (1988) admittedly rough criteria for small, medium, and large effect sizes in terms of values of $\Delta$ and values of

### TABLE 5.1
#### Approximate Relationships Among Some Measures of Effect Size

| $\Delta$ | $r_{pop}$ | $PS$ | $U_3(\%)$ |
|---|---|---|---|
| 0 | .000 | .500 | 50.0 |
| .1 | .050 | .528 | 54.0 |
| .2 | .100 | .556 | 57.9 |
| .3 | .148 | .584 | 61.8 |
| .4 | .196 | .611 | 65.5 |
| .5 | .243 | .638 | 69.1 |
| .6 | .287 | .664 | 72.6 |
| .7 | .330 | .690 | 75.8 |
| .8 | .371 | .714 | 78.8 |
| .9 | .410 | .738 | 81.6 |
| 1.0 | .447 | .760 | 84.1 |
| 1.5 | .600 | .856 | 93.3 |
| 2.0 | .707 | .921 | 97.7 |
| 2.5 | .781 | .962 | 99.4 |
| 3.0 | .832 | .983 | 99.9 |
| 3.4 | .862 | .992 | >99.95 |

$r_{pop}$. Due to the relationships among many measures of effect size, we can now also apply Cohen's criteria to the $PS$ and $U_3$. Categorized as small effect sizes ($\Delta \leq .20$, $r_{pop} \leq .10$) would be $PS \leq .56$ and $U_3 \leq 57.9\%$. Medium values ($\Delta = .50$, $r_{pop} = .243$) would be $PS = .638$ and $U_3 = 69.1\%$. Large values ($\Delta \geq .8$, $r_{pop} \geq .371$) would be $PS \geq .714$ and $U_3 \geq 78.8\%$.

## APPLICATION TO CULTURAL EFFECT SIZE

Three of the measures of effect size that have been discussed thus far in this book have been applied to the comparison of two cultures (Matsumoto, Grissom, & Dinnel, 2001). Among many other differences between participants in the United States ($n_{US} = 182$) and in Japan ($n_{JP} = 161$) that had been reported in a previous study (Kleinknecht, Dinnel, Kleinknecht, Hiruma, & Hirada, 1997), the Japanese had statistically significantly higher mean scores than the US participants on a scale of Embarrassability, t(341) = 4.33, $p < .001$; a scale of Social Anxiety, t(341) = 2.96, $p < .01$; and a scale of Social Interaction Anxiety, t(341) = 3.713, $p < .001$. To demonstrate that statistically significant differences, or even so-called "highly" statistically significant differences, do not necessarily translate to very large, or even large, effects of culture (cultural effect size), Matsumoto et al. (2001) estimated a standardized-difference effect size (Hedges' $g_{pop}$ of chap. 3), $r_{pop}$, and the $PS$ for these results. The $PS$ was estimated by $\hat{p}_{a>b}$ using Equation 5.2. Table 5.2 displays the results.

Values of $U_3$ are not included in Table 5.2 because $U_3$ assumes populations of equal size, a condition that is not met by the United States and Japan. Observe that the values in the last column are all below .5, suggesting that the members of Group a (USA) would tend to be outscored by the members of Group b (Japan) in paired comparisons of members of the two groups. Recall that when the $PS$ is based on $Pr(Y_a > Y_b)$ instead of the equally applicable $Pr(Y_b > Y_a)$, if the members

TABLE 5.2

Cultural Effect Size Estimates When Comparing the United States and Japan

| Scale | $\overline{Y}_{US}$ | $\overline{Y}_{JP}$ | p level | g | $r_{pb}$ | $\hat{p}_{a>b}$ |
|---|---|---|---|---|---|---|
| Embarrassability | 108.80 | 112.27 | < .001 | −.16 | .08 | .46 |
| Social anxiety | 83.65 | 93.50 | < .01 | −.34 | .17 | .41 |
| Social interaction anxiety | 26.36 | 31.50 | < .001 | −.41 | .20 | .38 |

Note. Adapted from "Do between-culture differences really mean that people are different? A look at some measures of cultural effect size," by D. Matsumoto, R. J. Grissom, and D. L. Dinnel, 2001, *Journal of Cross-Cultural Psychology, 32*, (No. 4), 478–490, p. 486. Copyright © 2001 by Sage Publications. Adapted with permission of Sage Publications.

of Group a tend to be outscored by the members of Group b, then the value of this *PS* gets smaller as the effect gets larger. Thus, the greater the effect, the more the current *PS* departs upward from .5 when Group a is superior and downward from .5 when Group b is superior.

Observe in Table 5.2 that, although the estimates of effect size for the two anxiety scales are between Cohen's (1988) criteria for small and medium effect sizes, the large sample sizes (182 and 161) have elevated the cultural mean differences to what some would call highly or very highly statistically significant differences on the basis of the impressively small *p* values. Moreover, although the cultural difference for Embarrassability might be considered by some to be highly statistically significant, the effect sizes are only in the category of small effects. Thus, it is possible for a cultural (or gender) stereotype that is based on a statistically significant difference actually to translate to a small effect of culture (or gender). Even a somewhat valid (statistically) stereotype may actually not apply to a large percentage of the stereotyped group and, therefore, may not be of much practical use, such as in the training of diplomats. Worse, of course, some stereotypes can do much personal and social harm.

### TECHNICAL NOTE 5.2: ESTIMATING EFFECT SIZES THROUGHOUT A DISTRIBUTION

Traditional measures of effect size might be insufficiently informative or even misleading when there is heteroscedasticity, nonhomomerity, or both. *Nonhomomerity* means inequality of shapes of the distributions. For example, suppose that a treatment causes some participants to score higher and some to score lower than they would have scored if they had been in the comparison group. In this case the treated group's variability will increase or decrease depending on whether it was the higher or lower scoring participants whose scores were increased or decreased by the treatment. However, although variability has been changed by the treatment in this example, the two groups' means and/or medians might remain nearly the same (which is possible but much less likely than the example that is presented in the next paragraph). In this case, if we estimate an effect size with $\bar{Y}_a - \bar{Y}_b$ or $Mdn_a - Mdn_b$ in the numerator, the estimate might be a value that is not far from zero although the treatment may have had a moderate or large effect on the tails even if there is not much of an effect on the center of the treated group's distribution. The effect on variability may have resulted from the treatment having "pulled" tails outward or having "pushed" tails inward.

In another case, the treatment may have an effect throughout a distribution, changing both the center and the tails of the treated group's distribution. In fact, it is common for the group with the higher mean also to have the greater variability. In this case, if we now consider a combined distribution that contains all of the scores of the treated and comparison groups, the proportions of the treated group's scores among the overall high scores and among the overall low scores can be different from what would be implied by an estimate of $\Delta$ or $U_3$. Hedges and Nowell (1995) provided a specific example. In this example, if $\Delta = +.3$, distributions are normal, and the variance of the treated population's scores is only 15% greater than the variance of the comparison population's scores, one would find approximately 2.5 times more treated participants' scores than comparison participants' scores in the top 5% of the combined distribution. For more discussion and examples consult Feingold (1992, 1995) and O'Brien (1988). Note that the kinds of results that have just been discussed can occur even under homoscedasticity if there is non-homomerity. To deal with the possibility of treatment effects that are not restricted to the centers of distributions, other measures of effect size have been proposed, such as the measures that are briefly introduced in the next two sections.

### Hedges–Friedman Method

Informative methods have been proposed for measuring effect size at places along a distribution in addition to its center. Such methods are necessarily more complex than the usual methods, so they have not been widely used. For example, Hedges and Friedman (1993), assuming normality, recommended the use of a standardized-difference effect size, $\Delta_\alpha$, at a portion of a tail beyond a fixed value, $Y_\alpha$, in a distribution of the combined scores from Populations a and b. The subscript alpha indicates that $Y_\alpha$ is the score at the $100\alpha$ percentile point of the combined distribution, and the value of alpha is chosen by the researcher according to which portion of the combined distribution is of interest. For example, if $\alpha = .25$, then $Y_\alpha$ is the score that has $100(.25)\% = 25\%$ of the scores above it.

One can then define

$$\Delta_\alpha = \frac{\mu_{\alpha a} - \mu_{\alpha b}}{\sigma_\alpha}, \qquad (5.7)$$

where $\mu_{\alpha a}$ and $\mu_{\alpha b}$ are the means of just those scores from Populations a and b, respectively, that are higher than $Y_\alpha$, and $\sigma_\alpha$ is the standard deviation of those scores in the combined distribution that are higher than $Y_\alpha$. Again, the value of $Y_\alpha$ is selected by the researcher as the score in the combined distribution that has $c\%$ of the scores above it. Computations of the estimates of values of the various $\Delta_\alpha$ are repeated for those values of $c$ that are of interest to the researcher. Extensive computational details can be found in the appendix of Hedges and Friedman (1993).

### Shift-Function Method

Doksum (1977) presented a graphical method for comparing two groups not only at the centers of their distributions but, more informatively, at various quantiles. Recall from chapter 1 that a quantile can be roughly defined as a score that is equal to or greater than a specified proportion of the scores in a distribution.

Recall also that the median is at the .50 quantile, which, if one divides a distribution into successive fourths (called *quartiles*), can also be said to be at the second quartile. If one divides a distribution into successive tenths, the quantiles are called *deciles*. The median is at the fifth decile. Doksum's (1977) method involves a series of shift functions, each shift function indicating how far the comparison sample's scores have to be moved (shifted) to reach the scores of the treated sample at a quantile of interest to the researcher. The method results in a graph of shift functions. In such a graph quantiles of the comparison sample's scores at their various $q$th quantile values, $Y_{qc}$, are plotted against the differences between the values of $Y_{qc}$ and $Y_{qt}$, which is the score of a treated participant at the treated sample's $q$th quantile. (A subscripted letter c refers to the comparison group and a subscripted letter t refers to the treated group.) Each shift function in this graph is thus given by $Y_{qt} - Y_{qc}$. The graph of shift functions describes whether a treatment becomes more or less effective as one observes along the comparison sample's distribution from its lower scoring to its higher scoring members.

For more detailed discussions consult Doksum (1977) and Wilcox (1995, 1996, 1997, 2003). Wilcox (1996) provided a Minitab macro for estimating shift functions and another for constructing a confidence interval for the difference between the two populations' deciles at any of the deciles throughout the comparison group's distribution. Wilcox (1997) also provided S-PLUS software functions for making robust inferences about shift functions and for constructing robust simultaneous confidence intervals for them. With regard to simultaneous confidence intervals, the confidence level, say .95, refers to one's level of confidence in the full set of intervals taken together, not separately. Thus, a 95% simultaneous confidence interval means that it is estimated that 95% of the time all of the involved intervals would contain the actual difference between the two populations' deciles.

### Other Graphical Estimators of Effect Sizes

It would be beyond the scope of this book to provide detailed discussions of additional graphical methods for estimating effect sizes at various points along a distribution. Such methods include the Wilk and Gnanadesikan (1968) *percentile comparison graph* and the *Tukey sum-difference graph* (Cleveland, 1985, 1988). The percentile comparison graph plots percentiles from one group's distribution against the same percentiles from the other group's distribution. Cleveland (1985) demonstrated the use of the percentile comparison graph for the cases of equal and unequal sample sizes. (When sample sizes are equal one only need plot the ordered raw scores from one group against the ordered raw scores from the other group.) A linear relationship between the two sets of percentiles or ordered raw scores would be consistent with the shift model that we previously discussed, and this would thus help justify the use of effect sizes that compare means (or medians). On the other hand, a nonlinear relationship would further justify the use of what we called the *probability of superiority* (*PS*). Consult Cleveland (1985) for discussion of how the Tukey sum-difference graph can shed further light on the appropriateness of the shift model.

Darlington (1973) presented an *ordinal dominance curve* for depicting the ordinal relationship between two sets of data, a graph that is similar to the percentile comparison graph. The proportion of the total area under the ordinal dominance curve corresponds to an estimate of the *PS*. This estimate can readily be made by inspection of the ordinal dominance curve as described by Darlington (1973), who also demonstrated other uses of the curve for comparing two groups.

The simplest example of graphic comparison of distributions is the depiction of two or more boxplots within the same figure for easy comparison. As mentioned in chapter 1, statistical software packages that produce such comparisons include Minitab, SAS, SPSS, STATA, and SYSTAT. However, simplicity sometimes comes at a price because more complex methods can be more informative. Trenkler (2002) presented a more complex boxplot method (quantile-boxplot) for comparing two or more distributions. Discussion of other complex methods can be found in Silverman (1986) and Izenman (1991).

## DEPENDENT GROUPS

The probability of superiority, *PS*, as previously defined and estimated in this chapter is not applicable to the dependent-groups design. In this case one can instead define and estimate a similar effect size that we label $PS_{dep}$;

$$PS_{dep} = PR(Y_{ib} > Y_{ia}),  \tag{5.8}$$

where $Y_{ib}$ is the score of an individual under Condition b and $Y_{ia}$ is the score of that same (or a related or matched) individual under Condition a. We use the repeated-measures (i.e., same individual) case for the remainder of this section.

The $PS_{dep}$ as defined in Equation 5.8 is the probability that within a randomly sampled pair of dependent scores (e.g., two scores from the same participant under two different conditions), the score obtained under Condition b will be greater than the score obtained under Condition a. Note the difference between the previously presented definition of the *PS* and the definition of the $PS_{dep}$. In the case of the $PS_{dep}$ one is estimating an effect size that would arise if, for each member of the sampled population, one could compare a member's score under Condition b to that same member's score under Condition a to observe which is greater.

To be concrete, one begins estimating $PS_{dep}$ by making, for each participant in the sample, such comparisons as comparing Jane Jones' score under Condition b with Jane Jones' score under Condition a. The estimate of $PS_{dep}$ is the proportion of all such within-participant comparisons in which a participant's score under Condition b is greater than that participant's score under Condition a. Ties are ignored in this method. For example, if there are $n = 100$ participants of whom 60 score higher under Condition b than they do under Condition a, the estimate of $PS_{dep}$ is $\hat{p}_{dep} = 60/100 = .60$. In the example that follows we define as a *win* for Condition b each instance in which a participant scores higher under Condition b than under Condition a. We use the letter $w$ for the total number of such wins for Condition b throughout the $n$ comparisons. Therefore,

$$\hat{p}_{dep} = w/n. \tag{5.9}$$

An example should make estimation of $PS_{dep}$ very clear. Recall the data of Table 2.1 in chapter 2 in which the weights of $n = 17$ anorectic girls are shown posttreatment ($Y_{ib}$) and pretreatment ($Y_{ia}$). Observe in Table 2.1 that 13 of the 17 girls weighed more posttreatment than they did pretreatment, so the number of wins for posttreatment weight is $w = 13$. (The four exceptions to weight gain were Participants 6, 7, 10, and 11; there were no tied posttreatment and pretreatment weights.) Therefore, $\hat{p}_{dep} = w/n = 13/17 = .76$. We thus estimate that for a randomly sampled member of a population of anorectic girls, of whom these 17 girls would be representative, there is a .76 probability of weight gain from pretreatment to posttreatment. Causal attribution of the weight gain to the effect of the specific treatment is subject to the limitations of the pretest–posttest design that were discussed in the last section of chapter 2.

Manual calculation of a confidence interval for $PS_{dep}$ is easiest in the extreme cases in which $w = 0, 1,$ or $n - 1$ (Wilcox, 1997). Somewhat more laborious manual calculation is also possible for all other values of $w$ by following the steps provided by Wilcox (1997) for Pratt's (1968) method. Wilcox (1997), who called $PS_{dep}$ simply $p$, also provided an S-PLUS software function for computing a confidence interval for $PS_{dep}$ for any value of $w$.

Hand (1992) discussed circumstances in which the $PS$ may not be the best measure of the probability that a certain treatment will be better than another treatment for a future treated individual and how the $PS_{dep}$ can be ideal for this purpose. Refer to Vargha and Delaney (2000) for further discussion of application of the $PS$ to the case of two dependent groups, and consult Brunner and Puri (2001) for extension to multiple groups and factorial designs. Note again that Hand (1992) and others do not use our $PS$ and $PS_{dep}$ notation. Authors vary in their notation for these probabilities.

## QUESTIONS

1. Define the *probability of superiority* for independent groups.

2. Interpret $PS = 0$, $PS = .5$, and $PS = 1$.
3. What is the meaning of the numerator in Equation 5.2, and what is the meaning of the denominator there?
4. What is the focus of researchers who prefer to use a $t$ test and to estimate a standardized difference between means, and what is the focus of researchers who prefers to use the $U$ test and estimate a $PS$?
5. What is the nature of a large-sample approximation for the $U$ test?
6. What was the original purpose of the $U$ test?
7. What is a shift model, and why might this model be unrealistic in many cases of behavioral research?
8. When might a shift model be more appropriate, and when might the $PS$ be more appropriate?
9. What is the effect of heteroscedasticity on the $U$ test and on the usual normal approximation for the $U$ test?
10. What is the common language effect size statistic?
11. What is a major implication of the existence of a monotonic, but not necessarily linear, relationship between a measure of a dependent variable and a latent variable that it is measuring in behavioral science?
12. Identify two assumptions of the common language effect size statistic.
13. If assumptions are satisfied, describe the extent of overlap between the two distributions when $PS = 0$, $PS = .5$, and $PS = 1$.
14. Define and discuss the purpose of the dominance measure of effect size.
15. Define Cohen's $U_3$, and list three requirements for its appropriate use.
16. Discuss the relationship between $U_3$ and the success percentage.
17. Describe ways in which traditional measures of effect size can be misleading when there is inequality of the variances or shapes of distributions for the two groups.
18. Define the probability of superiority in the case of dependent groups, and describe the procedure for estimating it.

# Chapter 6

# Effect Sizes
# for One-Way ANOVA Designs

## INTRODUCTION

The discussions in this and in the next chapter assume the fixed-effects model, in which the two or more levels of the independent variable that are being compared are all of the possible variations of the independent variable (e.g., female and male), or have been specifically chosen by the researcher to represent only those variations to which the results are to be generalized. For example, if ethnicity were the independent variable and there were, say, a white group and two specifically chosen non-white groups, the fixed-effects model is operative and the results should not be generalized to any nonwhite group that was not represented in the research. Methods for dependent groups are discussed in the last section of this chapter.

Note that the ANOVA F test assumes normality and homoscedasticity and that its statistical power and the accuracy of its obtained p levels can be reduced by violation of these assumptions. Consult Grissom (2000) and Wilcox (2003) for further discussion. Wilcox (2003) provided S-PLUS software functions for robust alternatives to the traditional ANOVA F test for both the independent- and the dependent-groups' cases. Wilcox and Keselman (2003a) further discussed robust ANOVA methods and software packages (SAS, S-PLUS, and R) for implementing them. We address the assumptions throughout this chapter.

## ANOVA RESULTS FOR THIS CHAPTER

For worked examples of the estimators of effect sizes that are presented in this chapter, we use ANOVA results from an unpublished study in which the levels of the independent variable were five methods of presentation of material to be learned and the dependent variable was the recall scores for that material (Wright, 1946; cited in McNemar, 1962). This study preceded the time when it was common for researchers to estimate effect size to complement an ANOVA. Nonstatistical details about this research do not concern us here. What one needs to know for the calculations in this chapter is presented in Table 6.1.

## A STANDARDIZED-DIFFERENCE MEASURE OF OVERALL EFFECT SIZE

The simplest measure of the overall effect size is given by

$$g_{mmpop} = \frac{\mu_{max} - \mu_{min}}{\sigma}, \qquad (6.1)$$

where $\mu_{max}$ and $\mu_{min}$ represent the highest and the lowest population means from the sampled populations, respectively, and $\sigma$ is the assumed common standard deviation within the populations, which is estimated by $MS_w^{\frac{1}{2}}$, where $MS_w$ is obtained from the software output for the $F$ test or calculated using a variation of the formula for pooling separate variances,

$$MS_w = \frac{(n_1 - 1)s_1^2 + ... + (n_k - 1)s_k^2}{N - k}. \qquad (6.2)$$

The estimator of the effect size that is given by Equation 6.1 is

$$g_{mm} = \frac{\overline{Y}_{max} - \overline{Y}_{min}}{MS_w^{\frac{1}{2}}}. \qquad (6.3)$$

(For a reminder of the distinction between $g$ [pooling] and $d$ [no pooling] estimators of standardized differences between means see the section Equal or Unequal Variances in chap. 3.) Applying the values from

### TABLE 6.1
#### Information Needed for the Calculations in Chapter 6

| $k = 5$: | Group 1 (n = 16) | Group 2 (n = 16) | Group 3 (n = 16) | Group 4 (n = 16) | Group 5 (n = 16) | Totals (N = 80) |
|---|---|---|---|---|---|---|
| Sample mean ($\overline{Y}_j$) | 3.56 | 6.38 | 9.12 | 10.75 | 13.44 | $\overline{Y}_{all} = 8.65$ |
| Sample standard deviation ($s_j$) | 2.25 | 2.79 | 3.82 | 2.98 | 3.36 | |

Notes. $SS_b = 937.82$, $SS_w = 714.38$, $SS_{tot} = 1,652.20$
$MS_b = 234.46$, $MS_w = 9.53$
$F(4,75) = 24.60$, $p < .001$.

Note.   The data are from "Spacing of practice in verbal learning and the maturation hypothesis," by S. T. Wright, 1946, unpublished master's thesis, Stanford University, Stanford, CA. Adapted with permission of S. T. Wright, now Suzanne Scott.

the current set of ANOVA results in Table 6.1 to Equation 6.3, one finds that $g_{mm} = (13.44 - 3.56) / 9.53^{1/2} = 3.20$. Thus, the highest and lowest population means are estimated to be 3.20 standard deviation units apart, if the standard deviation is assumed to be the same for each population that is represented in the study. Note that it is not always true that when the overall $F$ is statistically significant a test of $\overline{Y}_{max} - \overline{Y}_{min}$ will also yield statistical significance. Discussions of testing the statistical significance of $\overline{Y}_{max} - \overline{Y}_{min}$ and testing differences within other pairs of means among the k means are presented in a later section, Statistical Significance, Confidence Intervals, and Robustness. Note that the measure $g_{mmpop}$ should only be estimated in data analysis if the researcher can justify a genuine interest in it as a measure of overall effect size. The motivation for its use should not be the presentation of the obviously highest value of a $g$ possible. Not surprisingly for standardized-difference estimators of effect size, $g_{mm}$ tends to overestimate $g_{mmpop}$. This measure, and many others, can also be used to estimate needed sample size when planning research (Cohen, 1988; Maxwell & Delaney, 2004).

## A STANDARDIZED OVERALL EFFECT SIZE USING ALL MEANS

The $g_{mmpop}$ and $g_{mm}$ of Equations 6.1 and 6.3 ignore all of the means except the two most extreme means. There is a measure of overall effect size in a one-way ANOVA that uses all of the means. This effect size, which assumes homoscedasticity, is Cohen's (1988) $f$, a measure of a kind of standardized average effect in the population across all of the levels of the independent variable. Cohen's $f$ is given by

$$f = \frac{\sigma_\mu}{\sigma}, \tag{6.4}$$

where $\sigma_\mu$ is the standard deviation of all of the means of the populations that are represented by the samples (based on the deviation of each mean from the mean of all of the means, as in Equation 6.6), and $\sigma$ is the common (assumed) standard deviation within the populations. An estimator of $f$ is given by

$$\hat{f} = \frac{s_{\overline{Y}}}{MS_w^{1/2}}, \tag{6.5}$$

where $s_{\overline{Y}}$ is the standard deviation of the set of all of the $\overline{Y}$ values from $\overline{Y}_1$ to $\overline{Y}_k$. Thus, for equal sample sizes,

$$s_{\overline{Y}} = \left[ \frac{\sum \left( \overline{Y}_i - \overline{Y}_{all} \right)^2}{k-1} \right]^{1/2}, \tag{6.6}$$

where, as previously defined, $\overline{Y}_{all}$ is the mean of all sample means. In Equation 6.6 each $\overline{Y}_i - \overline{Y}_{all}$ reflects the effect of the $i$th level of the independent variable, so $s_{\overline{Y}}$ reflects a kind of average effect in the sample data across the levels of the independent variable. Therefore, $\hat{f}$ estimates the standardized average effect. Again, $MS_w$ can be found in software output from the overall ANOVA F test or calculated using Equation 6.2. Refer to Cohen (1988) for the case of unequal sample sizes. Applying the results from the recall study to Equation 6.6 we find that

$$
s_{\overline{Y}} = \left[ \frac{ \begin{array}{l} (3.56 - 8.65)^2 + (6.38 - 8.65)^2 + (9.12 - 8.65)^2 \\ +(10.75 - 8.65)^2 + (13.44 - 8.65)^2 \end{array} }{5 - 1} \right]^{\frac{1}{2}} = 3.828.
$$

Therefore, using Equation 6.5, $\hat{f} = 3.83 / 9.53^{\frac{1}{2}} = 1.24$. The average effect across the samples is 1.24 standard deviation units.

Although they have the same denominator, $g_{mm}$ should be expected to be greater than $\hat{f}$ because of the difference between their numerators. The numerator of $g_{mm}$ is the range of the means, whereas the numerator of $\hat{f}$ is the standard deviation of that same set of means, an obviously smaller number. In fact $g_{mm}$ is often two to four times larger than $\hat{f}$ (Cohen, 1988). Consistent with this typical result, for our data on recall $g_{mm}$ is more than 2.5 times greater than $\hat{f}$; $g_{mm}/\hat{f} = 3.20/1.24 = 2.58$.

Note that the estimator in Equation 6.5 is positively (i.e., upwardly) biased because the sample means in the numerator are likely to vary more than do the population means. An unbiased estimator of $f$ is

$$
f_{unbiased} = \left[ \frac{k-1}{N}(F - 1) \right]^{\frac{1}{2}}. \tag{6.7}
$$

Refer to Maxwell and Delaney (2004) for further discussion. Applying Equation 6.7 to the data in Table 6.1 yields $f_{unbiased} = \left[ \frac{5-1}{80}(24.60 - 1) \right]^{\frac{1}{2}} = 1.09$. Note that this estimate for $f$ is lower than the one produced by Equation 6.5, as it should be. Consult Steiger (2004) for additional treatment of measures of overall standardized effect size in ANOVA.

## STRENGTH OF ASSOCIATION

Recall from the section The Coefficient of Determination in chapter 4 that in the two-group case, $r^2_{pb}$, has traditionally been used to estimate the proportion of the total variance in the dependent variable that is associated with variation in the independent variable. Somewhat similar estimators of effect size have traditionally been used for one-way ANOVA designs in which $k > 2$. These estimators are intended to reflect strength of association on a scale ranging from 0 (*no association*) to 1 (*maximum association*).

## ETA SQUARED ($\eta^2$)

A parameter that measures the proportion of the variance in the population that is accounted for by variation in the treatment is $\eta^2$. A traditional but especially problematic estimator of the strength-of-association parameter, $\eta^2$, is $\hat{\eta}^2$:

$$\hat{\eta}^2 = \frac{SS_b}{SS_{tot}}. \qquad (6.8)$$

The numerator of Equation 6.8 reflects variability that is attributable to variation in the independent variable and the denominator reflects total variability. The original name for $\eta$ itself was the *correlation ratio*, but this name has since come to be used by some also for $\eta^2$. When the independent variable is quantitative $\eta$ represents the correlation between the independent variable and the dependent variable, but, unlike $r_{pop}$, $\eta$ reflects a curvilinear as well as a linear relationship in that case. When there are two groups $\eta$ has the same absolute size as $r_{pop}$. Also, the previously discussed Cohen's (1988) $f$ is related to $\eta^2$; $f = [\eta^2/(1 - \eta^2)]^{1/2}$.

A major flaw of $\hat{\eta}^2$ as an estimator of strength of association is that it is positively biased; that is, it tends to overestimate $\eta^2$. This estimator tends to overestimate because its numerator, $SS_b$, is inflated by some error variability. Bias is less for larger sample sizes and for larger values of $\eta^2$. In the next section we discuss ways to reduce the positive bias in estimating $\eta^2$. For further discussion of such bias consult P. Snyder and Lawson (1993) and Maxwell and Delaney (2004).

## EPSILON SQUARED ($\varepsilon^2$) AND OMEGA SQUARED ($\omega^2$)

A somewhat less biased alternative estimator of $\eta^2$ is $\hat{\varepsilon}^2$, and a more nearly unbiased estimator is $\hat{\omega}^2$; consult Keselman (1975). The equations are (Ezekiel, 1930):

$$\hat{\varepsilon}^2 = \frac{SS_b - (k-1)MS_w}{SS_{tot}}, \qquad (6.9)$$

and Hays' (1994)

$$\hat{\omega}^2 = \frac{SS_b - (k-1)MS_w}{SS_{tot} + MS_w}. \tag{6.10}$$

We assume equal sample sizes and homoscedasticity. Software output for the ANOVA $F$ test might include $\hat{\varepsilon}^2$ and/or $\hat{\omega}^2$. However, manual calculation is easy (demonstrated later) because the $SS$ and $MS_w$ values are available from output even if these estimators are not.

Comparing the numerators of Equations 6.9 and 6.10 with the numerator of Equation 6.8 for $\hat{\eta}^2$, observe that Equations 6.9 and 6.10 attempt to compensate for the fact that $\hat{\eta}^2$ tends to overestimate $\eta^2$ by reducing the numerator of the estimators by $(k-1)MS_w$. Equation 6.10 goes even further in attempting to reduce the overestimation by also adding $MS_w$ to the denominator. The $\hat{\omega}^2$ estimator is now more widely used than is $\hat{\varepsilon}^2$.

A statistically significant overall $F$ can be taken as evidence that $\hat{\omega}^2$ is significantly greater than 0. However, confidence intervals are especially important here because of the high sampling variability of the estimators (Maxwell, Camp, & Arvey, 1981). For example, R. M. Carroll and Nordholm (1975) found great sampling variability even when $N = 90$ and $k = 3$. Of course, high sampling variability results in estimates often being much above or much below the effect size that is being estimated.

For rough purposes approximate confidence limits for $\eta^2$ based on $\hat{\omega}^2$ can be obtained using graphs (called *nomographs*) that can be found in Abu Libdeh (1984). Refer to Venables (1975) for an advanced discussion. Assuming normality and, especially, homoscedasticity, the use of noncentral distributions is appropriate for constructing such confidence intervals. Therefore, as was discussed in the section on noncentral distributions in chapter 3, software is required for their construction, so no example of manual calculation is presented here. Refer to Fidler and Thompson (2001) for a demonstration of the use of SPSS to construct a confidence interval for $\eta^2$ that is based on a noncentral distribution. Also consult Smithson (2003) and Steiger (2004) for further discussion of such confidence intervals. At the time of this writing Michael Smithson provides SPSS, SAS, S-PLUS, and R scripts for computing confidence intervals. These scripts can be accessed at http://www.anu.edu.au/psychology/staff/mike/Index.html. STATISTICA can also produce such confidence intervals.

Note that as a measure of a proportion (of total variance of the dependent variable that is associated with variation of the independent variable) the value of $\eta^2$ cannot be below 0, but inspection of Equations 6.9 and 6.10 reveals that the values of the estimators $\hat{\varepsilon}^2$ and $\hat{\omega}^2$ can themselves be below 0. Hays (1994), who had earlier introduced $\hat{\omega}^2$, recommended that when the value of this estimator is below 0 the value should be reported as 0. However, some meta-analysts are concerned that replacing negative estimates with zeros might cause an additional positive bias in an estimate that is based on averaging estimates in a meta-analysis. Similarly, Fidler and Thompson (2001) argued that any obtained negative value should be reported as such instead of converting it to 0 so that the full width of a confidence interval can be reported. Of course, when a negative value is reported, a reader of a research report has an opportunity to interpret it as 0 if one so chooses. Consult Susskind and Howland (1980) and Vaughan and Corballis (1969) for further discussions of this issue.

For an example of $\hat{\omega}^2$ we apply the results from the recall study (Table 6.1) to Equation 6.10 to find that

$$\hat{\omega}^2 = \frac{937.82 - (5-1)9.53}{1,652.20 + 9.53} = .54.$$

Therefore, we estimate that 54% of the variability of the recall scores is attributable to varying the method of presentation of the material that is to be learned. This estimation is subject to the limitations that are discussed later in this chapter in the section entitled Evaluation of Criticisms of Estimators of Strength of Association. For discussions of application of $\hat{\omega}^2$ to analysis of covariance and to multivariate designs refer to Olejnik and Algina (2000).

## STRENGTH OF ASSOCIATION FOR SPECIFIC COMPARISONS

Estimation of the strength of association within just two of the $k$ groups at a time may be called *estimation of a specific, focused, or simple-effects strength of association*. Such estimation provides more detailed information than do the previously discussed estimators of overall strength of association. To make such a focused estimate one can use

$$\hat{\omega}^2_{comp} = \frac{SS_{comp} - MS_w}{SS_{tot} + MS_w}, \tag{6.11}$$

where the subscript *comp* represents a comparison (between two groups). The symbol $SS_{contrast}$ is sometimes used instead of $SS_{comp}$. (Often *comparison* refers to two means, whereas *contrast* refers to more than two means, as is shown in the next paragraph.) Observe the similarity between Equations 6.10 and 6.11. In Equation 6.11 $SS_{comp}$ replaces the $SS_b$ of Equation 6.10, and the $(k - 1)$ of Equation 6.10 is now $2 - 1 = 1$ in Equation 6.11 because one is now involving only two groups. To find $SS_{comp}$ in the present case of making a simple comparison involving two of the $k$ means, $\overline{Y}_i$ and $\overline{Y}_j$, use

$$SS_{comp} = \frac{\left(\overline{Y}_i - \overline{Y}_j\right)^2}{\dfrac{1}{n_i} + \dfrac{1}{n_j}}. \tag{6.12}$$

Consult Olejnik and Algina (2000) for a more general formulation and a worked example of Equation 6.12 that involves the case of a complex comparison (often simply called a contrast), such as comparing the mean of a control group with the overall mean of two or more combined treatment groups.

In the research on recall two of the five group means were $\overline{Y}_i = 10.75$ and $\overline{Y}_j = 6.38$. Using these two means for an example and using that study's ANOVA results that are presented in Table 6.1, we apply Equation 6.12 to find that in this example $SS_{comp} = (10.75 - 6.38)^2 / (1/16 + 1/16) = 152.78$. Now applying Equation 6.11, we find that $\hat{\omega}^2_{comp} = (152.78 - 9.53) / (1,652.20 + 9.53) = .09$. Therefore, we estimate (subject to the limitations that are discussed in the next section) that 9% of the variability of the recall scores is attributable to whether presentation method $i$ or presentation method $j$ is used for learning the material that is to be recalled. Consult Keppel (1991), Maxwell et al. (1981), Olejnik and Algina (2000), and Vaughan and Corballis (1969) for further discussions of estimating strength of association for specific comparisons.

## EVALUATION OF CRITICISMS OF ESTIMATORS OF STRENGTH OF ASSOCIATION

The estimators $\hat{\eta}^2$, $\hat{\varepsilon}^2$, and $\hat{\omega}^2$ are all called estimators of strength of association, variance accounted for, or proportion of variance explained (POV). We will call such estimators POV estimators in the remainder of this chapter. (When $k = 2$ these POV estimators are similar, but not identical, to $r^2_{pb}$, the sample coefficient of determination that was discussed in chap. 4.) Such estimators and the $\eta^2$ that they estimate share some of the criticisms of $r^2_{pb}$ and $r^2_{pop}$ that have appeared in the literature and that were discussed in chapter 4. We very briefly review and evaluate these criticisms and evaluate some others. Note that we repeatedly state in this book that no effect size or estimator is without one or more limitations. Furthermore, some of the limitations of $\eta^2$ and its estimators are also applicable to measures of the standardized difference between means, $\Delta$ and $g_{pop}$, and their estimators. Also, some of the limitations are more of a problem for meta-analysis than for the underlying primary research that is the focus of this book. (For an argument that these estimators, unlike $r^2$, do not actually estimate $POV_{pop}$, consult Murray and Dosser, 1987.)

First, recall from the section The Coefficient of Determination in chapter 4 that effect sizes that involve squaring values that would otherwise be below 1 yield values that are often closer to 0 than 1 in the human sciences. A consequence of this that is sometimes pointed out in the literature is a possible undervaluing of the importance of the result. A statistically inexperienced reader of a research report or summary, one who is familiar with little more than the 0% to 100% scale of percentages, will not likely be familiar with the range of typical values of estimates of a standardized-difference effect size or POV effect size.

Therefore, if, say, the estimate from an obtained $d$ is that $\Delta = .5$, a value that is approximately equivalent to $\omega^2 = .05$, such a statistically inexperienced reader will likely be more impressed by the effect of the independent variable if an estimated $\Delta = .5$ is reported than if an estimated $POV = .05$ is reported. (Note that the magnitudes of an estimate of $POV$ and an estimate of $\Delta$ depend in part on sample size; consult Barnette & McLean, 2002, and Onwuegbuzie & Levin, 2003.)

The just-noted criticism of the $POV$ approach to effect size is less applicable the more statistical knowledge that the intended readership of a research report has and the more the author of a report does to disabuse readers of incorrect interpretation of the results. Indeed, the more warnings about this limitation that appear in articles and books, the less susceptibility there will be to such undervaluing. On the other hand, a low value for an estimate of $POV$ can be informative in alerting us to the need to (a) search for additional independent variables that might contribute to determining values of the dependent variable and/or (b) improve control of extraneous variables that contribute to error variability in the research and thereby lower an estimate of the $POV$.

Second, also recall from chapter 4 and from earlier in this chapter that measures of effect size (but not necessarily their estimates) that involve squaring are directionless; they cannot be negative, rendering them typically useless for averaging in meta-analysis. The inappropriateness of averaging estimates of $POV$ across studies can be readily seen by recognizing that the same value for the estimate would be obtained in two studies if all of the values of the terms in Equations 6.8, 6.9, or 6.10 were the same in both studies even if the rank order of the $k$ means were opposite in these studies. An example of this situation would be one in which the most, intermediate, and least effective treatments in Study 1 were Treatments a, b, and c, respectively, whereas the ranking of effectiveness in Study 2 was Treatments c, b, and a, respectively. The two $POV$ estimates would be the same although the two studies produced opposite results. This is more a problem for a meta-analyst than for a primary researcher. However, this limitation reminds one again that research reports should include means for all samples, rendering it easier to interpret results in the context of the results from other related studies.

Third, a criticism that is sometimes raised is easy to accommodate. Namely, unlike a typical standardized-difference effect size for $k = 2$, the most commonly used $POV$ effect size for $k > 2$ designs (estimated by Equations 6.8, 6.9, or 6.10) is *global*, that is, it provides information about the overall association between the independent and dependent variables but it does not provide information about specific comparisons within the $k$ levels of the independent variable. This limitation can be avoided by applying the less commonly used Equation 6.11 to two samples at a time from the $k$ samples.

Fourth, an additional criticism is related to the first criticism. Recall from the section The Coefficient of Determination in chapter 4 that human behavior (e.g., the dependent variable) is multiply determined; that is, it is influenced by a variety of genetic and background experiential variables (both kinds being extraneous variables in much research). Therefore, it is usually unreasonable to expect that any single independent variable is going to contribute a very large proportion of what determines variability of the dependent variable (Ahadi & Diener, 1989; O'Grady, 1982). Again, more statistically experienced consumers of research reports will take multiple determination and typical sizes of estimates of POVs into account when interpreting an estimate of a POV. However, again, those readers of reports who are inexperienced in statistics might merely note that an estimated POV is not very far above 0% and often mistakenly conclude that the effect, therefore, must be of little practical importance. In fact a small-appearing estimate of POV might actually be important and might also be typical of the effect of independent variables in the human sciences. Again, a report of research can deal with this possible problem by tailoring the Discussion section to the level of statistical knowledge of the readership.

Fifth, the literature includes another criticism of the POV measure that is applied under the fixed-effects model; namely, its magnitude depends on which of the possible levels of the independent variable are selected by the researcher for the study. For example, including an extreme level, such as a no-treatment control group (a strong manipulation), can increase the estimate. Note, however, that standardized-difference effect sizes are similarly dependent on the range of difference between the two levels of the independent variable that are being compared, because this difference influences the magnitude of the numerator of the measure or its estimator. For example, one is likely to obtain a larger value of an estimate of a POV or standardized-difference effect size if one compares a high dose of a drug with a zero dose than if one compares two intermediate doses. This criticism can be countered if the researcher chooses the levels of the independent variable sensibly and limits the interpretation of the results only to those levels, as is required under the fixed-effects model. In applied research a researcher's "sensible" choice of levels of the independent variable would be those that are comparable to the levels that are currently used or ones that are likely to be adopted in practice. Note too by inspecting the numerators of Equations 6.9 and 6.10 that an estimate of overall POV is also affected by the number of levels of the independent variable, $k$; consult F. Snyder and Lawson (1993) and Barnette and McLean (2002).

As is the case for other kinds of effect sizes, estimates of POV will be reduced by unreliable measurement of the dependent variable or by unreliable measurement, unreliable recording, or unreliable manipulation of the independent variable, all of which was discussed in chapter 4. The estimate of the POV can be no greater than, and likely often much less than, the product of $r_{xx}$ and $r_{yy}$, which are the reliability coefficients (chap. 4) of the independent variable and dependent variable, respectively. In many cases the reliability of the independent variable will not be known. However, if we assume that for a manipulated independent variable $r_{xx} = 1$, or nearly so, then the estimate of the *POV* will have an upper limit at or slightly below the value of $r_{yy}$. The lower the reliabilities, the greater the contribution of error variance to the total variance of the data and, therefore, the lower the proportion of total variance of the data that is associated with variation of the independent variable. (Observe that the denominators of Equations 6.9, 6.10, and 6.11 become greater the greater the error variability.) Also, as was previously stated, estimators of *POV* assume homoscedasticity, and they can especially overestimate *POV* when there is heteroscedasticity and unequal sample sizes (R. M. Carroll & Nordholm, 1975). This is reason enough to be cautious about comparing estimates of *POV* from studies with different sample sizes (Murray & Dosser, 1987).

Finally, analysis of data occurs in a context of design characteristics that can influence the results (Wilson & Lipsey, 2001). Therefore, when interpreting results and when comparing them with those from other studies, one should be cognizant of the research design and context that gave rise to those results. As P. Snyder and Lawson (1993) cautiously noted, a researcher should not simply report that an independent variable accounted for an estimated *P*% of the variance of the measure of the dependent variable. Instead, a researcher should report, subject to the other limitations that have been discussed, that it is estimated that *P*% of the variance of the measure of the dependent variable is accounted for when *n* of the kind of participants who were used are assigned to each of the *k* levels of the independent variable that were used. Refer to Onwuegbuzie and Levin (2003) and the many references therein for further discussions of the influence of numerous characteristics of research designs on effect sizes. Olejnik and Algina (2003) discussed generalized *POV* measures that are applicable to a variety of designs.

There is extensive literature on estimating a *POV*. Good starting points for a search of this literature are articles by Fern and Monroe (1996), O'Grady (1982), Olejnik and Algina (2000), Richardson (1996), P. Snyder and Lawson (1993), Vaughan and Corballis (1969), and the other articles that have been cited in this chapter. Also consult the references that are footnoted by Keppel (1991). In the next section we consider standardized-difference measures of effect size that focus on comparisons between two groups at a time from the set of *k* groups. This is an informative approach that also addresses the third criticism of measures of *POV* that was already discussed. Hunter and Schmidt (2004) discussed their objection to *POV* measures.

## STANDARDIZED-DIFFERENCE EFFECT SIZES FOR TWO OF *k* MEANS AT A TIME

When an estimator of a standardized-difference effect size involves the mean ($\overline{Y}_c$) of a control, placebo, or standard-treatment comparison group and the mean of any one of the other groups ($\overline{Y}_i$), and homoscedasticity is not assumed, it is sensible to use the standard deviation of such a comparison group, $s_c$, for standardizing the mean difference to obtain

$$d_{comp} = \frac{\overline{Y}_i - \overline{Y}_c}{s_c}. \tag{6.13}$$

Alternatively, if one assumes homoscedasticity of the two populations whose samples are involved in the comparison, the pooled standard deviation from these two samples, $s_p$, may be used instead to find

$$g_p = \frac{\overline{Y}_i - \overline{Y}_j}{s_p}, \tag{6.14}$$

where $j$ can represent a control or any other kind of group. If one assumes homoscedasticity of all of the $k$ populations, the best standard deviation by which to divide the difference between any two of the means, including $\overline{Y}_i - \overline{Y}_c$, is the standard deviation that is based on pooling the within-group variances of all $k$ groups, $MS_w^{\frac{1}{2}}$, producing

$$g_{msw} = \frac{\overline{Y}_i - \overline{Y}_j}{MS_w^{\frac{1}{2}}}. \tag{6.15}$$

Again, to find $MS_w^{\frac{1}{2}}$ take the square root of the value of $MS_w$ that is found in the ANOVA software output or take the square root of the $MS_w$ that has been calculated from Equation 6.2. As is discussed in the next section, Worked Examples, each of the estimators in Equations 6.13, 6.14, and 6.15 has a somewhat different interpretation.

A problem may occur when applying Equation 6.14 to more than one of the possible pairs of the $k$ means. To some extent differences among the two or more values of $g_p$ may arise merely from varying values of $s_i$ from comparison to comparison, even if the same $\overline{Y}_j$, say, $\overline{Y}_c$, is used for each $g_p$. Even when there is homoscedasticity (a characteristic of populations, not samples), sampling variability of values of $s_i^2$ can cause great variation in the different $s_i^2$ values that contribute to the pooling of an $s_i^2$ and an $s_j^2$ for each $g_p$. Such sampling variability should be taken into account when interpreting differences among the values of $g_p$. For further discussion of limitations of $d$ (and $g$) types of estimators of effect sizes, see the last section of chapter 7.

## WORKED EXAMPLES

We use the results in Table 6.1 from the research on recall to demonstrate calculation of all of the estimators that were presented in the previous section. For calculation using Equations 6.13 and 6.14 we use

$\overline{Y}_2 = 6.38$ for $\overline{Y}_i$ and $\overline{Y}_5 = 13.44$ for $\overline{Y}_c$ and $\overline{Y}_j$. Therefore, $s_c$ is $s_5 = 3.36$ and $s_p$ is based on pooling the variances of Samples 2 and 5, in which $s_2^2 = 2.79^2 = 7.78$ and $s_5^2 = 3.36^2 = 11.29$. Values of $s^2$ for each sample can be obtained from software output or from an equation for manual calculation; $s^2 = [(\Sigma Y^2) - n(\overline{Y}^2)] / (n - 1)$. (Calculation of $s^2$ using this equation is demonstrated in chap. 7 in the Classificatory Factors Only section.) We previously reported that $MS_w = 9.53$ for the current data on recall.

One pools the variances $s_2^2 = 7.78$ and $s_5^2 = 11.29$ to find $s_p^2$ using Equation 6.16;

$$s_p^2 = \frac{(n_i - 1)s_i^2 + (n_j - 1)s_j^2}{n_i + n_j - 2}. \tag{6.16}$$

Using Equation 6.16,
$s_p^2 = [(16 - 1)7.78 + (16 - 1)11.29] / (16 + 16 - 2) = 9.54$ and $s_p = 9.54^{1/2} = 3.09$.

Applying the needed previously noted values to Equations 6.13, 6.14, and 6.15 one finds that $d_{comp} = (6.38 - 13.44) / 3.36 = -2.10$, $g_p = (6.38 - 13.44) / 3.09 = -2.28$, and $g_{msw} = (6.38 - 13.44) / 9.53^{1/2} = -2.29$.

From the value of $d_{comp}$ we estimate that, with regard to the comparison population's distribution and standard deviation, the mean of Population $i$ is 2.10 standard deviation units below the mean of the comparison population. From the value of $g_p$ we estimate that, with regard to the distribution of Population $j$ and a common standard deviation for Populations $i$ and $j$, the mean of Population $i$ is 2.28 standard deviation units below the mean of Population $j$. Finally, from the value of $g_{msw}$ we estimate that, with regard to the distribution of Population $j$ and a common standard deviation for all five of the involved populations, the mean of Population $i$ is 2.29 standard deviation units below the mean of Population $j$.

If one assumes normality for the two compared populations, one can interpret the results in terms of an estimation of what percentage of the members of one population score higher or lower than the average-scoring members of the other population. (Refer to the second section of chap. 3 for a refresher on this topic.) A researcher should decide a priori which pair or pairs of means are of interest and then choose among Equations 6.13, 6.14, and 6.15 based on whether homoscedasticity is to be assumed. Any estimator that is calculated must then be reported.

## STATISTICAL SIGNIFICANCE, CONFIDENCE INTERVALS, AND ROBUSTNESS

Before considering standardized differences between means we discuss methods for unstandardized differences between means. Recall from the opening sections of chapters 2 and 3 that inferences about unstandardized differences between means can be especially informative when the dependent variable is scaled in familiar units such as weight lost or gained, ounces of alcohol or number of cigarettes consumed, days abstinent or absent, or dollars spent. Bond et al. (2003) argued for routine use of unstandardized differences in such cases and demonstrated a method for their use in meta-analysis.

Tests of the statistical significance of all of the $\bar{Y}_i - \bar{Y}_j$ pairings, including $\bar{Y}_{max} - \bar{Y}_{min}$, and construction of confidence intervals that are based on all of these differences (simultaneous confidence intervals) are often conducted using John Tukey's honestly statistically different (HSD) test of pairwise comparisons. This method is widely available in software packages. Note that when using some methods of pairwise comparisons, such as Tukey's HSD method, it is customary but perhaps unwise in terms of loss of statistical power to have conducted a previous omnibus (overall) $F$ test. Tukey's method is a substitute for, not a follow-up to, an omnibus test. (The well-known Scheffé method, which is not discussed here, and Dayton's, 2003, method, which is discussed here, are exceptions.) Consult Bernhardson (1975) and Wilcox (2003) for elaboration of this issue of problematic prior omnibus $F$ testing.

Additionally, the results of an omnibus $F$ test may not be consistent with those of Tukey's HSD test. The omnibus $F$ may be significant even when none of the pairwise comparisons is significant and vice versa. The researcher's initial research hypothesis or hypotheses should determine whether to use an omnibus $F$ test and omnibus estimator of effect size or pairwise comparisons of means and their related specific (focused) effect sizes.

The procedures for the Tukey method for such pairwise significance testing and construction of confidence intervals, including modifications for unequal sample size and heteroscedasticity, are explained in detail in Maxwell and Delaney (2004). The Tukey method that we discuss here, which is also known as the wholly significantly different (WSD) method, is included in some major software packages. Note that the Tukey method that is relevant to this section is not the same and not interchangeable with a method that is known as the Tukey-b method.

In their simulation study of the robustness of several methods for making pairwise comparisons under various conditions of violation of assumptions, Cribbie and Keselman (2003a) found that the Tukey method can be outperformed by a hybrid method in terms of control of Type I error and power, at least under the conditions that were studied. The hybrid method, which came to be known as the REGWQ procedure, is based on modification and remodification of the once-popular Newman–Keuls method. Consult Cribbie and Keselman (2003a) for discussion and references regarding the history of the REGWQ method. Cribbie and Keselman (2003a) found that applying the REGWQ method to the Welch (1938) version of the $t$ statistic controlled Type I error well. When there was moderate skew power was higher when using the original Welch $t$, but when skew was great power was higher when using the Yuen (1974) version of the Welch $t$ that uses trimmed means and Winsorized variances, a version that was discussed in chapter 2 of this book.

Note that computer simulations (known as Monte Carlo studies) of the robustness of a statistical procedure cannot examine all possible conditions of violations of assumptions. Therefore, where there is no mathematical theory to inform about the robustness of a procedure, the best that a simulation study can do is to simulate a reasonable variety of conditions under which a statistical procedure might be applied by a researcher. Among the variables and combinations of variables that a good simulation, such as those by Cribbie and Keselman (2003a) and others, simulate are $k$, $N$, variation of $n$ across samples, extent of heteroscedasticity, pairings of unequal values of $n$ and unequal values of $\sigma^2$, pattern of means of the involved populations, shapes of the distributions in the populations, and, in the case of pairwise comparisons, whether and what kind of preceding omnibus test has been applied. Refer to Sawilowsky (2003) for additional criteria for an appropriate Monte Carlo simulation.

In the case of planned comparisons between each mean and the mean of a baseline group (i.e., a control, placebo, or standard-treatment group as in the numerator of Equation 6.13), the Dunnett many-one method may be used for significance testing and construction of simultaneous confidence intervals for all of the values of $\mu_i - \mu_c$. The procedure, which assumes homoscedasticity, can be found in Maxwell and Delaney (2004). Note that the Dunnett many-one method is not the same and is not for the same purpose as the Dunnett T3 method.

In applied research one might be interested in pairwise comparisons of the mean of the best-performing group (not known a priori) with each of the other groups. The Dunnett many-one method for planned comparisons is not applicable to this case. However, Hsu's (1996) modification of the many-one method is applicable, assuming homoscedasticity, for testing each such difference and constructing a confidence interval for each one. Refer to Maxwell and Delaney (2004) for additional detailed discussion.

Wilcox (2003) provided discussions and S-PLUS software functions for a variety of newer robust methods that compete with the Tukey method, including comparing pairwise medians instead of means. For another approach that is based on comparing medians, refer to Bonett and Price (2002). For a fundamentally different approach that is based on a reformulation of the traditional null hypothesis refer to Shaffer (2002).

Note that if a researcher is interested in the relative magnitudes of all of the means of the populations that are represented in the design, methods of pairwise comparisons, such as Tukey's method, can produce intransitive (i.e., contradictory) results. For example, suppose that there are three groups, so that one can test $H_0: \mu_1 = \mu_2$, $H_0: \mu_2 = \mu_3$, and $H_0: \mu_1 = \mu_3$. Unfortunately, it is possible for a method of pairwise comparisons to produce intransitive results, such as seeming to indicate that $\mu_1 = \mu_2, \mu_2 = \mu_3$, and, contradictorily, $\mu_1 > \mu_3$. Of course, such a suggested pattern of means cannot be true.

Dayton (2003) provided a method for making inferences about the true pattern of the means of the involved populations. The method is intended to be applicable to the case of homoscedasticity or the case in which the pattern of the magnitudes of the variances in the populations is the same as the pattern of the means in the populations, which is likely common. The required sample sizes at a given effect size to attain a given level of statistical power for detecting the true pattern of these means depends on the nature of this pattern (see Cribbie & Keselman, 2003b; consult Table 3 in Dayton, 2003). For some patterns the required sample sizes are very large, but they are not as large as would be required for tests such as Tukey's HSD test to detect the true pattern. Construction of confidence intervals is not possible within Dayton's (2003) procedure. Also, this method, unlike Tukey's, should be preceded by an omnibus test (a *protected procedure*) to improve its accuracy in detecting the pattern of means (Cribbie & Keselman, 2003b).

Dayton's method generally appears to be robust to nonnormality (Cribbie & Keselman, 2003a; Dayton, 2003) and to heteroscedasticity in most cases (Cribbie & Keselman, 2003b). Although Cribbie and Keselman (2003a) concluded from their simulations that Dayton's method generally provided good control of Type I error and good power, more simulation research may be needed before a definitive conclusion can be reached regarding the overall performance of the method under heteroscedasticity. Dayton (2003) too was cautious about his method in this regard. Computations can be implemented using Microsoft Excel alone or together with special software. Refer to Dayton (2003) for details.

Maxwell (2004) discussed the often ignored power implications of methods of multiple comparisons, distinguishing among *power for a specific comparison, any-pair power* to detect at least one pairwise difference, and *all-pairs power* to detect all true differences within pairs of means. Low specific-comparison power can result in inconsistent results across studies even when any-pair power is adequate. Maxwell's (2004) results indicate that extremely large sample sizes, large multi-center studies, or meta-analyses might be required to deal with this problem. He made numerous other recommendations, including the increased use of confidence intervals.

We turn our attention now from unstandardized to standardized differences between means. Approximate confidence intervals for $\Delta$, the standardized difference between population means, can be obtained, assuming homoscedasticity, by dividing the lower and upper limits of the confidence interval for each pairwise difference between population means by $MS_w^{\frac{1}{2}}$. Refer to Steiger (1999) for software for constructing exact confidence intervals for a standardized–difference effect size (as estimated by $g_p$ of our Equation 6.14) that arises from planned contrasts when sample sizes are equal. The exact confidence intervals use noncentral distributions. Steiger and Fouladi (1997) and Smithson (2003) illustrated the method. Consult Steiger (2004) for further discussion. Refer to Bird (2002) for a discussion of the likely differences in widths of exact and approximate confidence intervals.

Bird (2002) also presented an approximate method for construction of a confidence interval for $\Delta$ that is based on the usual (i.e., central) $t$ distribution. (Assuming normality, an exact confidence interval would require the use of the noncentral $t$ distribution that was discussed in chap. 3.) This method also assumes homoscedasticity by using the square root of $MS_w$ from the ANOVA results to standardize the difference between the two means of interest. This method appears generally to provide fairly close approximation to the nominal confidence level (e.g., 95%). A simulation study indicated that the actual confidence level (called the *probability coverage*) departs downward somewhat from the nominal level the greater the true value of $\Delta$—and even more so the smaller the number of groups. For example, when there were only two groups in the entire design and $\Delta = 0$, the probability coverage for a 95% confidence interval was indeed found to be .950, but when $\Delta = 1.6$, the probability coverage was actually .911. However, the latter coverage improved from .911 to .929 when there was a total of four groups in the design (Algina & Keselman, 2003). Also consult Algina and Keselman (2003) for a method and a SAS/IML program for constructing an exact confidence interval for $\Delta$, assuming homoscedasticity. This method provides the option to pool all variances in the design or just the variances of the two groups that are involved in the effect size. At the time of this writing Kevin Bird and his colleagues offer free software for constructing approximate confidence intervals for standardized or unstandardized contrasts, planned or unplanned, from between-groups or within-groups designs. This software is available at http://www.psy.unsw.edu.au/research/PSY.htm.

Refer to Keselman, Cribbie, and Wilcox (2002) for a method of paired comparisons of trimmed means that controls Type I error when sample sizes are unequal and there is nonnormality and heteroscedasticity. (Trimmed means were discussed in chap. 1 of this book.) Also, as was discussed for the $k = 2$ case in chapter 3, there are additional, rarely used estimators of standardized-difference effect sizes that may be more resistant to heteroscedasticity than the estimators that have been discussed in this section. These estimators involve alternatives to the use of mean differences in the numerators and alternatives to standard deviations in the denominators. For further discussions refer to the sections Tentative Recommendations and Additional Standardized-Difference Effect Sizes When There are Outliers in chapter 3 and to Grissom and Kim (2001).

For discussions of effect sizes for multivariate designs, consult Olejnik and Algina (2000) and Smithson (2003). For a measure of effect size for two or more groups in a randomized longitudinal design, refer to Maxwell (1998). Rosenthal et al. (2000) provided an alternative treatment of effect sizes in terms of correlational contrasts for one-way and factorial designs. Maxwell and Delaney (2004) also discussed this topic. Timm (2004) proposed the *ubiquitous effect size index* as an alternative to correlational effect sizes for exploratory experiments. Timm's (2004) method is applicable to omnibus $F$ tests or tests on contrasts. This method assumes homoscedasticity and reduces to Hedges' $g$ in the case of two equal sized groups.

For the case in which two groups at a time from multiple groups are compared, Wilcox (2003) discussed and provided S-PLUS software functions for estimation of what we called in chapter 5 the *PS* (probability of superiority) and the *DM* (dominance measure). Consult Vargha and Delaney (2000) and Brunner and Puri (2001) for extensions of what we called the *PS* to multiple-group and factorial designs.

## WITHIN-GROUPS DESIGNS AND FURTHER READING

Recall from the Dependent Groups section in chapter 3 that the choice of a standardizer for an effect size depends on the nature of the population to which one intends to generalize the results. The choice of standardizer in the estimator must be consistent with the nature of the variability within this targeted population. However, in this regard, primary researchers, who directly estimate effect sizes from raw data, unlike meta-analysts, do not have to be concerned about the inflation of estimates of standardized-difference effect sizes. Such inflation by a meta-analyst would be attributable to the use of invalid formulas, instead of the valid formulas in the case of within-groups designs, for converting values of $t$ or $F$ to an estimate of effect size (cf. Cortina & Nouri, 2000).

For one-way ANOVA within-groups designs (e.g., repeated-measures designs), primary researchers can use the same equations that were presented in this chapter for the independent-groups design to calculate standardized-difference effect-size indicators. If a repeated-measures design has involved a pretest, the pretest mean ($\overline{Y}_{pre}$) can be one of any two compared means, and the standard deviation may be $s_{pre}$, $s_p$, or $MS_w^{1/2}$. The latter two standardizers assume homoscedasticity with regard either to the two compared groups or to all of the groups, respectively. (Statistical software may not automatically generate $s_{pre}$, $s_p$, or $MS_w^{1/2}$ when it computes a within-groups ANOVA. However, such software does allow one to compute the variance of data within a single condition of the design. Therefore, one may use the variances so generated to calculate $MS_w^{1/2}$ and $s_p$ using Equations 6.2 and 6.16, respectively.) Consult Algina and Keselman (2003) for a method and a SAS/IML program for constructing an approximate confidence interval for a standardized-difference effect size under homoscedasticity or heteroscedasticity in a within-groups design.

For methods for making all pairwise comparisons (planned or unplanned) of the $\overline{Y}_i - \overline{Y}_j$ differences for dependent data, including the construction of simultaneous confidence intervals, refer to Maxwell and Delaney's (2004) and Wilcox's (2003) discussions of a Bonferroni method (historically, Bonferroni–Dunn method). Also consult Algina and Keselman (2003) for a method for constructing confidence intervals for pairwise comparisons.

The Tukey method (HSD or WSD) is not recommended for significance testing and the construction of confidence intervals in the case of dependent data because, as is not the case for the Bonferroni–Dunn method, the Tukey method might not maintain family-wise error rate (e.g., $\alpha_{FW} < .05$) unless the sphericity assumption is satisfied. (Of the several ways to define *sphericity*, the simplest considers the variance of the difference scores, $Y_i - Y_j$, with respect to compared levels $i$ and $j$. Sphericity is satisfied when the population variances of such difference scores are the same for all such pairs of levels.) Because tests of sphericity may not have sufficient power to detect its absence, it is best to use methods that do not assume sphericity (e.g., it is better to use a multivariate than a univariate approach to designs with dependent groups). Refer to Maxwell and Delaney (2004) for further discussion of sphericity.

Finally, with regard to unstandardized differences, Wilcox (2003) discussed and provided S-PLUS software functions for newer robust methods for pairwise comparisons in the case of dependent groups. Refer to Wilcox and Keselman (2002b) for simulations of the effectiveness of bootstrap methods to deal with the problem of controlling Type I error when outliers are either simply removed or formally trimmed when conducting all pairwise comparisons of the locations (e.g., trimmed means) of one specific group and each of the other groups (another many-one procedure) in the case of dependent data. Dayton's (2003) method and suggested software (both discussed in the previous section) for detecting the pattern of relationships among the means of the populations are also applicable to the case of dependent groups. Wilcox and Keselman (2003b) discussed the application of modified one-step M-estimators (that were discussed in our chap. 4) to one-way repeated-measures ANOVA. We turn our attention now to *POV*.

To estimate overall *POV* in a one-way ANOVA design with dependent groups, one can use (Dodd & Schultz, 1973; also refer to Olejnik & Algina, 2000)

$$\omega^2 = \frac{(k-1)(MS_{effect} - MS_{t \times s})}{SS_{tot} + MS_{sub}}, \qquad (6.17)$$

where $k$ is the number of treatment levels, $MS_{effect}$ is the mean square for the main effect of treatment, $MS_{t \times s}$ is the mean square for Treatment × Subject interaction, $SS_{tot}$ is the total sum of squares, and $MS_{sub}$ is the mean square for subjects. If software does not produce this estimate directly calculation is done manually by obtaining the needed values from output. The approach underlying Equation 6.17 treats a one-way dependent-groups ANOVA as if it were a two-way design in which the main factor is Treatment, the other factor is Subjects, and the error term is the mean square for interaction.

With regard to areas of research in which the same independent variable is studied in between-groups and within-groups designs it has been argued that a partial *POV* should be estimated instead of the usual *POV* for a within-groups design. The purpose is to render a *POV* from a within-groups design comparable to one from a between-groups design by eliminating subject variability from total variability. Keppel (1991) provided the relevant formulas. For a contrary view refer to Maxwell and Delaney (2004). Partial *POV* is discussed in chapter 7.

We demonstrate the application of Equation 6.17 using data that preceded the introduction of $\omega^2$ as a measure of *POV*. The dependent variable was visual acuity, and the treatments were three distances at which the target was viewed by four participants (Walker, 1947; cited in McNemar, 1962). Substantive details of the research and possible alternative analyses of the data do not concern us here. The values that are required for Equation 6.17 (directly or indirectly) are $k = 3$, $SS_{effect} = 1{,}095.50$, $SS_{t \times s} = 596.50$, $n = 4$, $SS_{tot} = 2{,}290.25$, and $SS_{sub} = 598.25$. The value of F is significant at $p < .05$. Dividing the values of $SS$ by the appropriate degrees of freedom to obtain the required values of $MS$, we find that

$$\omega^2 = \frac{(3-1)\left[\dfrac{1{,}095.50}{3-1} - \dfrac{596.50}{(3-1)(4-1)}\right]}{2{,}290.25 + \dfrac{598.25}{4-1}} = .36.$$

Therefore, we estimate that the distance at which the target is viewed accounts for 36% of the variance in acuity scores, under the conditions in which the research was conducted. Note that the effect had to be relatively strong for the F to have attained significance at $p < .05$ with only four participants.

Rosenthal et al. (2000) presented an alternative treatment of effect sizes for one-way and factorial dependent-group designs in terms of correlational types of contrasts (also discussed by Maxwell & Delaney, 2004). For further discussions of various topics of this chapter, consult Olejnik and Algina (2000), Cortina and Nouri (2000), and Hedges and Olkin (1985). Hunter and Schmidt (2004) presented a strong case for the use of dependent-groups designs. For extension of what we call the *PS* measure to dependent multiple groups in one-way and factorial designs consult Vargha and Delaney (2000) and Brunner and Puri (2001). We consider effect sizes for factorial designs in the next chapter.

## QUESTIONS

1. Define the *fixed effects model*, and state to whom may one generalize the results from such design?
2. Name two assumptions, other than independence, of the F test in an ANOVA, and state two possible consequences of violating these assumptions.
3. Why bother to test for the significance of the difference between the greatest and the smallest of the sample means if the overall F test is significant?
4. Define Cohen's *f* conceptually, stating why it is an effect size.
5. In which direction is the estimator in Equation 6.5 biased, and why?
6. Why is the sample eta squared a problematic estimator of the eta-squared parameter?
7. How do the sample epsilon squared and omega squared attempt to reduce biased estimation, and which is less biased?
8. How does one determine if omega squared is statistically significantly greater than 0?
9. Why are confidence intervals especially important for estimators of POV?
10. Discuss the rationale for reporting negative estimates of POV instead of reporting them as 0.
11. List those limitations or criticisms of POV and its estimators that might apply and those that would not apply to standardized differences between means.
12. How does unreliability of scores affect estimates of POV?
13. What would be more accurate wording in a Results section of a research report than merely stating that the independent variable accounted for an estimated P% of the variance of the dependent variable?
14. Name three choices for the standardizer of a standardized difference between two of k means, and when would each choice be appropriate?
15. Why should one be cautious when interpreting differences among the values of the estimator in Equation 6.14?
16. In which circumstance are statistical inferences and confidence intervals about unstandardized differences between two means especially informative?
17. Why might it be unwise to precede Tukey's HSD method with an omnibus F test?
18. Are the results of an omnibus F test and applications of the Tukey HSD test always consistent? Explain.
19. Describe in general terms the nature of a good Monte Carlo study of the robustness of a statistical test.
20. What is the purpose of the Dunnett many-one method?

138 CHAPTER 6

21. Give an example of intransitive results in multiple comparisons of three means that differs from the one in the text.

22. What assumption is being made if one constructs a confidence interval for the standardized difference between two of $k$ population means by dividing the upper and lower limits of the confidence interval for the unstandardized pairwise difference by $MS_w^{1/2}$? Answer using more than one word.

23. List the numbers of the formulas in this chapter for between-groups standardized mean differences that would also be applicable to within-groups designs.

# Chapter 7

# Effect Sizes for Factorial Designs

## INTRODUCTION

In this chapter we discuss a variety of estimators of standardized-difference and strength-of-association effect sizes for factorial designs with fixed-effects factors. Prior to the section on within-groups designs the discussion and examples involve only between-groups factors. The discussions of estimators of standardized differences are much influenced by the seminal work of Cortina and Nouri (2000) and Olejnik and Algina (2000). We add some alternative approaches and some of our own perspectives, focusing on assumptions, the nature of the populations to which results are to be generalized, and pairwise comparisons.

We call the factor with respect to which one estimates an effect size the *targeted factor*. We call any other factor in the design a *peripheral factor*. If later in the analysis of the same set of data a researcher estimates an effect size with respect to a factor that had previously been a peripheral factor, the roles and labels for this factor and the previously targeted factor are reversed. A peripheral factor is also called an *off factor* (Cortina & Nouri, 2000; Maxwell & Delaney, 2004).

The appropriate procedures for estimating an effect size from a factorial design depend in part on whether targeted and peripheral factors are extrinsic or intrinsic. *Extrinsic factors* are factors that do not ordinarily or naturally vary in the population to which the results are to be generalized. Extrinsic factors are often manipulated factors that are treatment variables imposed on the participants. *Intrinsic factors* are those that do naturally vary in the population to which the results are to be generalized—factors such as gender, ethnicity, or occupational or educational level. Intrinsic factors are typically *classificatory factors* (which is the label that we use in this chapter), which are also called *subject factors, grouping factors, stratified factors, organismic factors*, or *individual-difference factors*. Refer to Maxwell and Delaney (2004) for further discussion of the distinction between extrinsic and intrinsic factors.

An extremely important consideration when choosing a method for estimating a standardized difference or *POV* (proportion of variance explained) effect size with regard to a targeted factor is whether the peripheral factor is extrinsic or intrinsic. As we soon explain, when a peripheral factor is extrinsic one generally will want to choose a method in which variability in the data that is attributable to that factor is held constant (making no contribution to the standardizer or to the total variability that is to be accounted for). When a peripheral factor is intrinsic one generally will want to choose a method in which variability that is attributable to the peripheral factor is permitted to contribute to the magnitude of the standardizer or to the total variance for some estimated proportion of which the targeted factor accounts.

In practical terms, when deciding the role that a peripheral factor is to play the researcher must consider the nature of the population with respect to which the estimate of effect size is to be made. If a peripheral factor does not typically vary in the population that is of interest (usually a variable that is manipulated in research but not in nature), one will choose a method that ignores variability in the data that is attributable to the peripheral factor. If a peripheral factor does typically vary in the population that is of interest (often a classificatory factor such as gender) one will choose a method in which variability that is attributable to such a peripheral factor is permitted to contribute to the standardizer or to total variability. We address this issue as we discuss each of the estimators of effect size in this chapter. For further discussions of the role of what we call a peripheral factor, consult Cortina and Nouri (2000), Gillett (2003), Glass et al. (1981), Maxwell and Delaney (2004), and Olejnik and Algina (2000).

## STRENGTH OF ASSOCIATION: PROPORTION
## OF VARIANCE EXPLAINED

Estimation of $\eta^2_{pop}$ (the eta squared *POV* of chap. 6) is more complicated with regard to factorial designs than is the case with the one-way design, even in the simplest case, which we assume here, in which all sample sizes are equal. In general, for the effect of some factor or the effect of interaction, when the peripheral factors are intrinsic one can estimate *POV* using

$$\hat{\omega}^2 = \frac{SS_{effect} - \left(df_{effect} MS_w\right)}{SS_{tot} + MS_w}. \tag{7.1}$$

All *MS*, *SS*, and *df* values are available or can be calculated from the ANOVA *F*-test software output. With regard to the main effect of Factor A, $SS_{effect} = SS_A$ and $df_{effect} = a - 1$, in which *a* is the number of levels of Factor A. With regard to the main effect of Factor B, substitute B and *b* (i.e., the number of levels of Factor B) for A and *a* in the previous sentence, and so forth for the main effect of any other factor in the design.

With regard to the interaction effect in a two-way design, $SS_{\text{effect}} = SS_{AB}$ and $df_{\text{effect}} = (a - 1)(b - 1)$. In the later Illustrative Worked Examples section we apply Equation 7.1 using an example that is integrated with examples of estimating standardized differences between means, $\Delta$ and $g_{\text{pop}}$, for the same data. References for estimation of effect sizes for designs that are not covered in this chapter, including higer order designs, are provided later in the Additional Designs and Measures section.

Equation 7.1 provides an estimate of the proportion of the total variance of the measure of the dependent variable that is accounted for by an independent variable (or by interaction as another example in the factorial case), as does Equation 6.9 in chapter 6 for the one-way design. However, in this case of factorial designs there can be more sources of variance than in the one-way case because of the contributions made to total variance by one or more additional factors and interactions. An effect of, say, Factor A might yield a different value of $\hat{\omega}^2$ if it is researched in the context of a one-way design instead of a factorial design, in which there will be more sources of variance that account for the total variance. As stated previously, estimates of effect size must be interpreted in the context of the design whose results produced the estimate. A method that was intended to render estimates of *POV* from factorial designs comparable to those from one-way designs is discussed in the next section.

For a method for correcting for overestimation of *POV* by omega squared in nested designs, in which each level of a factor is combined with only one level of another factor, consult Wampold and Serlin (2000). Also refer to a series of articles that debate the matter (Crits-Christoph, Tu, & Gallop, 2003; Serlin, Wampold, & Levin, 2003; Siemer & Joormann, 2003a, 2003b). The designs in this chapter are not nested but crossed designs, in which each level of a factor is combined with each level of another factor, as shown later in Tables 7.1 through 7.5.

## PARTIAL $\hat{\omega}^2$

An alternative conceptualization of estimation of *POV* from factorial designs modifies Equation 7.1 so as to attempt to eliminate the contribution that any extrinsic peripheral factor may make to total variance. The resulting measure is called a *partial POV*. Whereas a *POV* measures the strength of an effect relative to the total variability from error and from all effects, a partial *POV* measures the strength of an effect relative to variability that is not attributable to other effects. The excluded effects are those that would not be present if the levels of the targeted factor had been researched in a one-way design. For this purpose partial eta squared and partial omega squared, the latter being less biased (chap. 6), have been traditionally used. Partial omega squared, $\hat{\omega}^2_{\text{partial}}$, for any effect is given by

$$\hat{\omega}^2_{\text{partial}} = \frac{SS_{\text{effect}} - \left(df_{\text{effect}} MS_w\right)}{SS_{\text{effect}} + \left(N - df_{\text{effect}}\right)MS_w}, \qquad (7.2)$$

where $N$ is the total sample size and calculation is again a matter of simple arithmetic because all of the needed values are available from the output from the ANOVA $F$ test. Again we defer introducing a worked example until the later section Illustrative Worked Examples so that discussion of the example can be integrated with discussion of worked examples of other estimators of effect size for the same set of data.

A research report must make clear whether a reported estimate of *POV* is based on the overall $\hat{\omega}^2$ or $\hat{\omega}^2_{\text{partial}}$. Unfortunately, because values of estimates of overall *POV* and of partial *POV* can be very different, the more so the more complex a design, some textbooks and some software may be unclear or incorrect about which of the two estimators it is discussing or outputting (Levine & Hullett, 2002). One serious consequence of such confusion would be misleading meta-analyses in which the meta-analysts are unknowingly integrating sets of two different kinds of estimates of *POV*. If a report of primary research provides a formula for the estimate of *POV*, readers should examine the denominator to observe if Equation 7.1 or 7.2 is being used.

## COMPARING VALUES OF $\hat{\omega}^2$

A researcher who wants to interpret the relative values of the two or more estimates of *POV* (or partial *POV*) for the various effects in a factorial study should proceed with caution or consider giving up the idea. First, it is not necessarily true that a value of $\hat{\omega}^2_{\text{effect}}$ whose corresponding $F$ is statistically significant represents a greater *POV* than one whose corresponding $F$ is not statistically significant. The two $F$ tests might simply have differed in statistical power. Also, a larger significant $F$ does not necessarily indicate that its corresponding $POV_{\text{pop}}$ is greater than the $POV_{\text{pop}}$ corresponding to a smaller significant $F$. The issue is that estimates of $POV_{\text{pop}}$ have great sampling variability, so they are quite imprecise (R. M. Carroll & Nordholm, 1975).

In the case of levels of continuous independent variables (e.g., $a$ levels of drug dosage and $b$ levels of treatment duration or intensity), any apparent difference in estimated values of *POV* (or values of $d$ or $g$) for two factors may merely reflect a difference in the strengths of manipulation of the two factors. This problem is related to the problem of restricted range, as was discussed in chapter 4. Moreover, in many cases it may not be meaningful to compare two strengths of manipulation; this would be an "apples versus oranges" comparison. For example, suppose that Factor A is duration of psychotherapy and Factor B is dose of antidepressive drug. What range of weeks of therapy would represent a manipulation whose strength is comparable to a certain range of milligrams of the drug? On the other hand, if the levels of each of the two compared factors represent standard levels of these factors in clinical practice, it might be more justifiable to compare the two estimates of *POV* or of Δ. Furthermore, because estimates of *POV* have great sampling variability, even if two strengths of manipulation were comparable it would be difficult to generalize about the difference between two values of *POV* merely by comparing the two estimates.

Note that the great sampling variability of estimates of *POV* argues for the use of confidence intervals for *POV*s. Also, as Olejnik and Algina (2000) pointed out, one should not compare estimates of partial *POV* for two factors in the same study because, as can be observed in Equation 7.2, the denominator of an estimate of partial *POV* can have a different value for each factor (different sources of variability). For a similar reason one should not ordinarily compare estimates of *POV* for the effect of a given factor from two studies that do not use the same peripheral factors and the same levels of these peripheral factors.

Ronis (1981) discussed ways to render manipulations in studies comparable. The Ronis (1981) method for comparing values of estimated *POV* applies only to factorial designs with two levels per factor. Fowler (1987) provided a method that can be applied to larger designs and is applicable to within-groups as well as between-groups designs, but it is very complicated. Cohen (1973) recommended that one use partial *POV*s if one wants to compare the estimates of *POV*s that are obtained by different studies of the same number of levels of the same targeted factor when that factor has been combined with peripheral factors that differ across the studies. For further discussions consult Cohen (1973), Keppel (1991), Keren and Lewis (1979), Levine and Hullett (2002), Maxwell and Delaney (2004), Maxwell et al. (1981), Olejnik and Algina (2000), and Susskind and Howland (1980). Different research designs can produce greatly varying estimates of *POV*, rendering comparisons or meta-analyses of estimates of *POV* problematic if they do not take the different research features into account. Because such comparisons or meta-analyses across different designs might be misleading, Olejnik and Algina (2003) provided dozens of formulas for estimated generalized eta squared and omega squared that are intended to provide comparable estimators across a great variety of research designs. Similarly, Gillett (2003) provided formulas for rendering standardized-difference estimators of effect size from factorial designs comparable to those from single-factor designs.

## RATIOS OF ESTIMATES OF EFFECT SIZE

One should also be very cautious about deciding on the relative importance of two factors by inspecting the ratio of their estimates of effect size. The ratio of values of $\hat{\omega}^2$ for two factors can be very different from the ratio of two estimates of standardized-difference effect size for these two factors. Therefore, these two kinds of estimators can provide different perspectives on the relative effect sizes of the two factors. Maxwell et al. (1981) provided an example in which the ratio of the two $\hat{\omega}^2$ values is approximately 4:1, which might lead some to conclude that one factor is roughly four times more important than the other factor. Such an interpretation would fail to take into account the relative strengths of manipulation of the two factors and the likely great sampling variabilities of the estimates, as were previously discussed. Moreover, in this example those authors found that the ratio of two standardized-difference estimates for those same two factors is not approximately 4:1 but instead 2:1, providing a quantitatively, if not qualitatively, somewhat different perspective on the relative importance of the two factors. We soon turn our attention to effect sizes involving standardized differences in factorial designs.

## DESIGNS AND RESULTS FOR THIS CHAPTER

Tables 7.1 through 7.5 illustrate the designs and results that are discussed in the remainder of this chapter.

The meaning of the superscript asterisks in the notation for the column variances in Table 7.3 is explained where these variances are relevant in the later section Manipulated Targeted Factor and Intrinsic Peripheral Factor.

**TABLE 7.1**

**A 2 × 2 Design With Two Extrinsic Factors**

|          | Factor A  |           |
| -------- | --------- | --------- |
| Factor B | Therapy 1 | Therapy 2 |
| Drug     | Cell 1    | Cell 2    |
| No drug  | Cell 3    | Cell 4    |
|          | $\bar{Y}_1$ | $\bar{Y}_2$ |

**TABLE 7.2**

**A 3 × 2 Design With an Extrinsic and an Intrinsic Factor**

|          | Factor A    |             |             |
| -------- | ----------- | ----------- | ----------- |
| Factor B | Treatment 1 | Treatment 2 | Treatment 3 |
| Female   | Cell 1      | Cell 2      | Cell 3      |
| Male     | Cell 4      | Cell 5      | Cell 6      |

## TABLE 7.3

**Hypothetical Results From a 2 × 2 Design With One Extrinsic and One Intrinsic Factor**

| Factor B | Treatment 1 | Treatment 2 | |
|---|---|---|---|
| | | *Factor A* | |
| Female | 1, 1, 1, 1, 2, 2, 2, 2, 3, 4 | 2, 2, 3, 3, 3, 3, 3, 4, 4, 4 | |
| | $\bar{Y}_{11} = 1.9$ | $\bar{Y}_{21} = 3.1$ | $\bar{Y}_{.1} = 2.5$ |
| | $s_{11}^2 = .989$ | $s_{21}^2 = .544$ | $s_{.1}^2 = 1.105$ |
| Male | 1, 1, 2, 2, 2, 2, 2, 2, 3, 4 | 1, 2, 2, 3, 3, 3, 3, 4, 4, 4 | |
| | $\bar{Y}_{12} = 2.1$ | $\bar{Y}_{22} = 2.9$ | $\bar{Y}_{.2} = 2.5$ |
| | $s_{12}^2 = .767$ | $s_{22}^2 = .989$ | $s_{.2}^2 = 1.000$ |
| | $\bar{Y}_{1.} = 2.0$ | $\bar{Y}_{2.} = 3.0$ | |
| | $s_{1.}^{*2} = .842$ | $s_{2.}^{*2} = .737$ | |

## TABLE 7.4

**ANOVA Output for the Data in Table 7.3**

| Source | SS | df | MS | F | p |
|---|---|---|---|---|---|
| A | 10.000 | 1 | 10.000 | 12.16 | .002 |
| B | 0.000 | 1 | 0.000 | 0.00 | 1.000 |
| A × B | 0.400 | 1 | 0.400 | 0.049 | .497 |
| Within | 29.600 | 36 | 0.822 | | |

## TABLE 7.5

**A 3 × 2 × 2 Design With One Extrinsic and Two Intrinsic Factors**

| Factor B | | Treatment 1 | Treatment 2 | Treatment 3 |
|---|---|---|---|---|
| | | | *Factor A* | |
| Female | White | Cell 1 | Cell 2 | Cell 3 |
| | Non-white | Cell 4 | Cell 5 | Cell 6 |
| Male | White | Cell 7 | Cell 8 | Cell 9 |
| | Non-white | Cell 10 | Cell 11 | Cell 12 |

## MANIPULATED FACTORS ONLY

The appropriate procedure for calculating an estimate of a standardized-difference effect size that involves two means at a time in a factorial design depends in part on whether the targeted factor is manipulated or classificatory and whether the peripheral factor is extrinsic or intrinsic. To focus on the main ideas we first and mostly consider the two-way design. Suppose that each factor is a manipulated factor, as in Table 7.1, so that the peripheral factor is extrinsic. Suppose further that we want to compare Psychotherapies 1 and 2 overall, so the numerator of the standardized difference is $\bar{Y}_{1.} - \bar{Y}_{2.}$, where 1 and 2 represent columns 1 and 2 and the dot reminds us that we are considering column 1 (or 2) period, over all rows, not just a part of column 1 or a part of column 2 in combination with any particular row (i.e., not a cell of the table). These two means are thus column marginal means. Therefore, in this example Factor A is the targeted factor and Factor B is the peripheral factor. As in chapters 3 and 6, in this chapter we use $d$ to denote estimators whose standardizers are based on taking the square root of the variance of one group, and we use $g$ to denote estimators whose standardizers are based on taking the square root of two or more pooled variances (i.e., the pooling-based standardizers $s_p$ and $MS_w^{\frac{1}{2}}$ of chap. 6). (Note that we have placed the subscript for the column factor ahead of the subscript for the row factor, whereas the more common notation in factorial ANOVA places the subscript for a row ahead of the subscript for a column. However, in this chapter we are beginning with the case in which the targeted factor is a column factor and we want to be consistent with the notation used by two of the major sources on effect sizes to which we refer readers. These sources place the subscript for the targeted factor first.)

Recall that the choice of a standardizer by which to divide the difference between means to calculate a $d$ or $g$ from a factorial design depends on one's conception of the population to which one wants to generalize the results. Suppose that one wants to generalize the results to a population that does not naturally vary with respect to the peripheral factor. Such will often (not always) be the case when each factor is a manipulated factor. In this case the peripheral factor would not contribute to variability in the measure of the dependent variable in the population, so one should not let it contribute to the magnitude of the standardizer that is used to calculate the estimate of effect size. Such additional variability in sample data from a peripheral factor that is assumed not to vary in the population would lower the value of the estimate of effect size by inflating the standardizer in its denominator. There are options for choice of standardizer in this case. (Note that in the case of clinical problems for which the psychotherapy and the drug therapy at hand are sometimes combined in practice, Table 7.1 and this example may not provide an example of a peripheral factor that does not vary in the population of interest to the researcher. If so, the discussion and methods in this section would not apply.)

First, suppose that both factors in a two-way design have a combined control group (e.g., cell 3 in Table 7.1 if Therapy 1 were actually No Therapy) and that homoscedasticity of the variances across the margins of the peripheral factor is not assumed. By homoscedasticity across the margins of the peripheral factor we mean equality of the variances of the populations that are represented by each level of the peripheral factor over all of the levels of the targeted factor. In Table 7.1 the example of such homoscedasticity would be equality of variances of a population that receives the drug (represented by the combined participants in cells 1 and 2) and a population that does not receive the drug (represented by the combined participants in cells 3 and 4)—that is, homoscedasticity of the population row margin variances in the present case. (Although the factors in Table 7.3 do not represent the current example of estimation of effect size, $s_{.1}^2$ and $s_{.2}^2$ in that table exemplify row marginal sample variances that estimate the population variances to whose homoscedasticity we are now referring.) In this section we do not interrupt the development of the discussion by demonstrating estimation of effect size when such peripheral-factor marginal homoscedasticity is assumed because the method is the same as the one that we demonstrate later using Equation 7.20 in the section Within-Groups Factorial Designs.

When such peripheral-factor marginal homoscedasticity is not assumed one may want to use the standard deviation of the group that is a control group with respect to both factors as the standardizer, $s_c$. For example, in Table 7.1 if Therapy 1 were in fact No Therapy (control or placebo), one may want to use the standard deviation of cell 3 (a No-Therapy No-Drug cell in this case) as the standardizer. This method would also be applicable if, instead of a control-group cell, the design included a cell that represented a standard (in practice) combination of a level of Factor A and a level of Factor B, a standard-treatment comparison group. In either of these cases we label the estimate of $\Delta$ as $d_{comp}$ (*comp* for comparison group) and use

$$d_{comp} = \frac{\overline{Y}_{1.} - \overline{Y}_{2.}}{s_c}. \tag{7.3}$$

If instead one assumes homoscedasticity for all of the populations that are represented by all of the cells in the design, an option for a standardizer in this case would be to use the pooled standard deviation, $MS_w^{1/2}$, of all of the groups, resulting in the estimator

$$g_{msw} = \frac{\overline{Y}_{1.} - \overline{Y}_{2.}}{MS_w^{1/2}}. \tag{7.4}$$

Note that the method of Equation 7.4 does not deflate $g$ by inflating the standardizer because $MS_w$ is based on pooling the within-cell $SS$ values, and within each cell no factor in the design is varying, including the peripheral factor. Therefore, the peripheral factor is not contributing to the magnitude of the standardizer, just as we are assuming in this section that it does not contribute to variability in the population of interest. Equations 7.3 and 7.4, with appropriately changed subscripts, can also be used to compare the means of two levels of the manipulated factor that had previously been designated as a peripheral factor, but thereafter becomes a newly targeted factor, using the same reasoning as before. In this case the previously targeted factor now becomes the peripheral factor. Worked examples using Equations 7.3 and 7.4 are presented later in the section Within-Groups Factorial Designs, where their application is also appropriate.

## MANIPULATED TARGETED FACTOR
## AND INTRINSIC PERIPHERAL FACTOR

Suppose now the case of Table 7.2, in which there is a manipulated and an intrinsic classificatory factor, and that one wants to calculate an estimate of effect size for two levels of the manipulated factor. Unlike the previous case of Table 7.1, in this case the intrinsic factor, Gender, does vary in the population so one might now want to let the part of variability in the measure of the dependent variable that is attributable to the intrinsic factor also contribute to the standardizer. First, in this case there is an option for choice of a standardizer if there is a control condition (or standard-treatment comparison condition), say, Treatment 1 in Table 7.2 if Treatment 1 were actually No Treatment. In this case one might want to use for the standardizer the overall $s$ of the control groups across the levels of the peripheral factor (overall $s$ of cells 1 and 4 combined). In our example in which Treatment 1 of Table 7.2 is the control condition, this standardizer would be $s_{1.}$, the marginal $s$ of column 1. Using this method one is collapsing (combining) the levels of the peripheral factor so that for the moment the design is equivalent to a one-way design in which the targeted treatment factor is the only factor. This method does not assume homoscedasticity because it does not pool variances (i.e., cells 1 and 4 are being considered to represent one group). Also, because the standardizer is based on a now-combined group of women and men, it reflects any gender-based variability of the measure of the dependent variable in the population. This method yields as an estimate of effect size

$$d_{comp^*} = \frac{\overline{Y}_{1.} - \overline{Y}_{2.}}{s_{1.}}. \tag{7.5}$$

When there are more than two levels of the targeted manipulated factor, as is the case in Table 7.2, the numerical subscripts in Equation 7.5 vary depending on which column represents the control (or standard-treatment) condition and which column contains the groups (level) with which it is being compared.

If the targeted factor is represented by the rows instead of the columns of a table, the dots in Equation 7.5 precede the numerical subscripts (e.g., $s_{1.}$ become $s_{.1}$) and *row* replaces *column* in the previous discussion. A definitional equation, Equation 7.15, for $s_{.1}$ (the row case) is provided later in the section Classificatory Factors Only using notation that is not yet needed. Computational formulas and some worked examples are also provided there.

Despite whether there is a control or standard-treatment level there is an alternative more complex standardizer for the present design and purpose. This standardizer, which assumes homoscedasticity of all of the populations that are involved in the estimate, was introduced by Nouri and Greenberg (1995) and also presented by Cortina and Nouri (2000). The method involves a special kind of pooling from cells that is consistent with the goal of this section to let variability in the measure of the dependent variable that is attributable to the peripheral factor contribute to the magnitude of the standardizer. One first calculates, separately for each of the two variances that are later going to be entered into a modified version of the formula for pooling,

$$s_{t.}^{*2} = \frac{\Sigma\left(n_{tp} - 1\right)s_{tp}^{2} + \Sigma n_{tp}\left(\bar{Y}_{tp} - \bar{Y}_{t.}\right)^{2}}{n_{t.} - 1}, \tag{7.6}$$

where *t* stands for targeted, *p* stands for peripheral, *tp* stands for a cell at the *t*th level of the targeted factor and the *p*th level of the peripheral factor, and *t.* stands for a level of the targeted factor over the levels of the peripheral factor, which is at a margin of a table (e.g., the margin of column 1 or column 2 in Table 7.2). The asterisk indicates a special kind of variance that has had variability that is attributable to the peripheral factor "added back" to it. The summation in Equation 7.6 is undertaken over the levels of the peripheral factor, there being two such levels in the case of Table 7.2. Observe that Equation 7.6 begins before the plus sign as if it were going to be the usual formula for pooling variances, but the expression in the numerator after the plus sign adds the now appropriate portion of variability that is attributable to the peripheral factor. Therefore, we denote the resulting standardizer that is presented in Equation 7.7 by $s_{msw+}$.

Equation 7.6 yields the overall variance of all participants who were subjected to a level within the targeted factor that is of interest to the researcher for the purpose of estimating an effect size that involves that level. This variance is the variance of all such participants as if they were combined into just one larger group at that level of the targeted factor, ignoring the subgroupings that are based on the peripheral factor. This variance serves the purpose of being comparable to the variance that would be obtained if that level of the targeted factor had been studied in a one-way design. The estimate of effect size that will result from this approach will thus be comparable to an estimate that would arise from such a one-way design.

Again, Equation 7.6 is calculated twice, once each for the two compared levels of the targeted factor, to find the special kind of $s_{1.}^2$ and $s_{2.}^2$ (in this example), $s_{1.}^{*2}$ and $s_{2.}^{*2}$, to enter into the pooling formula 7.7 below for the standardizer,

$$ s_{msw+} = \left[ \frac{(n_{1.} - 1)s_{1.}^{*2} + (n_{2.} - 1)s_{2.}^{*2}}{n_{1.} + n_{2.} - 2} \right]^{\frac{1}{2}}. \qquad (7.7) $$

The resulting estimator is then given by

$$ g_{msw+} = \frac{\overline{Y}_{1.} - \overline{Y}_{2.}}{s_{msw+}}. \qquad (7.8) $$

As previously stated, the numerical subscripts and the sequence of the numerical and dot parts of a subscript depend, respectively, on (a) which two levels of a multi-leveled targeted factor are being compared (e.g., columns 1 and 2, 1 and 3, or 2 and 3), and (b) whether the targeted factor is represented by the rows or columns of the table. Refer to Olejnik and Algina (2000) for another approach for this case. Having developed the reasoning behind various approaches and equations we now turn to worked examples.

## ILLUSTRATIVE WORKED EXAMPLES

Table 7.3 depicts hypothetical data in a simplified version of Table 7.2 in which there are now only two levels of the targeted manipulated factor that is represented by the columns. The cells' raw scores are degrees of respondents' endorsement of an attitudinal statement with respect to a 4-point rating scale ranging from *strongly disagree* to *strongly agree*. The treatments represent alternative wording for the attitudinal statement. It is supposed that 20 women and 20 men were randomly assigned, 10 each to each treatment. The table includes cell and marginal values of $\overline{Y}$ and $s^2$. Because the contrived data are presented only for the purpose of illustrating calculations, we assume homoscedasticity as needed.

Before we begin estimating effect sizes some comments are in order about the example at hand. First, although rating-scale items are typically used in combination with other such items on the same topic to form summated rating scales, our example that uses just one rating-scale item is nonetheless relevant because a rating-scale item is sometimes used alone to address a specific question (Penfield, 2003). Second, although some (e.g., Cliff, 1993) have recommended using ordinal methods (such as what we call the *PS* in our chaps. 5 and 9) to analyze data from rating scales, many researchers still use parametric methods involving means for the data from such scales, and parametric methods are still being developed for them (Penfield, 2003). However, violation of the assumption of normality in the case of data from rating scales may be especially problematic the fewer the number of categories, the smaller the sample size, and the more extreme the mean rating in the population (Penfield, 2003). Nonetheless, we use hypothetical data from a rating scale here because they provide a simple example for calculations.

Suppose first that Treatment 1 in Table 7.3 is a control (or standard-treatment) level and, as was discussed in the previous section, one wants to estimate an effect size from a standardized $\overline{Y}_{1.} - \overline{Y}_{2.}$ that would be comparable to an estimate that would arise from a design in which treatment were the only factor. In this case one can standardize using the overall $s$ of the control group in Table 7.3, $(s_{1.}^{*2})^{1/2} = (.842)^{1/2} = .918$. The overall $s$ of a column is the $s$ of a group consisting of all of the participants in all of the cells of that column (with column data treated as if it were one set of data). As should be clear from our previous explanation of the variance that Equation 7.6 yields, this overall $s$ is not the square root of the mean of the variances of cells 1 and 3 in the current example that involves Table 7.3. That is, this overall $s$ is not $[(.989 + .767)/2]^{1/2}$. Applying Equation 7.3, which is applicable in this case, we find that $d_{\text{comp}} = (2.0 - 3.0) / .918 = -1.09$. Therefore, we estimate that, with respect to the control population's distribution and $\sigma$, the mean of the control population is 1.09 standard deviations below the mean of the population that receives Treatment 2.

Next, regardless of the existence of a control level, if we assume homoscedasticity of all of the involved populations we can use the special pooling method of Equations 7.6 and 7.7 as the first steps toward standardizing the difference between $\overline{Y}_{1.}$ and $\overline{Y}_{2.}$ in Table 7.3 with the method of Equation 7.8. First we apply the results of column 1 to Equation 7.6 to find

$$s_{1.}^{*2} = \frac{[(10-1).989] + [(10-1).767] + \left[10(1.9-2.0)^2\right] + \left[10(2.1-2.0)^2\right]}{20-1} = .842.$$

We then apply the results of column 2 to Equation 7.6 to find

$$s_{2.}^{*2} = \frac{[(10-1).544] + [(10-1).989] + \left[10(3.1-3.0)^2\right] + \left[10(2.9-3.0)^2\right]}{20-1} = .737.$$

Applying the two preceding results to Equation 7.7 we find the standardizer

$$s_{msw+} = \left[ \frac{(20-1).842 + (20-1).737}{20+20-2} \right]^{\frac{1}{2}} = .889.$$

Applying the difference between the two targeted column means, 2.0 and 3.0, and the standardizer, .889, to Equation 7.8 we find that $g_{msw+} = (2.0 - 3.0) / .889 = -1.12$. We, therefore, estimate that the mean of the population that receives Treatment 1 is 1.12 standard deviations below the mean of the population that receives Treatment 2, where the standard deviation is assumed to be a value common to the involved populations. Observe that the result, $g_{msw+} = -1.12$, is close to the previous result, $d_{comp} = -1.09$. Such similarity of results is attributable to the fact that the sample variances in the cells happen not to be as different in the case of the contrived data of Table 7.3 as they might well be in the case of real data.

The output from any ANOVA software (like that presented in Table 7.4) provides needed information to proceed with some additional interpretation and estimation of effect sizes for the data in Table 7.3. Output did not provide the total $SS$ directly, so we find from Table 7.4 that $SS_{tot} = SS_A + SS_B + SS_{AB} + SS_w = 10 + 0 + .400 + 29.600 = 40.000$. Observe in Table 7.3 that the marginal means of the Female and Male rows happen to be equal (both 2.5), so obviously $d$ or $g = 0$ in such a case regardless of which standardizer is used. For the targeted Treatment factor, A, observe in Table 7.4 that $F = 12.16$ and $p = .002$, so we have evidence of a statistically significant difference between the marginal means (a main effect) of Treatments 1 and 2.

Before we estimate a POV and a partial POV for Treatment Factor A from the results in Table 7.4 the reader is encouraged to reflect on the extent of difference one might expect between these two estimates in this case of hypothetical data in which $SS_B = 0$ and $MS_{AB}$ is unusually small. Now applying the ANOVA results to Equation 7.1 we find that $\hat{\omega}^2 = [10 - 1(.822)] / (40 + .822) = .22$. Applying the output results to Equation 7.2 we find that $\hat{\omega}^2_{partial} = [10 - 1(.822)] / [10 + (40 - 1).822] = .22$. Recalling the discussion of the difference between $\hat{\omega}^2$ and $\hat{\omega}^2_{partial}$ early in this chapter one should expect the two estimates to be very similar in the case of the hypothetical data of Table 7.3 because Factor B happened to contribute no variability to these data (output $SS_B = 0$). Interaction (statistically insignificant in this example) contributed just enough variability to the data (output $SS_{AB} = .400$) to cause a very slight difference in the magnitudes of the two kinds of estimates of a POV, but rounding to two decimal places renders $\hat{\omega}^2$ equal to $\hat{\omega}^2_{partial}$ in this example. We conclude, subject to the previously discussed limitations of measures of POV, that the Treatment factor is estimated to account for 22% of the variance in the scores under the specific research conditions.

## COMPARISONS OF LEVELS OF A MANIPULATED FACTOR
## AT ONE LEVEL OF A PERIPHERAL FACTOR

Suppose now that one wants a standardized comparison of two levels of a manipulated factor at one level of a peripheral factor at a time. For example, with regard to Table 7.2, suppose that one wants to compare Treatment 1 and Treatment 2 separately only for women or only for men. Thus, one would be interested in an estimate of effect size involving two values of $\overline{Y}_{tp}$ (i.e., two cells, such as cells 1 and 2) where, again, $t$ stands for a level of the targeted factor and $p$ stands for a level of the peripheral factor. Such separate comparisons are especially appropriate if there is an interaction between the targeted manipulated and peripheral factors. (Again, there may really be an interaction regardless of the result of a possibly low-powered $F$ test for interaction.).

If, say, one wants to standardize the difference between the means of cells 1 and 2 in Table 7.2 ($\overline{Y}_{11}$ and $\overline{Y}_{21}$, respectively) and Treatment 1 is a control level or standard-treatment comparison level, then one can standardize the mean difference using the standard deviation of cell 1, $s_{cell}$, if one is not assuming homoscedasticity. In this case the estimator is

$$d_{level} = \frac{\overline{Y}_{11} - \overline{Y}_{21}}{s_{cell}}. \qquad (7.9)$$

Of course, the subscripts for the two values of $\overline{Y}$ in Equation 7.9 change depending on which two levels of the targeted manipulated factor are involved in the comparison and at which level of the peripheral factor the comparison takes place. (Recall that in the Manipulated Factors Only section we explained why we adopted notation in which the subscript for a column precedes the subscript for a row.)

For a numerical example for this case suppose that one wants to make a standardized comparison of the means of Treatments 1 and 2 in Table 7.3 separately for men and women, and suppose further that Treatment 1 is a control level. We demonstrate the method by applying Equation 7.9 to the results in the Male row of Table 7.3. In this case the numerator of Equation 7.9 becomes ($\overline{Y}_{12} - \overline{Y}_{22}$), and $d_{level} = (2.1 - 2.9) / (.767)^{1/2} = -.91$. (Table 7.3 shows that the sample variance in the cell for Male–Treatment 1 is .767.) Therefore, with respect to the Male–Control population's distribution and $\sigma$, it is estimated that the mean of the Male–Treatment 2 population is approximately .91 of a standard deviation above the mean of the Male–Control population. If these are the kinds of populations that the researcher is seeking to address, then the method of Equation 7.9 is an appropriate one. Again, the method of estimation that is chosen must be consistent with the kind of effect-size parameter that the researcher wants to estimate and the assumptions (e.g., homoscedasticity) that are made about the involved populations.

There are alternatives to the aforementioned procedure. If one assumes homoscedasticity with regard to the two populations whose sample (cell) means are being compared, one can calculate the standardizer by pooling the two involved values of $s^2_{cell}$. For an example now involving cells 1 and 2 of Table 7.3 the standardizer, $s_{pcells}$, is given by a version of the general Equation 6.14 in chapter 6 for pooling two variances,

$$s_{pcells} = \left[ \frac{(n_{11} - 1)s^2_{11} + (n_{21} - 1)s^2_{21}}{n_{11} + n_{21} - 2} \right]^{\frac{1}{2}}. \tag{7.10}$$

Equation 7.10 results in the estimator

$$g_{level} = \frac{\overline{Y}_{11} - \overline{Y}_{21}}{s_{pcells}}. \tag{7.11}$$

Now applying the results in the Female row of Table 7.3 to Equation 7.10 we find

$$s_{pcells} = \left[ \frac{(10-1).989 + (10-1).544}{10 + 10 - 2} \right]^{\frac{1}{2}} = .875.$$

Therefore, Equation 7.11 yields $g_{level} = (1.9 - 3.1) / .875 = -1.37$. We estimate that, with regard to the Female–Treatment 2 population's distribution and $\sigma$, which is assumed to be the same as the Female–Treatment 1 population's $\sigma$, the mean of the latter population is 1.37 $\sigma$ units below the mean of the former population.

If there is only one manipulated factor, as is the case in Table 7.3, and if one assumes homoscedasticity with regard to all of the populations that are represented by the cells in the design, one can use $MS^{\frac{1}{2}}_w$ as the standardizer for our purpose. The resulting estimator when comparing $\overline{Y}_{11} - \overline{Y}_{21}$ is then given by

$$g_{levelmsw} = \frac{\overline{Y}_{11} - \overline{Y}_{21}}{MS^{\frac{1}{2}}_w}. \tag{7.12}$$

Using $MS_w$ from the ANOVA output that was reported in Table 7.4 of the previous section, applying the results in the Female row of Table 7.3 to Equation 7.12 yields $g_{levelmsw} = (1.9 - 3.1) / (.822)^{\frac{1}{2}} = -1.32$. We estimate that the mean of the Female–Treatment 1 population is 1.32 $\sigma$ units lower than the mean of the Female–Treatment 2 population, where $\sigma$ is assumed to be common for all of the populations that are represented in the design.

Note that under homoscedasticity of all represented populations $MS_w^{\frac{1}{2}}$ provides a better estimate of the common $\sigma$ within all of these populations than does $s_{pcells}$, resulting in a $g$ that is a better estimator of $g_{pop}$. However, there is greater risk that the assumption of homoscedasticity is wrong, or more seriously wrong, when one assumes that four or more populations that involve combined levels of manipulated and classificatory factors are homoscedastic (as could be the case in Tables 7.2 or 7.5) than when one assumes that two populations at the same level of a classificatory factor are homoscedastic. Note also that the method of Equation 7.12 is not applicable when there is more than one manipulated factor. Olejnik and Algina (2000) provided discussion of this somewhat more complicated case.

## TARGETED CLASSIFICATORY FACTOR AND EXTRINSIC PERIPHERAL FACTOR

Suppose now that one wants to standardize a comparison between two levels of an intrinsic factor (a classificatory factor here) when there are one or more extrinsic peripheral factors and there are no or any number of additional intrinsic factors. When gender is the targeted classificatory factor, Tables 7.2, 7.3, and 7.5 illustrate the simplest of such designs. We will consider the cases that are represented by Tables 7.2 and 7.3, in which the numerator of the estimator is $(\overline{Y}_{.1} - \overline{Y}_{.2})$, which is the difference between the marginal means of the Female row and Male row in our example. The difference between these two means is 0 in the case of Table 7.3, so we focus on the calculation of an appropriate standardizer.

Suppose further that one wants to examine the mean for one gender in relation to the mean and distribution of scores of the other gender. For example, suppose that one wants to calculate by how many standard deviation units the marginal sample mean of the males ($\overline{Y}_{.2}$) is below or above the marginal sample mean of the females ($\overline{Y}_{.1}$), where the standard deviation unit is the $s$ for the distribution of scores for the females. If the peripheral factor (treatment in this case) does not ordinarily vary in the population it is an extrinsic factor. In this case one would not want to use for the standardizer the square root of the variance of the row for the females, $s_{.1}^2$ in Tables 7.2 or 7.3, which would reflect variability that is attributable to treatment. Instead one can standardize using the square root of the variance obtained from pooling the variances of all of the cells for the females (cells 1, 2, and 3 in Table 7.2 or cells 1 and 2 in Table 7.3) to find $s_{pcells}$, where again $p$ stands for pooled. Within these cells treatment does not vary so variance within a cell is not influenced by variation in the manipulated peripheral factor. One can use the following version of the pooling formula to pool the cell variances.

$$s_{pcells} = \left[ \frac{\Sigma \left[ (n_{cell} - 1)s_{cell}^2 \right]}{\Sigma (n_{cell} - 1)} \right]^{\frac{1}{2}}. \tag{7.13}$$

The summation in Equation 7.13 is conducted over the levels of the peripheral factor. If an example involves a table such as Table 7.2, the summation would be over cells 1, 2, and 3. The resulting estimator is

$$g_{classp} = \frac{\overline{Y}_{.1} - \overline{Y}_{.2}}{s_{pcells}}, \tag{7.14}$$

where again *class* stands for classificatory. This method assumes homoscedasticity of the populations whose samples' cell variances are being pooled.

For simplicity we again use the data of Table 7.3 for the case and the purpose that we have been discussing, and we suppose that one wants to standardize the difference between the marginal means of the rows for the females and males in such a table. In such a case of a 2 × 2 table, Equation 7.13 reduces to Equation 7.10 and yields, just as we found when Equation 7.10 was applied to the data of Table 7.3,

$$s_{pcells} = \left[ \frac{(10-1).989 + (10-1).544}{(10-1) + (10-1)} \right]^{\frac{1}{2}} = .875.$$

In this case of a two-way design, if one assumes homoscedasticity of all of the populations that are represented by the cells in the table (as was previously discussed, this is a riskier assumption than the previous one) one can use $MS_w^{\frac{1}{2}}$ as the standardizer to find an estimator for a comparison of the marginal means of two levels of a classificatory factor. We would label such an estimator $g_{classmsw}$. If there are one or more classificatory factors in addition to the targeted classificatory factor, as in Table 7.5, refer to Olejnik and Algina (2000) for a modification of the standardizer.

## CLASSIFICATORY FACTORS ONLY

Suppose now that the column factor in Table 7.2 were not treatment (manipulated) but ethnicity, so that the design there now consisted only of classificatory factors, gender and ethnicity. Suppose also that one wants to standardize the overall mean difference between females and males (gender targeted, ethnicity peripheral, for the moment)—that is, the difference between the means of the rows for females and males, $\overline{Y}_{.1} - \overline{Y}_{.2}$, in the now revised Table 7.2. Again, there are alternative standardizers for this purpose.

Consider first the case in which one wants to calculate by how many standard deviation units the marginal mean for the males ($\overline{Y}_{.2}$) is below or above the females' marginal mean ($\overline{Y}_{.1}$), with regard to the overall distribution of the females' scores. In this case, unlike the case in the previous section, in many instances the peripheral factor, ethnicity, does naturally vary in the population that is of interest (an intrinsic factor). Therefore, one should now want the standardizer to reflect variability that is attributable to ethnicity. Thus, for our purpose the overall $s$ of all of the females' scores can be used for the standardizer. In the case of the modified version of Table 7.2, this standardizer is the square root of the marginal variance of row 1, $(s_{.1}^2)^{1/2}$. This standardizer is defined by (but not yet conveniently calculated by) an equation that is based on deviation scores,

$$
s_{.1} = \left[ \frac{\Sigma\left(Y_{itp} - \overline{Y}_{.1}\right)^2}{n_{.1} - 1} \right]^{1/2} , \tag{7.15}
$$

where, in this example, $Y_{itp}$ is an $i$th raw score in a cell of the row (or column in other examples) whose marginal $s$ is to be the standardizer, the summation is over all such raw scores in this row, $t$ is the level of the targeted factor on which the standardizer is based (female level here), and $p$ is a level of the peripheral factor; $p = 1, 2,$ and $3$ in Table 7.2. The resulting estimator is then

$$
d_{class} = \frac{\overline{Y}_{.1} - \overline{Y}_{.2}}{s_{.1}} . \tag{7.16}
$$

The method that underlies Equation 7.16 does not assume homoscedasticity with regard to the two populations that are being compared. However, because the subpopulations (i.e., the ethnic subpopulations in this example) may have unequal variances, a more accurate estimation of the overall population's standard deviation that the standardizer is estimating may be had if the proportions of the participants in each subsample correspond to their proportions in the overall population. For example, if ethnic Subpopulation a constitutes, say, 13% of the population, then ideally 13% of the participants should be from Ethnic Group a. If the subpopulations also differ in their means (often the case when variances differ), then choosing subsample sizes to match the proportions in the subpopulations will also make the mean of each of the two targeted levels that are being compared (e.g., male and female) a more accurate estimate of the mean of its population. A subsample should not have more or less influence on the standard deviation or mean of the overall sample than it has in the population. Thus, appropriate sampling will improve the numerator and denominator of Equation 7.16 as estimators.

An easy way to calculate the standardizer that is defined by Equation 7.15 for this case would be to use any statistical software to create a data file consisting of all of the $n_{.t}$ (i.e., $n_{.1}$ in our example) raw scores as if all of the scores in the row that produces the standardizer constituted a single group. One would then compute the $s$ for this group of scores. This $s_{.t}$ ($s_{.1}$ in our example) should derive from the square root of the unbiased $s^2$ (i.e., using $n-1$, not n, in the denominator). This $s_{.t}$ can also be calculated from another formula for s; in the present case $s_{.1} = [ [(\Sigma Y_{itp}^2) - n_{.1} (\bar{Y}_{.1}^2)] / (n_{.1} - 1) ]^{\frac{1}{2}}$.

For simplicity we use the data of Table 7.3 to demonstrate the calculation of $s_{.1}$, pretending now, to fit our case, that the columns there represent a peripheral classificatory factor, such as ethnicity, instead of a treatment factor. First, from the kind of data file that was just described for all of the scores in the standardizer's row, software output yielded $s_{.1}^2 = 1.105$, so $s_{.1} = 1.105^{\frac{1}{2}} = 1.051$. Using the alternative formula from the previous paragraph we confirm that

$$s_{.1} = \left[ \frac{\begin{array}{l} 1^2 + 1^2 + 1^2 + 1^2 + 2^2 + 2^2 + 2^2 + 2^2 + 3^2 + 4^2 + 2^2 \\ + 2^2 + 3^2 + 3^2 + 3^2 + 3^2 + 3^2 + 4^2 + 4^2 + 4^2 - 20(2.5^2) \end{array}}{20 - 1} \right]^{\frac{1}{2}} = 1.051.$$

Note that $d_{class}$ of Equation 7.16 is comparable to a $d$ that would arise from a one-way design in which the targeted classificatory factor were the only independent variable in the design. To illustrate another standardizer that would accomplish this purpose, we again use the example of gender as the targeted factor. In our present modified version of Table 7.2, in which ethnicity is a peripheral column factor replacing the treatment factor, one can base one's standardizer on the pooled row margin variances, $s_{.1}^2$ and $s_{.2}^2$, each one of which reflects variability attributable to ethnicity as the population would. We pool using Equation 7.17 (shown next) that is another version of the general formula for pooling two variances. We denote the resulting standardizer $s_{classp}$, where again $p$ denotes pooled. This method assumes homoscedasticity of the populations that are represented by the two compared levels of the targeted factor. Again, as was discussed regarding the method that underlies Equation 7.16, ideally the proportions of the participants in each subsample (e.g., proportions of ethnic groups) should be equal to their proportions in the population. The current standardizer is

$$s_{classp} = \left[ \frac{(n_{.1} - 1)s_{.1}^2 + (n_{.2} - 1)s_{.2}^2}{n_{.1} + n_{.2} - 2} \right]^{1/2}. \tag{7.17}$$

The resulting estimator is then given by

$$g_{classp}^* = \frac{\overline{Y}_{.1} - \overline{Y}_{.2}}{s_{classp}}. \tag{7.18}$$

The asterisk is applied to the $g$ of Equation 7.18 to distinguish it from the $g$ of Equation 7.14. Continuing to use the modified version of Table 7.3 in which the column factor is now a peripheral classificatory factor instead of a treatment factor, we already know from the preceding calculation that $s_{.1}^2 = 1.105$. After creating a data file for the data of row 2 (Male row) as was previously described for the data of row 1, we find that software output yields $s_{.2}^2 = 1.000$. Therefore, using Equation 7.17 for the standardizer we find that

$$s_{classp} = \left[ \frac{(20 - 1)1.105 + (20 - 1)1.000}{20 + 20 - 2} \right]^{1/2} = 1.026.$$

There is an alternative method for calculating $s_{classp}$ that is applicable when there are two or more levels of the targeted classificatory factor and all cell sample sizes are equal. In this case one can use output from ANOVA software to calculate, for entry into Equation 7.18,

$$s_{classp} = \left[ \frac{SS_{tot} - SS_{tc}}{N - k_{tc}} \right]^{1/2}, \tag{7.19}$$

where $SS_{tc}$ is the $SS$ for the targeted classificatory factor, $N$ is the total sample size, and $k_{tc}$ is the number of levels of the targeted classificatory factor (Olejnik & Algina, 2000). Observe in the numerator of Equation 7.19 that variability that is attributable to the targeted factor is subtracted from total variability leaving only variability that is attributable to the peripheral factor, which, as was previously discussed, is appropriate in the case considered here.

In the ANOVA summarizing Table 7.4, for our example that uses the data in the revised Table 7.3, $SS_{tc}$ is $SS_B$, $N = 40$, and $k_{tc} = 2$. In Table 7.4 we observe for the data of Table 7.3 that, by summing all $SS$ values, $SS_{tot} = 40.000$, and $SS_B = 0.000$. Applying Equation 7.19 we thus find that $s_{classp} = [(40.000 - 0.000) / (40 - 2)]^{1/2} = 1.026$. This value agrees with the previous value for $s_{classp}$ that was calculated from files for data from separate rows instead of ANOVA output.

We do not proceed to calculate an estimate of effect size that is based on the standardized difference between the row marginal means for the data of the modified Table 7.3 because $\overline{Y}_{.1} - \overline{Y}_{.2} = 0$ in that table. However, the method, and also the interpretation when the mean difference is not 0, should be clear from the previous worked examples and discussions. Again, when selecting from a variety of possible standardizers for an estimator, one should make a choice that is based on one's decision regarding which version of the effect-size parameter the sample $d$ or $g$ is to be estimating. As we have observed, each standardizer and its resulting $d$ or $g$ has a somewhat different purpose and/or underlying assumption about homoscedasticity.

## STATISTICAL INFERENCE AND FURTHER READING

Smithson (2001) discussed the use of SPSS to construct an exact confidence interval for $\eta^2$, whole or partial, and for a related effect size that is proportional to Cohen's (1988) $f$, which we discussed in chapter 6. Fidler and Thompson (2001) further illustrated application of Smithson's (2001) method to an $a \times b$ design. Smithson (2003) demonstrated the construction of confidence intervals for partial $\eta^2$ and related measures. Also refer to Steiger (2004). STATISTICA can also be used to construct an exact confidence interval for $\eta^2$ for the factorial design at hand. Estimation of $POV$ in complex designs was discussed by Dodd and Schultz (1973), Dwyer (1974), and Vaughan and Corballis (1969). Olejnik and Algina (2000) discussed estimation of $POV$ in designs with covariates and split-plot designs (both also discussed by Maxwell & Delaney, 2004) and in multivariate designs.

Bird (2002) discussed methods, under the assumptions of normality and homoscedasticity, for constructing individual and simultaneous confidence intervals for standardized differences between means and the implementation of these methods using readily available software. At the time of this writing Kevin Bird and his colleagues provide free software for constructing approximate confidence intervals for standardized and unstandardized contrasts, planned or unplanned, for factorial designs with a between-groups and a within-groups factor. Analyses of more complex factorial designs are possible, but in such cases construction of simultaneous confidence intervals is more difficult. This software is available at http://www.psy.unsw.edu.au/reasearch/PSY.htm. Steiger and Fouladi (1997) discussed the construction of exact confidence intervals. Also consult Steiger (2004). Note that in the case of ordinal data, such as those from rating scales, a different approach may have to be developed for the construction of confidence intervals for the difference between two means (Penfield, 2003).

As mentioned in chapter 6, an approximate confidence interval for a standardized difference between means can be constructed by dividing the limits that are obtained for the unstandardized difference by $MS_w^{1/2}$. This method assumes homoscedasticity. Under heteroscedasticity it would be problematic to define the population to which such a confidence interval would apply. Also, recall from our earlier discussion that when $MS_w^{\frac{1}{2}}$ is the standardizer in a factorial design one is not permitting variability that is attributable to a peripheral factor to contribute to the standardizer. Therefore, the use of $MS_w^{\frac{1}{2}}$ would not be appropriate if the peripheral factor is a classificatory one that varies in the population that is of interest.

In the already noted case in which a classificatory peripheral factor varies in the population (intrinsic factor), Maxwell and Delaney (2004) recommended that the standardizer be obtained by calculating the square root of the variance that results from adding the $SS$ values from all sources other than the targeted manipulated factor and then dividing by the degrees of freedom that are associated with these included sources. For example, suppose that one wants a standardizer for the difference between the two treatment means in Table 7.3 (marginal column means) and that the variability that is attributable to the peripheral factor of gender is to contribute to the standardizer. Using all of the values of $SS$ and of $df$ for the data in Table 7.3 that are presented in Table 7.4, except for those for the targeted factor of treatment (Factor A), the standardizer is given by $[\ SS_B + SS_{AB} + SS_w)\ /\ (df_B + df_{AB} + df_w)]^{\frac{1}{2}} = [\ (.000 + .400 + 29.600)\ /\ (1 + 1 + 36)\ ]^{\frac{1}{2}} = .889.$

As discussed in chapters 2 and 3, when the dependent variable is measured in familiar units, analysis of data in terms of "raw" (i.e., unstandardized) differences between means can be very informative and readily interpreted (Bond et al., 2003). Of course it is routine to conduct tests of significance and construct simultaneous confidence intervals involving comparisons within pairs of means whose differences are not standardized (Bird, 2002; Maxwell & Delaney, 2004). The latter coauthors discussed methods for the homoscedastic or heteroscedastic cases. The procedure that is generally known as the Bonferroni method (more appropriately, the Bonferroni–Dunn method) can be used to make planned pairwise comparisons. (However, unless there is only a small number of comparisons, one might be concerned about the loss of statistical power for each comparison.) Alternatively, the Tukey HSD method (which is the same as WSD but not the same as Tukey-b) is applicable. Wilcox (2003) discussed and provided S-PLUS software functions for less known robust methods for pairwise comparisons (more generally, linear contrasts) and construction of simultaneous confidence intervals involving the pairs of means of interest.

Abelson and Prentice (1997) and Olejnik and Algina (2000) presented methods for calculating an estimator of effect size for interaction. Maxwell and Delaney (2004) discussed methods for testing the statistical significance of the differences among the cell means that are involved in a factor that might or might not be interacting with another factor. Such cellwise comparisons test for simple effects. A comparison of marginal means (testing main effects) when there is interaction merely provides an overall (i.e., an average) comparison of levels of the targeted factor. Such a comparison, or estimation of an effect size that is based on such a comparison, can be misleading because when there is an interaction a difference between targeted marginal means does not reflect a constant difference between cell means at levels of the targeted factor at each level of a peripheral factor. For example, the difference between the column marginal means in Table 7.3 is $2.0 - 3.0 = -1.0$. However, the difference between mean scores under Treatments 1 and 2 for females is not $-1.0$ but $1.9 - 3.1 = -1.2$, and the difference between mean scores under Treatments 1 and 2 for males is also not $-1.0$ but $2.1 - 2.9 = -.8$. The difference between the column marginal means is the mean of these two differences; $[(-1.2) + (-.8)] / 2 = -1.0$. If the interaction had been statistically significant for the data of Table 7.3 one could infer that the difference between $-1.2$ and $-.8$ were thereby statistically significant.

Note, however, that an interaction implies a statistically significant difference between simple effects, but the fact that a simple effect is found to be statistically significant while another simple effect involving the same targeted factor is not statistically significant does not imply an interaction. For example, suppose that in Table 7.3 the difference in females' mean scores under Treatments 1 and 2 (i.e., $1.9 - 3.1 = -1.2$) were statistically significant but that the difference in males' mean scores under Treatments 1 and 2 (i.e., $2.1 - 2.9 = -.8$) were not statistically significant. Such a result would not necessarily indicate an interaction. Estimation of standardized-difference effect sizes for the kind of cellwise comparisons at hand was discussed in the section Comparisons of Levels of a Manipulated Factor at One Level of a Peripheral Factor.

Aside from the statistical issues, in research that has theoretical implications explaining an interaction would be of great importance. Note in this regard that whether main effects, simple effects, and/or interactions are found to be statistically significant might depend on the researcher's choice of measure. Two measures might seem to be representing the same underlying construct when, in fact, they might be measuring somewhat different constructs. For further discussion and debate on this and related issues refer to Sawilowsky and Fahoome (2003).

Maxwell and Delaney (2004) and the references therein provided detailed discussions of the issue of interaction, including alternative approaches, confidence intervals for the standardized and unstandardized population differences between the cell means, and a measure of strength of association for interaction contrasts. Timm's (2004) *ubiquitous study effect size index*, which, as we mentioned in chapter 6, assumes homoscedasticity, is applicable to $F$ tests and tests of contrasts in exploratory studies that use factorial designs. Brunner and Puri (2001) extended the application of what we call the *PS* measure of effect size (discussed in our chap. 5) to factorial designs.

## WITHIN-GROUPS FACTORIAL DESIGNS

In the case of factorial designs with only within-groups factors primary researchers can usually conceptualize and estimate a standardized difference between means using the same reasoning and the same methods that were presented using Equations 7.3 and 7.4 in the earlier Manipulated Factors Only section. Note that there is not literally a $MS_w$ in designs with only within-group factors, but it is valid here to apply Equation 7.4 as if the data had come from a between-subjects design. There is variability within each cell of a within-groups design, as there is within each cell of a between-subjects design, and the subject variables that underlie population variability will be reflected by this variability in both types of designs (cf. Olejnik & Algina, 2000). (In the section Within-Groups Designs and Further Reading in chapter 6, we presented instructions for using statistical software packages to calculate standardizers in the case of one-way within-groups designs. Those instructions are also applicable to the denominators of Equations 7.3 and 7.4.) Typically a within-groups factor will be a manipulated rather than a classificatory one because researchers often subject the same participant to different levels of treatment at different times but typically cannot vary the classification of a person (e.g., gender or ethnicity). (Exceptions in which a within-groups factor might be considered to be classificatory would include research that collects data before and after a participant-initiated change of political affiliation, religion, or gender.)

In the case of within-groups factorial designs, variability that is attributable to the peripheral manipulated factor should not contribute to the variability that is reflected by the standardizer if the peripheral manipulated factor does not vary in the population of interest, as it typically does not. For an example, suppose now that in Table 7.3 Treatment 1 and Treatment 2 were the absence and presence, respectively, of a new drug for Alzheimer's disease, drug A, with Factor A being a within-groups factor. Suppose also that in Table 7.3 Factor B were not gender but instead the absence (row 1) or presence (row 2) of a very different new kind of drug for Alzheimer's disease, drug B, with Factor B also being a within-groups factor. The data in Table 7.3 might represent the patients' scores on a short test of memory or the number of symptoms remaining after treatment with one or the other drug, a combination of the two drugs, or no drug. Because of our purpose here we do not discuss methodological issues (other than supposing counterbalancing) in this hypothetical research, but instead we proceed directly to demonstrating alternative estimators of a standardized difference between means for the case of within-groups factorial designs.

Using Factor A for the targeted factor and supposing now that cell 1 represents a control or standard-treatment comparison group (a control or placebo condition in this example of the revised factors in Table 7.3), we first apply Equation 7.3 to the data to find that $d_{comp} = (2.00 - 3.00) / .989^{1/2} = -1.01$. If we assume homoscedasticity of all four populations of scores that are represented in the design (cells 1 through 4), and recalling from Table 7.4 that we found that $MS_w = .822$ for the data of Table 7.3, we can alternatively apply Equation 7.4 to find that $g_{msw} = (2.00 - 3.00) / .822^{1/2} = -1.10$.

Finally, if we now assume homoscedasticity with regard to the marginal variances of peripheral Factor B, we can standardize using the square root of the pooled variances in the margins of rows 1 and 2; $s_{.1}^2 = 1.105$ and $s_{.2}^2 = 1.000$. Because the sample sizes for the two rows are the same, the pooled variance is merely the mean of the two variances; $s_{prm}^2 = (1.105 + 1.000) / 2 = 1.053$, where $p$, as before, denotes pooled and $rm$ denotes repeated measures. The standardizer is then $s_{prm} = 1.053^{1/2} = 1.026$. The estimator for our purpose is given by

$$g_{prm} = \frac{\overline{Y}_{1.} - \overline{Y}_{2.}}{s_{prm}}. \quad (7.20)$$

For the data at hand $g_{prm} = (2.00 - 3.00) / 1.026 = -.97$. Note that the results from applying Equations 7.3, 7.4, and 7.20 are not very different in the artificial case of the data of Table 7.3 because the variances in that table are not as different as they are likely to be in the case of real data. Again, the choice of standardizer is based on the assumptions that the researcher makes about the variances of the involved populations. The interpretation of the estimates in terms of population parameters and distributions should be clear from the earlier discussions.

For further discussions of Equations 7.3 and 7.4 and of the basis of Equation 7.20, review the earlier Manipulated Factors Only section. Olejnik and Algina (2000) provided discussions, and more worked examples of estimation of standardized effect sizes for within-group factorial designs. Maxwell and Delaney (2004) discussed construction of confidence intervals for the difference between marginal means and for the difference between cell means within the framework of a multivariate approach to two-way within-groups designs. Bird (2002) provided an example of the use of SPSS to construct simultaneous confidence intervals for standardized effect sizes, assuming homoscedasticity, from a design with one within-groups factor and one between-groups factor (split-plot design). Approximate individual and simultaneous confidence intervals for such a design can be constructed, assuming homoscedasticity, using the currently downloadable free software, PSY, from Kevin Bird and his colleagues. This software and its web site were cited in the previous section. Consult Wilcox (2003) for discussions and S-PLUS functions for less known robust methods for pairwise comparisons for two-way within-groups designs. Brunner and Puri (2001) discussed extension of what we call the *PS* measure to within-groups factorial designs.

Maxwell and Delaney (2004) presented one of the various formulas that attempt to estimate *POV* for the main effect of the targeted factor in a within-groups factorial design. Their version of such a formula, a partial omega squared, renders the estimate comparable to what it would have been if the targeted factor had been manipulated in a one-way between-groups design. Research reports should be clear about which of the available conceptually different equations has been used to estimate

*POV* for a targeted factor in a within-groups factorial design so that the authors of the report, their readers, or later meta-analysts do not unwittingly compare or combine estimates of incomparable measures. For example, Maxwell and Delaney's (2004) formula partials out all effects except for the main effect of subjects, whereas other possible approaches might partial out all effects, including the main effect of subjects, or partial out no effects (an estimation of *POV*, not partial *POV*). Refer to Maxwell and Delaney (2004) and Olejnik and Algina (2003) for further discussions, and refer to this chapter's earlier section on partial omega squared for a brief refresher on partial *POV*. Earlier discussions were provided by Dodd and Schultz (1973), Olejnik and Algina (2000), and Susskind and Howland (1980).

The reader is referred to Maxwell and Delaney (2004) for detailed discussions of assumptions and of analyses of marginal means and interactions in the case of within-groups factorial designs. With regard to split-plot designs these authors again provided detailed discussion of those topics, the construction of confidence intervals for the variety of contrasts that are possible, and equations for estimation of partial omega squared for each kind of factor and for interaction. As was discussed in the previous paragraph, these equations for estimation of partial omega squared have a different conceptual basis and form from those that might be found elsewhere (cf. Olejnik & Algina, 2000). As we have previously mentioned, Hunter and Schmidt (2004) provided a strong endorsement of the use of within-groups designs.

Note that researchers often apply parametric statistical methods such as ANOVA to data that arise from rating scales by assigning ordered numerical values to the ordered categories. For example, the successive values 1, 2, 3, 4 (or 4, 3, 2, 1) might be assigned respectively to the categories *agree strongly*, *agree*, *disagree*, and *disagree strongly*. Therefore, many researchers would be inclined in such cases to apply the same methods that were applied in this section to the data of Table 7.3. However, the application of parametric methods (e.g., the use of means) to data from ordinal scales such as rating scales is controversial. Although such methods may not be problematic in terms of rates of Type I error, there may be more powerful methods, such as those that are discussed in chapter 9. Also, some do not consider the mean of a rating scale to be a meaningful statistic (but consult Penfield, 2003). We defer to the section Limitations of $r_{pb}$ for Ordinal Categorical Data in chapter 9 for discussion of the matter of parametric analysis of ordinal data such as those arising from rating scales.

## ADDITIONAL DESIGNS AND MEASURES

There are methods for calculating estimators of standardized mean differences available for various additional ANOVA designs. Discussions of these methods would be beyond the scope of this book, but the basic concepts and worked examples that have been presented here should prepare the reader to understand such methods, which are presented elsewhere. Cortina and Nouri (2000) and Olejnik and Algina (2000) discussed methods for $a \times b$, $a \times b \times c$, and analysis of covariance designs. The latter authors discussed methods related to split-plot designs (mix of between-groups and within-groups factors); also consult the previously cited article by Gillett (2003). Wilcox (2003) discussed and provided S-PLUS functions for robust linear contrasts for two-way split-plot designs. Kline (2004) discussed many of the topics of the current chapter.

For discussions of estimation of POV for designs with random factors or mixed random and fixed factors, consult Vaughan and Corballis (1969), Dodd and Schultz (1973), Olejnik and Algina (2000), and Maxwell and Delaney (2004). The latter authors also discussed estimation of POV and tests and construction of confidence intervals for differences between marginal means in the case of nested designs. For an alternative correlational approach to effect sizes for between-groups and within-groups factorial designs consult Rosenthal et al. (2000). Their approach was also discussed by Maxwell and Delaney (2004).

## LIMITATIONS AND RECOMMENDATIONS

We observed in this chapter that there can be more than one way to conceptualize and estimate an effect size even when faced with a given targeted factor and a given mix of manipulated and/or classificatory factors. Furthermore, there might be additional valid approaches, not discussed here, to choosing a method for designs that were discussed here. Moreover, sometimes in the literature there is outright disagreement about the appropriate method for a given purpose. There may be disagreement about how to estimate $\Delta$, how to estimate POV, and about whether $\Delta$ or POV is the more useful measure for a given set of data or for any set of data. Work on some of these topics is ongoing and more research is needed. Researchers should think carefully about the purpose of their research and of the nature of the populations of interest, as have been discussed in this book and in the references therein, before deciding on an appropriate measure and estimator.

Because varying methods can result in apparently conflicting results of estimation of effect sizes in the literature it is imperative that researchers make clear in their reports which method they have used. If this is done their readers and those who review the literature will not be unwittingly comparing or combining (i.e., meta-analysts) conceptually and computationally incomparable estimates of effect size. Authors of research reports should also consider reporting not just one kind of estimate of effect size but two or more defensible alternatively conceptualized estimates to provide themselves and their readers with alternative perspectives on the results. (We are aware of a dissenting opinion that holds that providing alternative estimators may only serve to confuse some readers of research reports.)

Because methodological and design features can contribute nearly as much to the magnitude of an estimate of effect size as does a targeted factor (Gillett, 2003; Olejnik & Algina, 2003; Wilson & Lipsey, 2001), researchers should be explicit in their reports' Method sections and have at least a brief comment in their Discussion sections about every characteristic of their study that could possibly influence the effect size. In their analysis of the effect of psychological, behavioral, and educational treatments Wilson and Lipsey (2001) estimated, as a first approximation, that the type of research design (randomized vs. nonrandomized, between-groups vs. within-groups) and choice of concrete measure of an abstract underlying dependent variable were the methodological features that correlated highest with estimates of effect size, but many other methodological features also correlated with these estimates. For example, as we observed in this chapter, estimates of effect size involving two levels of a targeted factor can vary depending on the nature of the peripheral factor (extrinsic or intrinsic). For further discussions of factors to which measures of effect size are sensitive, consult Onwuegbuzie and Levin (2003) and the references therein.

For another example of the influence of design features, we are aware of a thesis in which Experiment 1 was a between-groups study, Experiment 2 was a conceptual replication of that study using a within-groups design, and the results within the two versions of the study were both statistically significant, but in the opposite direction. Such a conflicting result from a between-groups and a within-groups study is not an isolated case. Consult Grice (1966), and Maxwell and Delaney (2004) and the references therein for further examples and discussion.

Also, estimates of effect size can vary depending on the extent of variability of the participants. For example, for a given pair of levels of a factor and a given dependent variable, effect sizes might be different for a population of college students and the possibly more variable general population. Therefore, one should be cautious about comparing effect sizes across studies that used samples from populations that might have differing variabilities on the dependent variable. Refer to Onwuegbuzie and Levin (2003) for further discussion. Again, by being explicit about all possibly relevant methodological characteristics of their research, authors of reports can facilitate interpretation of results and facilitate the work of meta-analysts who can systematically study the relationships between such methodological variables (moderator variables) and the magnitudes of estimates of effect size across studies.

## QUESTIONS

1. Distinguish between what the text calls a targeted factor and a peripheral factor.

2. Distinguish between an extrinsic factor and an intrinsic factor.

3. How does the distinction between extrinsic and intrinsic factors influence the procedure one adopts for estimating an effect size?

4. Are intrinsic factors always classificatory factors? Explain.

5. Why is estimation of the POV more complicated in the case of factorial designs than in the case of one-way designs?

6. What is the purpose of a partial POV?

7. Discuss why it is problematic to compare two values of an estimated POV based on the relative sizes of their values, of the values of their associated Fs, or of the values of significance levels attained by their Fs.

8. Why is it problematic to compare two estimates of partial POV for two factors in the same study?

9. Which two conditions should ordinarily be met if one wants to compare estimates of a POV for the same factor from different factorial studies?

10. Why is it problematic to interpret the relative importance of two factors by inspecting the ratio of their estimated POVs?

11. How do the nature of the targeted factor and the nature of the peripheral factor influence the choice of a procedure for estimating a standardized effect size?

12. How do the nature of one's assumption about homoscedasticity and the presence of a control group or standard-treatment comparison group influence one's choice of a standardizer?

13. What assumption underlies the use of Equation 7.6, and in simplest terms what is the nature of the variance that it produces?

14. Briefly describe three procedures for estimating a standardized difference between means at two levels of a manipulated factor at a given level of a peripheral factor, and how does one choose one procedure from these three?

15. Briefly describe how one estimates a standardized difference between means at two levels of an intrinsic factor when there is one or more extrinsic peripheral factors.

16. Discuss one procedure for estimating a standardized overall difference between means of a classificatory factor when the peripheral factor is intrinsic.

17. How might a difference between the proportions of various demographic subgroups in a sample and the proportions of those subgroups in the population influence the estimate of a standardized difference between means?

18. When would it be inappropriate to use the square root of $MS_w$ as a standardizer even when homoscedasticity of all involved populations is assumed?

19. Briefly describe the relationship between an interaction and simple effects.

20. What effect might one's choice of a measure for the dependent variable (when there are alternative measures) have on the results

of the various significance tests and estimates of effect size that emerge from a factorial ANOVA?

21. Why are Equations 7.3 and 7.4 typically applicable to within-groups designs?

22. What is the rationale for the use of Equation 7.20 in the case of within-group designs?

23. Discuss the roles that methodological and design features might play in the magnitude of an estimated effect size.

24. Considering the issues raised by Question 23, what information should be provided in the Method section of a research report?

# Chapter 8

# Effect Sizes
# for Categorical Variables

## BACKGROUND REVIEW

Readers who are very familiar with categorical variables, contingency tables, the chi-square ($\chi^2$) test of association, and related terminology might want to proceed directly to the last three paragraphs of this section. This chapter does not involve the chi-square test of goodness-of-fit.

Often in the behavioral and social sciences the two or more variables that are being related are categorical. An unordered categorical variable is also called a *nominal* or *qualitative variable* because its variations (categories) are names for qualities (characteristics). An experimental example of type of treatment as an unordered categorical variable is random assignment of participants to Treatments a, b, .... In this example the categorical independent variable is the type (category) of treatment. Common classificatory examples of categorical independent variables include gender: male and female and political affiliation: Democrat, Republican, or other. Note that the ordering of the categories in these examples is arbitrary, not meaningful. The categories in these examples could just as well have been considered in any other order. (In the next chapter we discuss only categorical variables that do represent a natural ordering, such as agree strongly, agree, disagree, and disagree strongly.) Note also that in such examples lumping minority political parties, minority religious groups, or minority ethnic groups, et cetera, into a catch-all "other" category is not intended to slight those groups; it would be purely a statistical consideration. Additional named categories (involving minority groups) of the independent variables in such examples may be used. However, no category should be used that is likely to be attained by no or few members of the samples. This problem is likely to occur if the researcher includes a category that represents a small minority of the population and the sampling method or size is inappropriate for sampling that minority sufficiently. Inferences from estimators of effect size may be impossible or problematic when there are too few participants in one or more of the categories. If the researcher wants to include minority groups an appropriate sampling method or size should be used to obtain sufficient numbers of members of these groups. When a categorical variable has only two possible values it is called a *dichotomous* or *binomial variable*. When more than two values are possible the variable is called *multinomial*.

When each of the variables in the research is categorical the data are usually presented in a table such as Table 8.1. In the simplest case only two variables are being studied, one variable being represented by the rows and the other by the columns of the table. In this case the table is called a two-way table. The general designation of a two-way table is $r \times c$ table, in which x means "by," and $r$ and $c$ stand for rows and columns, respectively. For a specific $r \times c$ table the letters $r$ and $c$ are replaced by the number of rows and the number of columns in that table, respectively; these numbers also correspond to the number of categories that the row and column variables have. In the simplest case the row variable has only two categories and the column variable has only two categories, resulting in the common $2 \times 2$ table that is also called a *fourfold table* because the table contains four cells. Two-way or multiway (i.e., more than two variables) tables are also called *cross-classification tables* or *contingency tables*. The cells of the cross-classification tables classify (categorize) each participant across two or more variables. Within each cell of the table is the number of participants that fall into the row category and the column category that the cell represents. Such data are called *cell counts* or *cell frequencies*.

The general purpose of a contingency table is to analyze the table's data to determine if there is a contingency (i.e., association or independence) between the variables. In a common example one might want to determine if participants' falling into the *client better* or *client not better* categories is contingent on which treatment category they were in. (Although *client better* vs. *client not better* is an example of an ordered categorical variable, the difference between ordered and unordered dependent variables is not important for us in the case of dichotomous dependent variables until chap. 9.) Note that in this example there is an

### TABLE 8.1
#### Frequencies of Outcomes After Treatment

| Therapy | Symptoms | | Totals |
| --- | --- | --- | --- |
| | Remain | Gone | |
| Psychotherapy | $f_{11} = 14$ | $f_{12} = 22$ | 36 |
| Drug Therapy | $f_{21} = 22$ | $f_{22} = 10$ | 32 |
| Totals | 36 | 32 | 68 |

independent variable (the type of treatment given) and a dependent variable (the outcome of better or not better), although we also consider examples in which the categorical variables need not be classifiable as independent variables or dependent variables. For example, in research that relates religious affiliation and political affiliation the researcher need not designate an independent variable and a dependent variable, although the researcher may have a theory of the relationship which does specify that, say, religious affiliation is the independent variable and political affiliation is the dependent variable. The total count for each row across the columns is placed at the right margin of the table, and the total count for each column across the rows is placed at the bottom margin of the table. The row totals and the column totals are each called *marginal totals*.

Table 8.1 is a 2 × 2 contingency table that is based on actual data. The clinical details are not relevant to our discussion of estimating an effect size for such data, but they would be very relevant to the researcher's interpretation and generalization of the results. For the purpose of the next section we assume for now that the data in Table 8.1 represent the fourfold categorizations of 68 former pain patients whose files had been sampled from a clinic that had provided either psychotherapy or drug therapy for a certain kind of pain. Such a method of research is called a *naturalistic* or *cross-sectional study*. In this method the researcher decides only the total number of participants to be sampled, not the row or column totals. These latter totals emerge naturally when the total sample is categorized. Naturalistic sampling is common in survey research.

In Table 8.1 the letter $f$ stands for frequency of occurrence in a cell, and the pair of subscripts for each cell stand for the row and column, respectively, that the cell frequency represents. For example, $f_{21}$ stands for the frequency with which participants are found in the cell representing the crossing of the second row and the first column, namely 22 of the 32 patients who received drug therapy. (Note that we are returning to standard notation in this chapter because for our present purposes we no longer have a reason for the atypical sequencing of column and row subscripts that we adopted and explained in chap. 7.)

The examples in this chapter involve independent samples. Refer to Fleiss, Levin, and Paik (2003) for discussion of the case of experiments that use matched samples. In that case participants are matched with respect to one or more attributes that are known to be, or are believed to be, related to the outcome variable. Each participant within each matched pair of individuals (or within each matched group of individuals in cases in which there are more than two treatments) is randomly assigned to one of the treatments. (Fleiss et al., 2003, discussed as *correlated binary data* the case of repeated measurements in longitudinal studies, in which each participant is categorized twice or more over time.) Also consult Fleiss et al. (2003) for discussion of cases in which there are missing data or in which some participants have been misclassified into the categories. The latter problem is related to the problem of unreliability of measurement that was discussed in chapter 4. Fleiss et al. (2003) also discussed measurement of interrater agreement in order to obtain an upper limit for the reliability of the categorizations.

## CHI-SQUARE TEST AND *Phi*

Note first that the statistical and effect-size procedures that are presented in this chapter for 2 × 2 tables are applied here only to originally discrete (i.e., truly or originally dichotomous) variables, not dichotomized variables. These procedures are problematic when the row or the column variable has been dichotomized by the researcher, say, into better versus not better categories from an originally continuous variable. For example, suppose that two therapies are to be compared for their effect on anxiety. Suppose further that two categories of anxiety are formed by the researcher categorizing patients as high or low anxiety using scores above or below the median (or some other cutpoint) respectively, on a continuous scale of anxiety. Such arbitrary dichotomizing might render the procedures in this chapter invalid because the results might depend not only on the relative effectiveness of the two therapies, as they should, but also on the arbitrary cutpoint the researcher decided to use to lump everyone below the cutpoint together as low anxiety and to lump everyone above the cutpoint together as high anxiety. If some other arbitrary cutpoints had been used, such as the lowest 25% of scores on the continuous anxiety test (low anxiety) and the highest 25% of scores (high anxiety), the results from statistical tests and estimation of effect size might differ from those arising from the equally arbitrary use of the median as the cutpoint. (However, refer to Sánchez-Meca, Marín-Martínez, & Chacón-Moscoso, 2003, for cases in which the choice of cutpoint seemed generally to have little influence on the biases and sampling variabilities of estimators of effect size.) When the dependent variable is a continuous variable methods that have been presented earlier throughout this book are more appropriate than dichotomizing.

The most common test of the statistical significance of the association between the row and column variables in a table such as Table 8.1 is the $\chi^2$ test of association. In general the degrees of freedom for this test is given by $df = (r-1)(c-1)$, which in the case of a 2 × 2 table yields $df = (2-1)(2-1) = 1$. However, whereas the $\chi^2$ test addresses the issue of whether or not there is an association, the emphasis in this book is on estimating the strength of this association with an appropriate estimator of effect size.

As we previously noted with regard to the $t$ statistic, the magnitude of $\chi^2$ does not necessarily indicate the strength of the association between the row and column variables. The numerical value of the $\chi^2$ statistic depends not only on the strength of association but also on the total sample size. Thus, if in a contingency table the pattern of the cell data were to remain the same (the same strength of association) but the sample size increased, $\chi^2$ would increase.

What is needed is a measure of the strength of the association between the row and column variables that is not affected, or less affected, by total sample size. One common such measure of effect size for a 2 × 2 table is the population correlation coefficient, $r_{pop}$. An $r_{pop}$ arising from a 2 × 2 table is called a population *phi* coefficient, $phi_{pop}$ in this book, estimated by the sample *phi*. (In the statistical literature what we denote in this book $phi_{pop}$ is usually denoted $\Phi$ and the estimator *phi* is usually denoted $\phi$. Although it is easier to conceive of $phi_{pop}$ as simply the special case of $r_{pop}$ when both X and Y are dichotomous, note first that $\chi^2$ can be considered to be a sum of squared effects;

$$\chi^2 = \sum \frac{(f_o - f_e)^2}{f_e}, \text{ where } f_o \text{ and } f_e \text{ are the observed frequencies and ex-}$$

pected frequencies, respectively, in a cell, and the summation is over all four cells. Therefore, $phi_{pop}$ can be considered to be a kind of average effect, the square root of an average of the squared effects. For formal expression of this parameter and further discussion consult Hays, 1994, and Liebetrau, 1983. It should not be surprising that $phi_{pop}$ is a kind of average because $r_{pop}$ too is a mean, the mean of products of z scores;

$$r_{pop} = \frac{\sum z_x z_y}{N}.) \text{ To calculate } phi \text{ for a 2} \times \text{2 table one can use the proce-}$$

dure that was outlined for this purpose in the section in chapter 4 on the binomial effect size display (BESD). However, *phi* can be calculated more simply using

$$phi - \left[\frac{\chi^2}{N}\right]^{\frac{1}{2}}, \tag{8.1}$$

where N is the total sample size. (Observe in Equation 8.1 how *phi*, as an estimator of effect size, compensates for the influence of sample size on $\chi^2$ by dividing $\chi^2$ by N.) For the purpose of applying *phi* to data from naturalistic sampling, one calculates an unadjusted $\chi^2$ using

$$\chi^2 = \frac{N(f_{11}f_{22} - f_{12}f_{21})^2}{n_{r1}n_{r2}n_{c1}n_{c2}}, \tag{8.2}$$

where $n_{r1}, n_{r2}, n_{c1}$, and $n_{c2}$, represent the number of participants in row 1, row 2, column 1, and column 2, respectively. (Note that we are adopting the recommendation of Fleiss et al., 2003, that the numerator of $\chi^2$ not be adjusted when calculating *phi*.)

For the data of Table 8.1, software and manual calculation yielded $\chi^2 = 6.06$ (for which $p = .013$), so $phi = (6.06/68)^{1/2} = .30$, a value that may be considered to be statistically significantly different from 0 at $p = .013$. Note that different software and different textbooks often use equations for $\chi^2$ that are different from Equation 8.2. Some superficially different looking equations for $\chi^2$ are actually functionally equivalent ones that yield identical results (e.g., our Equation 8.2 versus Equation 6.3 in Fleiss et al., 2003). Another difference between equations is a matter of adjusting or not adjusting the numerator of $\chi^2$ for the fact that its continuous theoretical distribution (used to obtain the significance level) is not perfectly represented by its actual discrete empirical sampling distribution. Again, to calculate *phi* the unadjusted $\chi^2$ is used as in Equation 8.2.

As an $r_{pop}$, $phi_{pop}$ theoretically ranges from $-1$ to $+1$. If phi is calculated as an $r$ using the method in the section on the BESD in chapter 4, the calculation will yield a signed value for any nonzero $r$, but, if we use Equation 8.1, which produces a square root, it may not be immediately clear whether *phi* is positive or negative. However, the sign of *phi* is a trivial result of the order in which the two columns or the two rows are arranged. For example, if Table 8.1 had drug therapy and its results in the first row and psychotherapy and its results in the second row, the sign of $r$, but not its size, would change. To interpret our obtained *phi* of .30 ($+$ or $-$?) note first that *symptom gone* is the better of the two outcome categories. Observe also that $22/36 = .61$ of the total psychotherapy patients attained this good outcome, whereas $10/32 = .31$ of the total patients in drug therapy attained it. Therefore, one now has the proper interpretation of the obtained *phi*. Because $\chi^2$ and, by implication, *phi* are statistically significant and a greater proportion of the psychotherapy patients than the drug patients are found in the better outcome category, one can conclude that psychotherapy is statistically significantly better than drug therapy in the particular clinical example of the data in Table 8.1.

Because one now has the proper interpretation of the results, the question of the sign of *phi* is unimportant. However, using the reasoning of chapter 4 regarding the sign of the point-biserial $r$, the reader should be able to see now that $r = phi$ is negative for the data in Table 8.1 using the usual kind of coding of the $X$ and $Y$ variables. If we were to code, say, row 1 as $X = 1$, row 2 as $X = 2$, column 1 as $Y = 1$, and column 2 as $Y = 2$, *phi* is negative because there is a tendency for those in the lower category of $X$ (i.e., row 1) to be in the higher category of $Y$ (i.e., column 2) and for those in the higher category of $X$ (i.e., row 2) to be in the lower category of $Y$ (i.e., column 1). This pattern of results defines a negative relationship between variables.

Unfortunately, the value of *phi* is not only influenced by the strength of association between the row and column variables, as it should be, but also by variation in the margin totals, as we discuss next, which can be detrimental to $phi_{pop}$ as a measure of effect size. Therefore, its use is recommended only in naturalistic research, wherein the researcher has chosen only the total sample size, not the row or column sample sizes, so that any variation between the two column totals or between the two row totals is natural rather than being based on the researcher's arbitrary choices of sample sizes. A *phi* arising from another study of the same two dichotomous variables but using a sampling method other than naturalistic sampling would not be comparable to a *phi* based on naturalistic sampling. Therefore, a meta-analyst should not simply average values of *phi* that arise from studies that used different sampling methods. Also, *phi* can only attain the extreme values of –1 or +1 (perfect correlations) when both variables are truly dichotomous and when the proportion of the total participants found in one or the other of the row margins is the same as the proportion of the total participants who are found in one or the other of the column margins.

The requirement about the equality of a row proportion and a column proportion to maintain the possibility of *phi* = +1 or –1 as an extreme limit is related to the problem of reduction of $r$ by unequal skew of an $X$ variable and a $Y$ variable that was discussed in the Assumptions of $r$ and $r_{pb}$ section in chapter 4. In naturalistic sampling a reduction of the absolute upper limit for *phi* due to the failure of a row proportion to equal a column proportion might merely be reflecting a natural phenomenon in the two populations instead of reflecting the researcher's arbitrary choice of the two sample sizes. Consult the treatments of *phi* in J. B. Carroll (1961), Cohen et al. (2002), and Haddock, Rindskopf, and Shadish (1998) for further discussions. J. B. Carroll (1961) provided an equation for the exact limits for *phi*, called $phi_{max}$, but he cautioned against the temptation to use $phi/phi_{max}$ as a kind of corrected *phi*. For our example, in Table 8.1 the proportions of the total 68 participants that are found in row 1, row 2, column 1, and column 2 are $36/68 = .53, 32/68 = .47, 36/68 = .53,$ and $32/68 = .47$, respectively. Note that the row and column marginal distributions in Table 8.1 happen to satisfy the proportionality criterion for a $2 \times 2$ table in which the absolute upper limit of *phi* is 1, although satisfying this criterion is not necessary in the case of naturalistic sampling. SPSS is among the statistical packages that calculate *phi*.

## NULL–COUNTERNULL INTERVAL FOR $Phi_{pop}$

Construction of an accurate confidence interval for $phi_{pop}$ can be complex, and there may be no entirely satisfactory method, especially for the sample sizes that are common in behavioral research and the more $phi_{pop}$ departs from 0. Refer to Fleiss et al. (2003) for discussion of a method for constructing an approximate confidence interval for $phi_{pop}$. Instead of constructing a confidence interval for $phi_{pop}$ we construct a null–counternull interval for $phi_{pop}$, which, as previously stated, is an

$r_{pop}$, using Equation 4.2 from chapter 4 to find the counternull value. We assume that the null-hypothesized value of $phi_{pop}$ is 0, so the null value of the interval is 0. Applying Equation 4.2 to the data in Table 8.1, $2\,phi\,/\,(1\,+\,3phi^2)^{1/2} = 2(-.30)\,/\,[1\,+\,3(-.30)^2]^{1/2} = -.53$. Therefore, the limits of the null–counternull interval for the data at hand are 0 and $-.53$. The result of $phi = -.30$ thus provides as much support for the null hypothesis that $phi_{pop} = 0$ as it would provide for a hypothesis that $phi_{pop} = -.53$ (a relatively large correlation).

## THE DIFFERENCE BETWEEN TWO PROPORTIONS

One important purpose of an effect size is to convey, if possible, the meaning of research results in the most understandable form for persons who have little or no knowledge of statistics, such as clients, patients, patient's caregivers and some educational, governmental, or health-insurance officials. For this purpose perhaps the simplest estimate of the association between the variables in a 2 × 2 table is the difference between two proportions, which estimates the difference between the probabilities of a given outcome in two independent populations. Unlike $phi_{pop}$, which requires naturalistic sampling, this measure of effect size requires either random assignment to one of the two treatment samples (an experimental study) or purposive sampling. In purposive sampling for two groups, the researcher samples a predetermined $N$ participants, $n_1$ of whom are those who have a certain characteristic and $n_2$ of whom have an alternative characteristic (e.g., males and females or past treatment with either Drug a or Drug b). The prospective and retrospective versions of purposive sampling are discussed later where needed in the Relative Risk and Number Needed to Treat section.

For an example, we again use the instructive data in Table 8.1, but now we assume that the participants had been randomly assigned to their treatment groups. Note that the sample sizes differ in Table 8.1 (36 and 32). Although one would typically expect equal sample sizes when assignment is random, random assignment does not strictly require equal sample sizes. In fact, all that is required for random assignment is that the total participants be randomly assigned to conditions, and not that sample sizes be equal. However, if the unequal sample sizes are attributable to attrition of participants, statistical inferences and estimation of effect sizes would be problematic unless the attrition were random.

The first step is to choose one of the two outcome categories to serve as what we call the *target category* or *target outcome*. From Table 8.1, one might use Symptoms Gone as the target category; we observe later that it does not matter which category of outcome is chosen for this purpose. The next step is to calculate the proportion of the total participants in Sample 1 (Treatment 1) who have that target outcome and the proportion of the total participants in Sample 2 (Treatment 2) who have that target outcome. In our example, .61 of the psychotherapy patients and

.31 of the drug therapy patients became free of their symptoms. One then finds the difference between these two proportions; in our case, .61 – .31 = .30. This sample result estimates that the probability that a member of the population that receives psychotherapy will be relieved of symptoms is .61 and the probability that a member of the population that receives drug therapy will be relieved of symptoms is .31. An even simpler interpretation is that the results estimate that of every 100 members of the population of those who are given psychotherapy for the symptoms at hand, 30 (i.e., 61 – 31 = 30) more patients will be relieved of these symptoms than would have been relieved of them had they been given the drug therapy instead.

We continue to use column 2 of Table 8.1 (Symptoms Gone) as our target category. Now call the proportion of the total participants in row 1 who fall into column 2 $p_1$, and call the proportion of the total participants in row 2 who fall into column 2 $p_2$. Therefore, our previously found proportions are $p_1 = .61$ and $p_2 = .31$.

Note that the absolute difference between the two proportions is the same as the absolute value of *phi* for the 2 × 2 table, both being equal to .30 for the data in Table 8.1. Recall from the section on the BESD in chapter 4 that, with regard to a table such as Table 8.1, $p_1$ and $p_2$ might be called the success proportions, and their difference will be equal to *phi* when the marginal totals in the table are uniform. (However, uniform marginal totals are unlikely under random assignment or naturalistic sampling.) Recall also that, as is often the case and as was illustrated in the section on the BESD, different kinds of measures of effect size can provide different perspectives on data. A *phi* = .30 might not seem to be very impressive to some, and the corresponding coefficient of determination of $r^2 = phi^2 = .30^2 = .09$ might seem to be even less impressive. However, a success proportion of .61 for one therapy that is nearly double the success proportion of .31 for another therapy seems to be very impressive. The difference between success proportions is commonly called the *risk difference*. Further discussions of the risk difference can be found in Rosenthal (2000) and Rosenthal et al. (2000).

Because the method in our example involved random assignment to treatments instead of naturalistic sampling, there are more appropriate approaches for estimating an effect size than an approach that is based on $\chi^2$ and *phi* (Fleiss et al., 2003; Wilcox, 1996). The recommended kind of approach is to focus directly on the difference between two proportions. Recall that a proportion, *p*, in a sample estimates a probability, *P*, in a population. The simplest and traditional approach is to test $H_0: P_1 = P_2$ against $H_{alt}: P_1 \neq P_2$ two-tailed, where $P_1$ and $P_2$ are estimated by $p_1$ and $p_2$, respectively. In general $P_i$ is the probability that a member of the population who has been assigned the treatment in row i will have the target outcome, and $P_j$ is the probability that a member of the population that has been assigned the treatment in row j will have the target outcome.

A researcher might choose to use the category that is represented by column 1 as the target category instead of using the category that is represented by column 2. The choice is of no statistical consequence because the same significance level will be attained when the difference between two proportions is based on column 1 as when it is based on column 2. Of course, finding that, say, the success rate (proportion) for Therapy i is statistically significantly higher than the success rate for Therapy j is equivalent to finding that the failure rate for Therapy i is statistically significantly lower than the failure rate for Therapy j. In Table 8.1 the failure outcome is represented in column 1.

There are competing methods for testing $H_0$: $P_1 = P_2$. Refer to Agresti (2002) and Fleiss et al. (2003) for very informative background discussion. Also consult Chan (1998), Chuang-Stein (2001), Martín Andrés and Herranz Tejedor (2004), and Röhmel and Mansmann (1999). Wilcox (1996) provided a Minitab macro for a method that was recommended as best by Storer and Kim (1990). (The Storer-Kim method has been modified by Skipka (2003) to attain slightly greater power.) A major controversy is whether such tests should be *conditional* or *unconditional*, which is a matter of the extent to which fixed margins in the contingency table determine the sampling distribution of the test statistic. For example, if each sample is a random sample from one or the other of two populations, and the samples are represented in the rows, then only the row margins are fixed and unconditional tests are applicable. Further discussion of the controversy is beyond the scope of this book, so we refer the reader to Agresti (2002). Manual calculation is also possible for the Storer-Kim method, but it is laborious. Therefore, we demonstrate a simpler traditional but less accurate method. The method is an example of what is called a *large-sample, approximate*, or *asymptotic* method because its accuracy increases as sample sizes $n_1$ and $n_2$ (e.g., the two row totals in Table 8.1) increase. We provide criteria for a large sample at the end of this section. After defining one additional concept we provide a detailed illustration of the method.

The mean proportion, $\bar{p}$, is the proportion of all participants (for both samples) that are found in the target category. In Table 8.1, in which column 2 represents the target category,

$$\bar{p} = \frac{f_{12} + f_{22}}{N} \tag{8.3}$$

where $N$ is the total sample size ($n_1 + n_2$). For Table 8.1, $\bar{p} = (22 + 10) / 68 = .47$, a value that one needs for the test of the current $H_0$. The mean proportion can also be called the *pooled estimate of P*, the overall population proportion of those who would be found in the target category. Because one initially assumes that $H_0$ is true, one assumes that $P_1 = P_2 = P$ and that, therefore, the best estimate of $P$ is obtained by pooling (averaging) $p_1$ and $p_2$ as in Equation 8.3.

Recall that to convert a statistic to a z (i.e., a standardized value) one divides the difference between that statistic and its mean by the standard deviation of that statistic. The statistic of interest here is $p_1 - p_2$, and the mean of this statistic upon repeated sampling of it, assuming as we are for now that $H_0$ is true, is 0. The standard deviation of the sampling distribution of values of $p_1 - p_2$, again assuming that $H_0$ is true, is shown in the denominator of Equation 8.4.

$$z_{p_1-p_2} = \frac{p_1 - p_2 - 0}{\left[\dfrac{\bar{p}(1-\bar{p})}{n_1} + \dfrac{\bar{p}(1-\bar{p})}{n_2}\right]^{1/2}}. \tag{8.4}$$

(We retained the value 0 in Equation 8.4 to make clear that the equation represents a kind of z, but we soon discuss a reason for replacing 0 with a correcting value.) The larger the sample sizes the closer the distribution of $z_{p_1-p_2}$ will approximate the normal curve. Using the previous calculations of $p_1$, $p_2$, and $\bar{p}$, the application of Equation 8.4 to the data in Table 8.1 yields

$$z_{p_1-p_2} = \frac{.61-.31-0}{\left[\dfrac{.47(1-.47)}{36} + \dfrac{.47(1-.47)}{32}\right]^{1/2}} = 2.47.$$

Referring $z = 2.47$ to a table of the normal curve one finds that this z and, therefore, $p_1 - p_2$ are statistically significantly different from 0 at an obtained significance level beyond .0136. Note that there is an adjustment of Equation 8.4 whereby 0 in the numerator is replaced by $.5(1/n_1 + 1/n_2)$ to produce a better approximation to the normal curve (Fleiss et al. 2003). Replacing 0 with this value in this example yields $z = 2.23$, a value that is statistically significant at an obtained significance level beyond .0258. We recommend use of this adjustment for the z test at hand. As a general rule the z test that we demonstrated may be used when all of the following are $\geq 5$: $n_1\bar{p}$, $n_1(1 - \bar{p})$, $n_2\bar{p}$, and $n_2(1 - \bar{p})$. For the data in Table 8.1, $n_1\bar{p} = 36(.47) = 16.92$, $n_1(1 - \bar{p}) = 36(1 - .47) = 19.08$, $n_2\bar{p} = 32(.47) = 15.04$, and $n_2(1 - \bar{p}) = 32(1 - .47) = 16.96$, all values greatly exceeding the criterion minimum of 5.

Refer to Fleiss et al. (2003) for a discussion of comparison of proportions from more than two independent samples. Recall from the discussion of multiple comparisons of means in the section on statistical significance in Chapter 6 that the methods (e.g., the Tukey HSD method) may result in contradictory evidence about the pairwise differences among the means (intransitivity). The same problem of intransitive results can occur when making pairwise comparisons from three or more proportions. For example, suppose that a third therapy were represented by a third row added to Table 8.1 (Therapy 3), so that one would now be interested in the proportion of patients whose symptoms are gone after Therapy 1, 2, or 3, that is, $P_1$, $P_2$, and $P_3$. Suppose further that one tested $H_0: P_1 = P_2$, $H_0: P_1 = P_3$, and $H_0: P_2 = P_3$ simply by applying the current method in this section (or some traditional competing method) three times. Even if we control for experimentwise error by using the Bonferroni–Dunn adjustment, say, by adopting the $.05/3 = .0167$ alpha level for each of the three tests, a problem of possible intransitivity remains.

An example of one of the possible sets of intransitive results from the three tests would be results that suggest the following contradictory relationships: $P_1 = P_2$, $P_2 = P_3$, and $P_1 > P_3$. Of course, such a pattern of values cannot be true in the three populations. A method for detecting the pattern of relationships among more than two proportions in independent populations has been proposed by Dayton (2003). The method is similar to Dayton's (2003) method that was discussed in chapter 6. The method can be implemented using Microsoft Excel with or without additional software programs. For details, consult Dayton (2003), who does not recommend his method for researchers who are interested in pairwise comparisons more than the overall pattern of the sizes of the proportions.

Fleiss et al. (2003) discussed the comparison of two proportions in the case of experiments that are called *noninferiority* trials, that seek evidence that a treatment is not worse than another treatment by a defined specified amount. These authors also discussed the comparison of proportions in the case of experiments that are called *equivalence trials*, which seek evidence that a treatment is neither better nor worse than another treatment by a specified amount. This method is best used when the researcher can make an informed decision about what minimal difference between the two proportions can be reasonably judged to be of no practical importance in a particular instance of research. This issue of selecting a minimally important difference was discussed further by Steiger (2004) in the context of continuous dependent variables. Steiger (2004) described the construction of a confidence interval (exact, if ANOVA assumptions are satisfied) for the purpose of observing whether it contains the selected minimal difference. StatXact software provides exact tests of equivalence, inferiority, and superiority when comparing two proportions in the independent- and dependent-groups cases. Although by definition an exact test provides an exact rate of Type I error, it is possible that an approximate method will be more powerful. An ideal method would yield very accurate $p$ levels while providing very high power (Skipka, 2003).

A repeated-measures version of the kind of experimental research that was discussed in this section is the crossover design. In this counterbalanced design each participant receives each of the two Treatments a and b, one at a time, in either the sequence ab for a randomly chosen one half of the participants or the sequence ba for the other half of the participants. The rows of a $2 \times 2$ table can then be labeled ab and ba, and the columns can be labeled a Better and b Better. Refer to Fleiss et al. (2003) for a discussion of the comparison of the proportion of times that Treatment a is better and the proportion of times that Treatment b is better.

## APPROXIMATE CONFIDENCE INTERVAL FOR $P_1 - P_2$

Again, for our purpose we demonstrate the simplest method for constructing a confidence interval for the difference between proportions (probabilities) in two independent populations, and then we provide references for more accurate but more complex methods. As is the case for approximate methods the accuracy of the following large-sample method increases with increasing sample sizes.

In general the simplest $(1 - \alpha)$ CI for $P_1 - P_2$ can be approximated by

$$CI_{p_1-p_2} : (p_1 - p_2) \pm ME, \tag{8.5}$$

where ME is the margin of error in using $p_1 - p_2$ to estimate $P_1 - P_2$.

$$ME = z^* s_{p_1-p_2}, \tag{8.6}$$

where $z^*$ is the positive value of z that has $\alpha/2$ of the area of the normal curve beyond it, and $s_{p_1-p_2}$ is the approximate standard deviation of the sampling distribution of the difference between $p_1$ and $p_2$. If one seeks the usual .95 CI (i.e., $(\alpha/2 = .05/2 = .025)$, then one will recall or observe in a table of the normal curve that $z^* = +1.96$.

Because we have already found evidence that $P_1 \neq P_2$, for the confidence interval we do not use the same equation for $s_{p_1-p_2}$ that was used in the denominator of Equation 8.4 when we tested $H_0: P_1 = P_2$. For the confidence interval we no longer pool $p_1$ and $p_2$ to estimate the previously supposed common value of $P_1 = P_2 = P$ that we assumed before we rejected $H_0$. Instead, we now estimate the different $P_1$ and $P_2$ values separately using $p_1$ and $p_2$ in the equation for $s_{p_1-p_2}$,

$$s_{p_1-p_2} = \left[ \frac{p_1(1-p_1)}{n_1} + \frac{p_2(1-p_2)}{n_2} \right]^{\frac{1}{2}}. \tag{8.7}$$

(One pools $p_1$ and $p_2$ for the significance test because one is then assuming the truth of $H_0$, but there is no such assumption when constructing a confidence interval.)

For the data in Table 8.1, $p_1 - p_2 = .61 - .31 = .30$, $z^* = +1.96$ because we are seeking a .95 CI, $1 - p_1 = 1 - .61 = .39$, $n_1 = 36$, $1 - p_2 = 1 - .31 = .69$, and $n_2 = 32$. Therefore, applying Equation 8.6, the *ME* that we subtract from and add to $p_1 - p_2$ is equal to $1.96[.61(1 - .61)/36 + .31(1 - .31)/32]^{1/2} = .23$. The limits of the confidence interval are thus $.30 \pm .23$. Therefore, we are approximately 95% confident that the interval from $.30 - .23 = .07$ to $.30 + .23 = .53$ contains the difference between $P_1$ and $P_2$. Unfortunately, as is often the case, the interval is rather wide. Nonetheless, the interval does not contain the value 0, a finding that is consistent with the result from testing $H_0: P_1 = P_2$. Note, however, that sometimes the result of a test of statistical significance at a specific alpha ($\alpha$) level and the $(1 - \alpha)$ *CI* for $P_1 - P_2$ do not produce consistent results. Refer to Fleiss et al. (2003) for discussion and references regarding such inconsistent results.

Efforts to construct a more accurate confidence interval for $P_1 - P_2$ have been ongoing for decades. Hauck and Anderson (1986) compared competing methods and found that the simple method used in Expression 8.5 and Equation 8.6 can result in an interval that, as wide as it can often be, actually tends to be inaccurately narrow. They recommended a correction for this method. Beal (1987) also compared competing methods and recommended and described a method for which Wilcox (1996) described manual calculation and provided a Minitab macro. Wilcox (2003) also provided an S-PLUS software function for constructing the confidence interval. Refer to Smithson (2003) for another large-sample method for constructing an approximate confidence interval for $P_1 - P_2$. StatXact software constructs an exact confidence interval for the independent- and dependent-groups cases. Also refer to the discussion and references in Agresti (2002) for both independent-groups and dependent-groups cases. Newcombe (1998) compared eleven methods and Martín Andrés and Herranz Tejedor (2003, 2004) discussed exact and approximate methods. Hou, Chiang, and Tai (2003) proposed, and justified by simulation studies, a method for construction of simultaneous confidence intervals in the case of multinomial proportions (i.e., the case of more than two possible categorical outcomes). Fleiss et al. (2003) and Cohen (1988) discussed and presented tables for estimating needed sample sizes for detecting a specified difference between $P_1$ and $P_2$.

Note that it would not be valid to construct a null–counternull interval for $P_1 - P_2$ using the methods for constructing such an interval that were appropriate earlier in this book because the distribution of $p_1 - p_2$ is not symmetrical. Also, consult Rosenthal (2000) for a modification of this measure. Recall that many, including Rosenthal (2000), called the difference between two proportions the *risk difference*, the reason for which is explained in the next section.

## RELATIVE RISK AND THE NUMBER NEEDED TO TREAT

Suppose that the data in Table 8.1 had arisen from research in which participants had been randomly assigned to Therapy 1 or Therapy 2, a supposition that is in fact true in the case of these data. In this case an effect size measure that is generally called the *relative risk* is applicable. We now turn to the development of this measure.

A certain difference between $P_1$ and $P_2$ may have more practical importance when the estimated $P$ values are both close to 0 or 1 than when they are both close to .5. For example, suppose that $P_1 = .010$ and $P_2 = .001$ or that $P_1 = .500$ and $P_2 = .491$. In both cases $P_1 - P_2 = .009$, but in the first case $P_1$ is 10 times greater than $P_2$, $(P_1/P_2 = .010/.001 = 10)$, and in the second case $P_1$ is only 1.018 times greater than $P_2$, $(P_1/P_2 = .500/.491 = 1.018)$. Thus, the ratio of the two probabilities can be very informative. For $2 \times 2$ tables the ratio of the two probabilities is the *RR* (which also is called *rate ratio* or *risk ratio*). The estimate of *RR*, *rr*, is calculated using the two sample proportions

$$rr = \frac{p_1}{p_2}.$$  (8.8)

As before, $p_1$ and $p_2$ represent the proportion of those participants in Samples 1 and 2, respectively, who fall into the target category, which again can be represented either by column 1 or column 2 in a table such as Table 8.1. For Table 8.1, if column 1 represents the target category then $rr_1 = (14/36)/(22/32) = .57$, and if column 2 represents the target category then $rr_2 = (22/36)/(10/32) = 1.96$. In the latter case there is an estimated nearly 2 to 1 greater probability of therapeutic success for psychotherapy than for drug therapy for the clinical problem at hand. (Because, as previously discussed, a given difference between $P_1$ and $P_2$ has different meanings at different values of $P_1$ and $P_2$, *RR* may be a more useful effect size for meta-analysts than $P_1 - P_2$, Fleiss, 1994.)

The name relative risk relates to medical research, in which the target category is classification of people as having a disease versus the other category of not having the disease. One sample has a presumed risk factor for the disease (e.g., smokers), and the other sample does not have this risk factor. However, because it seems strange to use the label *relative risk* when applying the ratio to a column, such as column 2 in Table 8.1, which represents a successful outcome of therapy, in such cases one can simply refer to *RR* and *rr* as success rate ratios, or as the ratio of two independent probabilities or the ratio of two independent proportions, respectively. For discussions of methods for constructing a confidence interval for the ratio of two probabilities, consult Bedrick (1987), Gart and Nam (1988), and Santner and Snell (1980). Refer to Smithson (2003) for a large-sample method for constructing an approximate confidence interval for the *RR*. A large-sample approximate confidence interval can be constructed for *RR* using the method that is demonstrated for $OR_{pop}$ in the section after the next section. StatXact software constructs an exact a confidence interval for the *RR*. Consult Agresti (2002) for further discussion. As we reiterate throughout this book all measures of effect size have some limitations. Refer to Fleiss (1994) for a discussion of limitations of $RR$ for research and meta-analysis.

One of the limitations of the $RR$ is that its different values depending on one's choice of placement of the two groups in the numerator and denominator can lead to different impressions of the result. The problem arises because, as a ratio of two proportions, the $RR$ or $rr$ can range from 0 to 1 if the group with the smaller proportion (lower risk) happens to be represented in the numerator, but they can range from 1 to ∞ if the group with the smaller proportion is represented in the denominator. The problem can be partially resolved by reporting the logarithm (common or natural) of $rr$ as an estimate of the logarithm of $RR$. When the smaller proportion is in the numerator log $rr$ can range from 0 to −∞, whereas when the larger proportion is in the numerator log $rr$ can range from 0 to +∞. The actual raw proportions should always be reported no matter how the $rr$ is reported. The value of the relative risk also varies depending on which of the two outcome categories it is based. For example, consider the case involving the two hospitals that provided coronary bypass surgery, an example that was discussed in the The Coefficient of Determination section in chapter 4. We observed previously that the estimated $RR$, based on the mortality percentages for the two hospitals, was 3.60%/1.40% = 2.57. On the other hand, looking at the survivability percentages for the two hospitals Breaugh (2003) noted that if one reverses the choice of which hospital's percentages are to appear in the numerator of the ratio, the success rate ratio for these data can be calculated as (100% − 1.40%) / (100% − 3.60%) = 1.02, a result that conveys a much smaller apparent effect of choice of hospital than does the risk ratio of 2.57. This example provides a compelling reason to present the results both ways. Rosenthal (2000) also presented an example in which the $RR$ can provide a misleading account of the results, and he presented a modification of the $RR$, based on the BESD, to correct the problem. Gigerenzer and Edwards (2003) discussed other measures that might be used when $RR$ might be misunderstood by patients or even by health professionals.

The $RR$ is applicable to data that arise from research that uses random assignment or from naturalistic or prospective research, but not from retrospective research. We previously defined naturalistic research. In prospective research the researcher selects $n_1$ participants who have a suspected risk factor (e.g., children whose parents have abused drugs) and $n_2$ participants who do not have the suspected risk factor. The two samples are tracked to determine the number from each sample who do and do not develop the target outcome (e.g., abuse drugs themselves). From the definition it should be clear why prospective research is also called *cohort, forward-going,* or *follow-up research*. On the other hand, in retrospective research (also called *case-control research*) the researcher selects $n_1$ participants who already exhibit the target outcome (the cases) and $n_2$ participants who do not exhibit the target outcome (the controls). The two samples are checked to see how many in each sample had or did not have the suspected risk factor. Refer to Fleiss et al. (2003) for discussions of a variety of sources of error that are possible in retrospective research and for methods to control or adjust for such errors.

A related measure of effect size in 2 × 2 tables in which one group is a treated group and the other is a control or otherwise treated group is the *number needed to treat, NNT*. The NNT can be defined informally as the number of people that would have to be given the treatment (instead of no treatment or the other treatment) per each such person who would be expected to benefit from it. The more effective a treatment is, relative to the control or competing treatment, the smaller the positive value of *NNT*, with *NNT* = 1 being the best result for a treatment. (Values between –1 and +1, exclusive, are problematic). When *NNT* = 1 every person who is subjected to the targeted treatment would be expected to benefit. Formally, in the case of comparing a treated group and a control group, the *NNT* parameter is defined as the reciprocal of the difference between the probability that a control participant will show no benefit (e.g., symptoms remain) and the probability that a treated person will show no benefit. This measure will be illustrated by pretending (for our present purpose of comparing a control group and a treated group) that row 2 of Table 8.1 represented a control group. The required probabilities are estimated by the relevant proportions in the table.

The estimate of the *NNT* parameter for the data in the now slightly revised Table 8.1 is given by the reciprocal of the difference between the proportion of participants in the control group whose symptoms remain (22/32 = .6875) and the proportion of the participants in the treated group whose symptoms remain (14/36 = .3889). The difference between these two proportions is .6875 − .3889 = .2986. Thus, $NNT_{est}$ = 1/.2986 = 3.35. Rounding to the nearest integer, we use $NNT_{est}$ = 3. We therefore estimate that we would need to treat approximately three people for each person who will benefit. For the case in which these results arise from the data of Table 8.1 as is (i.e., comparing two therapies) we would estimate that for every three patients treated with psychotherapy instead of drug therapy one person will become free of symptoms who would not have otherwise become free of symptoms. Note that the *NNT* measure can also be used in other areas such as education or organizational psychology (e.g., evaluating the costs-benefits of a remedial program for students or a training program for employees, in which, in both kinds of research, participants will be classified as attaining or not attaining mastery of a targeted skill.

The *NNT* effect size can be informative regarding the practical significance of results. Considering the estimated *NNT* in the context of the cost and risks of a treatment and the seriousness of the illness, or the seriousness of the lack of mastery of the skill, can aid in the decision about whether a treatment should be adopted. For example, one would not want to adopt a moderately expensive somewhat risky treatment when the $NNT_{est}$ is relatively large unless the disease were sufficiently serious.

The values of *NNT* that might seem to be useful for such decision-making are the upper and lower limits of a confidence interval for *NNT*.

Detailed discussions of the complex topics of significance testing for $NNT_{est}$ and confidence intervals for *NNT* are beyond the scope of this book. We will merely make some brief comments. First, if one were testing a traditional null hypothesis based on a hypothesis that the treatment has no effect, then one would be attempting a problematic test of $H_o$: $NNT = \infty$ or a problematic indirect test of significance by examining a confidence interval to observe if the interval contains the value $\infty$. (Less problematic would be constructing a confidence interval merely for providing some information about the precision of the estimate of *NNT*.) One approach to confidence intervals involves first constructing a confidence interval for the difference between the two populations' proportions (probabilities) that are involved in the definition of *NNT*, using one of the methods that were discussed in the previous section and by Fleiss, Levin, and Paik (2003). Then the reciprocals of the confidence limits satisfy the definition of the *NNT* and thus provide the limits for the *NNT*. There is another approach that is recommended by Schulzer and Mancini (1996), and these authors also discuss *NNT* in the context of treatments that harm some patients (*the number needed to harm, NNH*; Mancini and Schulzer, 1999). We are concerned, unless sample sizes are very large, that the various methods for constructing the confidence intervals might lead to greatly varying results, and, therefore, lead to inconsistent recommendations for practitioners. However, one must recognize that the *NNT* is a relatively new measure derived for 2 × 2 tables, and such tables have a long history of development of competing methods of analysis.

Note that some medical researchers attempt to resolve the problem of significance testing for the $NNT_{est}$ by applying a $\chi^2$ test of association or a *t* test (numerically coding the outcome categories) to the 2 × 2 table. Regarding the $\chi^2$ test, a better approach might be to test the significance of the difference between the two proportions as we previously discussed. Regarding the application of a *t* test to the data of a 2 × 2 table such as Table 8.1, issues arise concerning the facts that in such a case the dependent variable has only two values and is ordinal instead of continuous. For a discussion of the debate about these latter issues consult the section entitled "Limitations of $r_{pb}$ for Ordinal Categorical Data" in chapter 9.

Note also that, because the *NNT* varies with baseline risk, a point estimate and confidence limits for the *NNT* as estimated from prior research are most useful for a practitioner whose clients or patients are very similar to those who participated in the research from which the *NNT* was estimated. The baseline risk is estimated from the proportion of control participants who are classified as having the "bad" event (e.g., $22/32 = .6875$ in our presently revised Table 8.1). The lower the baseline risk the lower the justification might be for implementing the treatment, depending again on the seriousness of the illness and the overall costs of treatment. For an extensive discussion of the *NNT* and related measures refer to Sackett et al. (2000). Also consult Laupacis, Sackett, and Roberts (1988) and the many discussions of this and related topics that can be found in the online *British Medical Journal* (http://bmj.bmjjournals.com).

## THE ODDS RATIO

The final effect size for a 2 × 2 table that we discuss here is the *odds ratio*, which is a measure of how many times greater the odds are that a member of a certain population will fall into a certain category than the odds are that a member of another population will fall into that category. This effect size is applicable to research that uses random assignment, naturalistic research, prospective research, and retrospective research (Fleiss, 1994; Fleiss et al., 2003). Unlike the *phi* coefficient, the possible range of values of an odds ratio is not limited by the marginal distributions of the contingency table. Because we leave it to the interested reader to apply, as exercises, the methods of this and the next section to the data in Table 8.1, we illustrate this effect size with the naturalistic example in Table 8.2. A sample odds ratio provides an estimate of the ratio of (a) the odds that participants of a certain kind (e.g., women) attain a certain category (e.g., voting Democrat instead of voting Republican) and (b) those same odds for participants of another kind (e.g., men). An odds ratio can be calculated for any pair of categories of a variable (e.g., gender) that is being related to another pair of categories of another variable (e.g., political preference).

(For a formal definition of $OR_{pop}$, consider the common case in which categorization with respect to one of the two variables might be said to precede categorization with respect to the other variable. For examples, type of therapy precedes the symptoms–status outcome in Table 8.1 and being male or female precedes agreeing or disagreeing in Table 8.2. Now label a targeted outcome Category T (e.g., agree), the alternative outcome category being labeled *not* T. Then label a temporally preceding category [e.g., man] pc. Where *P* stands for probability, a measure of the odds that T will occur conditional on pc occurring is given by = $P(T|pc)$ / $P(\text{not } T|pc)$. Similarly, the odds that *T* will occur conditional on category pc not occurring [e.g., woman] is given by $Odds_{\text{not pc}} = P(T|\text{not pc}) / P(\text{not } T|\text{not pc})$. The ratio of these two odds in the population is the odds ratio, $OR_{pop} = Odds_{pc}/Odds_{\text{not pc}}$.)

In Table 8.2, as in Table 8.1, the cell values $f_{11}, f_{12}, f_{21}$, and $f_{22}$ represent the counts (frequencies) of participants in the first row and first column, first row and second column, second row and first column, and second row and second column, respectively. We use the category that is represented by column 1 as the target category. The sample odds that a participant who is in row 1 will be in column 1 instead of column 2 are

TABLE 8.2

**Gender Difference in Attitude Toward a Controversial Statement**

|  | *Agree* | *Disagree* |
|---|---|---|
| Men | $f_{11} = 10$ | $f_{12} = 13$ |
| Women | $f_{21} = 1$ | $f_{22} = 23$ |

given by $f_{11}/f_{12}$, which are approximately $10/13 = .77$, in the case of Table 8.2. In a study that is comparing two kinds of participants who are represented by the two rows in this example, one can evaluate these odds in relation to similarly calculated odds for participants who are in the second row. The odds that a participant in row 2 will be in column 1 instead of column 2 are given by $f_{21}/f_{22}$, which are approximately $1/23 = .04$, in the case of Table 8.2. The ratio of the two sample odds, denoted *OR*, is given by $(f_{11}/f_{12}) / (f_{21}/f_{22})$, which, because $(a/b) / (c/d) = (ad) / (bc)$, is equivalent to

$$OR = \frac{f_{11} f_{22}}{f_{12} f_{21}}. \qquad (8.9)$$

Note in Equation 8.9 that each cell frequency is being multiplied by the cell frequency that is diagonally across from it in a table such as Table 8.2. For this reason an odds ratio is also called a *cross-products ratio*. (Note also that odds are not the same as probabilities. We observed with regard to Table 8.2 that the odds that a man will be in the *agree* category are given by $10/13 = .77$. However, the probability that a man will be in the category *agree* is estimated by the proportion $10/23 = .43$, where 23 is the total number of men in the sample.)

Table 8.2 depicts actual data, but the example should be considered to be hypothetical because the column labels, row labels, and the title have been changed to suit the purpose of this section. A very important aspect of these data emerges if we relate the odds that a man will *agree* instead of disagree to the odds that a woman will *agree* instead of disagree with a controversial test statement that was presented to all participants by the researcher. Applying Equation 8.9, we find that $OR = 10(23) / 13(1) = 17.69$. We just found that the odds that a man will agree with the controversial statement are estimated to be nearly 18 times greater than the odds that a woman will agree with it. However, out of context this result can be somewhat misleading or incomplete, because if one inspects Table 8.2, which the researcher would be obliged to include in a research report, one also observes that in fact in the samples a majority of men (13 of 23) as well as a (larger) majority of women (23 of 24) disagree with the statement.

Both the sample $OR$ and the parameter $OR_{pop}$ range from zero to infinity, attaining either of these extreme values when one of the cell frequencies is zero. When there is no association between the row and column variables, $OR_{pop} = 1$. A zero cell frequency in the population (called a *structural zero*) would be unlikely because in most research in the behavioral and social sciences it would be unlikely that a researcher would include a variable into one of whose categories no member of the population falls. However, observe in the real data in Table 8.2 that we came very close to having a zero in sample cell$_{21}$, in which $f_{21} = 1$. In research in which $OR_{pop}$ would not likely be zero or infinity, a value of zero or infinity for the sample $OR$ would be unwelcome. When an empty cell in sample data does not reflect a zero population frequency for that cell, a solution for this problem of a mere sampling zero is required. One of the possible solutions would be to increase one's chance of adding an entry or entries to the empty cell by increasing total sample size by a fixed number. Another solution, which is common, is to adjust the sample $OR$ to $OR_{adj}$ by adding a very small constant to the frequency of each cell, not just to the empty one. Recommended such constants in the literature have been as small as $10^{-8}$ and as large as .5.

Refer to Agresti's (1990, 2002) discussions of the problem of the empty cell. Even when no cell frequency is zero, adding a constant, such as .5, has been recommended to improve $OR$ as an estimator of $OR_{pop}$. If a constant has been added to each cell, the researcher should report having done so and report $OR$ and the adjusted $OR$, $OR_{adj}$. Adding .5 to each cell in Table 8.2 changes $OR$ from 17.69 to 12.19, which is still impressively large. Note that adding a constant to each cell can sometimes actually cause $OR$ to provide an inaccurate estimate of $OR_{pop}$ and lower the power of a test of statistical significance of $OR$, which provides even more reason to report results with both $OR$ and $OR_{adj}$. Consult Agresti (2002) for discussions of adjustment methods that are less arbitrary than adding constants to cells.

Again, no measure of effect size is without limitations. Refer to Rosenthal (2000) for an illustration of results for which the odds ratio can be misleading and for his suggested modification (based on the BESD) of the odds ratio to correct the problem. For example, as was previously discussed with regard to $rr$ and $RR$, the possible range of values for $OR$ and $OR_{pop}$ is 0 to 1 or 1 to $\infty$ depending on which group is represented in the numerator or denominator. Again, the results can be presented both ways, or the result can be transformed to logarithms as before. For a review of criticisms and suggested modifications of odds ratios consult Fleiss et al. (2003), and for further discussions consult Agresti (2002), Fleiss (1994), Haddock et al. (1998), and the book on odds ratios by Rudas (1998).

The null hypothesis $H_0$: $OR_{pop} = 1$ can be tested approximately against the alternative hypothesis $H_{alt}$: $OR_{pop} \neq 1$ using the common corrected $\chi^2$ test of association (i.e., subtracting .5 in the numerator before squaring). This method becomes more accurate as the expected frequencies in each cell become larger. The method should not be used when any such expected frequency is below 5. The test statistic is

$$\chi^2 = \sum \frac{\left[\left|f_{rc} - (n_r n_c / N)\right| - .5\right]^2}{n_r n_c / N},$$

(8.10)

where the summation is over the four cells of the table, $f_{rc}$ is the observed frequency in a cell, and $n_r$ and $n_c$ are the total frequency for the particular row and the total frequency for a particular column that a given cell is in, respectively. The value $n_r n_c/N$ is the expected frequency for a given cell under the null hypothesis. (Note that, unlike the case in which $\chi^2$ is used to calculate *phi*, the numerator-adjusted Equation 8.10 should be used here.)

Applying the data in Table 8.2 to Equation 8.10 for manual calculation one finds that $\chi^2 = [ \,|10 - (23 \times 11/47) \,| - .5]^2 / (23 \times 11/47) + [ \,|13 - (23 \times 36/47)| - .5]^2 / (23 \times 36/47) + [ \,|1 - (24 \times 11/47)| - .5]^2 / (24 \times 11/47) + [ \,|23 - (24 \times 36/47)| - .5]^2 / (24 \times 36/47) = 8.05$. A table of critical values for $\chi^2$, which can be found in any textbook of introductory statistics, reveals that when $df = (r - 1)(c - 1) = (2 - 1)(2 - 1) = 1$, the value 8.05 is statistically significant beyond the .005 level. One has sufficient evidence that $OR_{pop}$ does not equal 1. Refer to Fleiss et al. (2003) for detailed discussion of approximate and exact $p$ values for this case. There are various methods for constructing a confidence interval for $OR_{pop}$, to which we turn in the next section.

## CONSTRUCTION OF CONFIDENCE INTERVALS FOR $OR_{pop}$

An approximate confidence interval for $OR_{pop}$ that is based on the normal distribution can be constructed indirectly. The larger the sample, the better the approximation. Again we present the simplest method for our purpose, and then we cite references for more accurate but more complex methods.

First, a confidence interval for the natural logarithm of $OR_{pop}$, *ln* $OR_{pop}$, is constructed because as sample size increases quicker approximation to a normal distribution is attained by the sampling distribution of *ln OR* than by the sampling distribution of *OR*. Then, the antilogarithms of the limits of this interval provide the limits of the confidence interval for $OR_{pop}$ itself. Adding the constant .5 to each cell frequency might reduce the bias in estimating *ln* $OR_{pop}$, so we use this adjustment. The limits of the $(1 - \alpha)$ *CI* for *ln* $OR_{pop}$ are approximated by

$$ln\ OR \pm z_{\alpha/2} S_{ln\ OR},$$

(8.11)

where $z_{\alpha/2}$ is the value of $z$ (the standard normal deviate) beyond which lies the upper $\alpha/2$ proportion of the area under the normal curve and $S_{ln\ OR}$

is the standard deviation (the standard error) of the sampling distribution of $ln\ OR$:

$$S_{ln\ OR} = \left[ \frac{1}{f_{11}+.5} + \frac{1}{f_{12}+.5} + \frac{1}{f_{21}+.5} + \frac{1}{f_{22}+.5} + \right]^{\frac{1}{2}}. \qquad (8.12)$$

Although the accuracy of this method is problematic for the relatively small sample sizes that are typical of behavioral research, compared to, say, epidemiological research (i.e., disease-incidence research), for illustrative purposes we will apply the method to the data at hand. Using the data in Table 8.2,

$$S_{ln\ OR} = \left[ \frac{1}{10+.5} + \frac{1}{13+.5} + \frac{1}{1+.5} + \frac{1}{23+.5} \right]^{\frac{1}{2}} = .937.$$

If seeking the usual $(1-\alpha) = (1-.05) = .95\ CI$, one uses $z_{\alpha/2} = 1.96$ because a total of .05 (i.e., .025 + .025) of the area of the normal curve lies in the tails beyond $z = \pm 1.96$. Therefore, the .95 confidence limits for $ln\ OR_{pop}$, based on $OR_{adj} = 12.19$ from the previous section, are $ln(12.19) \pm 1.96(.937)$, which are .664 and 4.337. The antilogarithms of .664 and 4.337 yield, as the .95 confidence limits for $OR_{pop}$ itself, 1.94 and 76.48.

Surprisingly, considering the vastness of the interval that we constructed for $OR_{pop}$ (1.94 to 76.48), the method that has been presented here will likely lead to a confidence interval that is too liberal; that is, it is narrower than the actual interval. For a better approximation a more complex traditional method is available (Cornfield, 1956; Gart & Thomas, 1972). Additional discussions of approximate and exact confidence intervals for $OR_{pop}$ can be found in Fleiss et al. (2003) and the references therein. Also consult Agresti (1990, 2002). SAS Version 9 and StatXact construct a confidence interval for $OR_{pop}$ in which the $1-\alpha$ confidence level (e.g., .95) is exact. The latter package includes software for both the independent-and dependent-groups cases.

If the null hypothesis that is being tested originally is $H_0$: $OR_{pop} = 1$ (i.e., no association), this is equivalent to testing $H_0$: $ln\ OR_{pop} = 0$. Therefore, because the distribution of $ln\ OR$ is symmetrical, one can also construct a null–counternull interval indirectly for $OR_{pop}$ using Equation 3.15 in chapter 3 by starting with such an interval for $ln\ OR_{pop}$. Recall from chapter 3 that the null value of the interval is the null-hypothesized value of the effect size ($ES$), which in this logarithmic case is 0, and the counternull value is 2 $ES$, which is 2 $ln(12.19) = 2(2.5) = 5$. Taking antilogarithms of 0 and 5, the null–counternull interval for $OR_{pop}$ itself ranges from 1 to 148.41, again a disappointingly wide interval.

Readers might be concerned about a null–counternull interval as wide ranging as 1 to 148.41. In this regard note that it is intrinsic to the null–counternull interval to grow wider the larger the obtained estimate of the effect size because its starting point is always the null-hypothesized value of $ES$ (usually the extreme value of $ES$ that indicates no association), and its endpoint, which, in the case of symmetrical sampling distributions, is twice the obtained value of the estimate of $ES$. Also, unlike a confidence interval, a null–counternull interval cannot be made narrower by increasing sample size.

Null–counternull intervals are simple to construct when estimators of an effect size are symmetrically distributed. In this book we used null–counternull intervals for cases in which there is no completely satisfactory method for constructing a confidence interval or for cases in which the methods for constructing confidence intervals are complex and presented well in references that we cite. However, the original intended uses of null–counternull intervals were to demonstrate that (a) a statistically significant attained $p$ level does not necessarily imply a large effect, and (b) a statistically insignificant $ES$ might provide as much evidence that $ES_{pop} = 2\ ES$ as it provides for the null hypothesis that $ES_{pop} = 0$ (Rosenthal et al., 2000). Using the data in Table 8.2 we found in the previous section that $\chi^2$ is statistically significant and that the estimate of effect size is moderately large, $OR_{adj} = 12.19$, estimating that the odds that a man will agree with the researcher's presented controversial statement are more than 12 times greater than the odds that a woman will agree with that statement. When possible, elaboration of results that involve a large estimate of effect size might be better undertaken by constructing a confidence interval for the effect size than by constructing a null–counternull interval for it that is likely to be very wide in the case of a large estimated effect size.

## TABLES LARGER THAN 2 × 2

It would be beyond the scope of this book to present a detailed discussion of measures of effect size for $r \times c$ tables that are larger than $2 \times 2$, which we call large $r \times c$ tables, or for tables that involve more than two categorical variables (multiway tables; e.g., Table 8.3). For example, if Table 8.2 had an additional column for the *no opinion* category it would be an example of a large $r \times c$ table (specifically, a $2 \times 3$ table). It will suffice to discuss two common methods, make some general comments, and provide references for detailed treatment of the possible methods.

One may begin analysis of data in a large $r \times c$ table with the usual $\chi^2$ test of association between the row and column variables with $df = (r - 1)(c - 1)$. The traditional measures of the overall strength of association between the row and column variables, when sampling has been naturalistic, are the contingency coefficient ($CC_{pop}$) and Cramér's $V_{pop}$, which are estimated by

$$CC = \left[ \frac{\chi^2}{\chi^2 + N} \right]^{\frac{1}{2}} , \tag{8.13}$$

### TABLE 8.3
### An Example of a Multiway Table

|  |  | Democrat | Republican | Other |
|---|---|---|---|---|
| White | Female |  |  |  |
|  | Male |  |  |  |
| Nonwhite | Female |  |  |  |
|  | Male |  |  |  |

and

$$V = \left[ \frac{\chi^2}{N \, min(r-1, c-1)} \right]^{\frac{1}{2}}, \qquad (8.14)$$

where $min(r-1, c-1)$ means the smaller of $r-1$ and $c-1$. Cramér's $V_{pop}$ ranges from 0 (no association) to 1 (maximum association). However, the upper limits of the $CC$ and $CC_{pop}$ are less than 1; and unless $r = c$, $V$ can equal 1 even when there is less than a maximum association between the row and column variables in the population. Refer to Siegel and Castellan (1988) for further discussion of this limitation of $V$. Observe that for $2 \times c$ (or $r \times 2$) tables $min(r-1, c-1) = 1$; therefore, $V = [\chi^2/N(1)]^{\frac{1}{2}}$ in this case, which is the *phi* coefficient. (As noted with regard to $phi_{pop}$ in the section Chi-Square Test and *Phi*, $V_{pop}$ is a kind of average effect, the square root of the mean of the squared standardized effects. For formal expressions for the parameters $CC_{pop}$ and $V_{pop}$ and further discussions, consult Hays, 1994, Liebetrau, 1983, and Smithson, 2003.) A value for $V$ is provided by SPSS.

Two or more values of the $CC$ should not be compared or averaged unless they arise from tables with the same number of rows and the same number of columns. Also, two or more values of $V$ should not be compared or averaged unless they arise from tables with the same $min(r, c)$. Refer to Smithson (2003) for methods for constructing a confidence interval for the $CC_{pop}$ and $V_{pop}$ using computing routines for some major software packages. StatXact and SPSS Exact calculate exact contingency coefficients.

The $CC_{pop}$ and Cramér's $V_{pop}$, as measures of the overall association between the two variables, are not as informative as are finer-grained indices of strength of association in a large $r \times c$ table. Also, it has been difficult for statisticians to develop a very satisfactory single index of the overall association. Refer to Agresti (1990, 2002) for discussions of several such indices for large $r \times c$ tables and of methods for partitioning such tables into smaller tables for more detailed $\chi^2$ analyses.

There are methods that attempt to pinpoint the source or sources of association in the subparts of a large $r \times c$ table. For example, consider that in any $r \times c$ table each sample has some proportion, $p$, of its members in the target category, where $p$ ranges from 0 to 1. If, say, $r$ represents the number of samples, there are $r$ such proportions. In the case of research that uses random assignment an unadjusted $\chi^2$ test (i.e., no constant subtracted in the numerator) with $df = r - 1$ can be used to test for the statistical significance of the differences, overall, of these $r$ proportions. The method was demonstrated by Fleiss et al. (2003). However, if this $\chi^2$ is statistically significant, it does not necessarily mean that each sample proportion is statistically significantly different from each other sample proportion. Therefore, the next task is to determine which proportions are statistically significantly different from which other proportions.

There are various methods for this task. References were provided by Fleiss et al. (2003), who demonstrated a method for an $r \times 2$ table. This method involves dividing all of the $r$ samples into two groups of samples, the $r_a$ group and the $r_b$ group. The overall proportion of all of the members of the $r_a$ group who fall into the target category is then compared to the overall proportion of all of the members of the $r_b$ group who fall into the target category. Another $\chi^2$ test with $df = 1$ is used for this purpose. Two additional $\chi^2$ tests are then conducted to determine if there is a statistically significant difference among the $r_a$ group of proportions ($df = r_a - 1$) and among the $r_b$ group of proportions ($df = r_b - 1$).

Note that the equations for the degrees of freedom for the last three $\chi^2$ tests assume that division of the total set of samples into the specific $r_a$ and $r_b$ groups of samples had been planned before the data had been collected. If the division into the two specific groups had not been planned before the data had been collected but was instead based on inspection of the data, the procedure that was just outlined is invalid and must be modified because it capitalizes on chance (a concept that was discussed in the section Tentative Recommendations in chap. 3). A simple solution to the problem is to use $df = r - 1$ for each of the last three $\chi^2$ tests instead of the previously stated $df = 1$, $df = r_a - 1$, and $df = r_b - 1$, respectively.

Simple descriptive aids to interpretation of the sample results in large $r \times c$ tables are tables or bar graphs showing the percentage of each kind of participant who fall into a target category of interest. For example, if Table 8.2 had a third no opinion column it would be informative to see a table or bar graph that depicts the percentages of men and women who fall into the categories of agree, disagree, and no opinion. Gliner, Morgan, and Harmon (2002) provided a specific example.

## ODDS RATIOS FOR LARGE $r \times c$ TABLES

Recall that an odds ratio applies to a $2 \times 2$ table. However, a researcher should not divide a large $r \times c$ table, step by step, into all possible $2 \times 2$

subtables to calculate a separate OR for each of these subtables. In this invalid method each cell would be involved in more than one $2 \times 2$ subtable and in more than one OR, resulting in much redundant information. The number of theoretically possible $2 \times 2$ subtables is $[r(r-1)/2][c(c-1)/2]$. However, Agresti (1990, 2002) provided a demonstration of the fact that using only cells in adjacent rows and adjacent columns results in a minimum number of ORs that serve as a sufficient descriptive fine-grained analysis of the association between the row and column variables for the sample data.

Goodman (1964, 1969) presented a method for constructing simultaneous confidence intervals for a full set of population ORs, but this method is too conservative for our interest in comparing only a nonredundant set of population ORs. (Simultaneous confidence intervals were defined in the section Shift-Function Method in chap. 5.) For a demonstration of a simpler procedure that produces narrower confidence intervals, refer to Wickens (1989). Consult Rudas (1998) for further discussion of odds ratios for $r \times c$ tables in general.

## MULTIWAY TABLES

Recall that contingency tables that relate more than two categorical variables, each of which consists of two or more categories, are called multiway tables. An example would be a table that relates the independent variables ethnicity and gender to the dependent variable political affiliation, although the variables do not have to be designated as independent variables or dependent variables. Table 8.3, a $2 \times 2 \times 3$ table, illustrates this hypothetical example.

It would be beyond the scope of this book to encapsulate the literature on effect sizes for multiway tables. Refer to the book by Wickens (1989) for an overview from the perspective of research in the social sciences. Those who consult that book should note that Wickens (1989) called some measures of effect size *association coefficients*. Rudas (1998) discussed odds ratios for tables in which there are two categories for each of more than two variables (called $2^k$ *tables*).

## RECOMMENDATIONS

When a researcher has undertaken naturalistic sampling, in which only the total number of participants has been chosen, and then the participants are classified with respect to two truly dichotomous variables in a $2 \times 2$ table, appropriate measures of effect size are the *phi* coefficient (taking into consideration its further limitations regarding meta-analysis), relative risk, and the odds ratio. In a study in which the researcher has randomly assigned the participants into two treatment groups to be classified in a $2 \times 2$ table, appropriate measures of effect size are the difference between two population probabilities (proportions), relative risk, and the odds ratio. The difference between two probabilities can also be used in the cases of prospective and retrospective sampling, and relative risk is also applicable to prospective sampling. These recommendations are summarized in Table 8.4.

Because very different perspectives on the results can be provided by the different measures of effect size, a research report should include values for estimates of the various appropriate measures. A research report should also include any contingency table on which a reported estimate of an effect size is based. Providing a contingency table is especially important to enable readers of the report to calculate other estimates of effect sizes if the researcher has not presented estimates for each of the appropriate measures and to enable readers to check the symmetry of the row and column marginal distributions. Consult Fleiss (1994) and Haddock, et al. (1998) for further discussions. For two-way tables that are larger than $2 \times 2$, if sampling has been naturalistic, researchers can report Cramér's $V$ with a cautionary remark about its limitations. A recommended approach when such a table has resulted from a study that used random assignment is to apply the method in Fleiss et al. (2003) for comparing multiple proportions.

There are many methods for analyzing data in contingency tables that are beyond the scope of discussion here. StatXact and LogXact are specialized statistical packages for such analyses. In chapter 9 we apply the measure that we called the probability of superiority (chap. 5) to contingency tables in which the two or more outcome categories have a meaningful order (e.g., participants categorized as worse, unchanged, or better after treatment or responses consisting of agree strongly, agree, disagree, and disagree strongly).

A problem of comparability of effect sizes arises when a meta-analyst encounters a combination of studies that used a continuous dependent variable measure, from which estimates of standardized-difference effect sizes can be calculated, and studies that dichotomized the same dependent variable measure and presented the data in a $2 \times 2$ table. However, there are methods for estimating a standardized-difference ef-

TABLE 8.4

Effect Sizes for 2 × 2 Tables

| Method of Categorization | Appropriate Effect Sizes | | | |
| --- | --- | --- | --- | --- |
| | $phi_{pop}$ | $P_1 - P_2$ | RR | $OR_{pop}$ |
| Naturalistic | Yes | No | Yes | Yes |
| Random Assignment | No | Yes | Yes | Yes |
| Prospective | No | Yes | Yes | Yes |
| Retrospective | No | Yes | No | Yes |

fect size from data in a 2 × 2 table so that results from the two kinds of studies can be combined in a meta-analysis (Sánchez-Meca et al., 2003). Alternatively, for this problem a meta-analyst might estimate the probability of superiority (*PS*) for continuous dependent variable measures and, as we demonstrate in the next chapter, apply the *PS* to the data in the 2 × 2 tables. The use of the *PS* in meta-analyses was discussed by Laird and Mosteller (1990) and Mosteller and Chalmers (1992).

## QUESTIONS

1. Name two synonyms for *unordered categorical variables*.
2. Distinguish between a nominal variable and an ordinal categorical variable, providing an example of each that is not in the text.
3. Define cross-classification table.
4. Why does a contingency table have that name?
5. Define *naturalistic sampling* and state one other name for it.
6. Misclassification is related to what common problem of measurement?
7. Why might the application of the methods for 2 × 2 tables in this chapter be problematic if applied to dichotomized variables instead of originally dichotomous variables?
8. Why is chi-square not an example of an effect size?
9. In which way is a *phi* coefficient a special case of the common Pearson *r*?
10. How does *phi*, as an effect size, compensate for the influence of sample size on chi-square?
11. How does one interpret a positive or negative value for *phi* in terms of the relationship between the two rows and the two columns?
12. If rows 1 and 2 are switched, or if columns 1 and 2 are switched, what would be the effect on a nonzero value of *phi*?
13. Why is *phi* only applicable to data that arise from naturalistic sampling?
14. For which kinds of sampling or assignment of participants is the difference between two proportions an appropriate effect size?
15. What do proportions in a representative sample estimate in a population?
16. When the difference between two proportions is transformed into a *z*, what influences how closely the distribution of such *z* values approximates the normal curve?
17. Provide a general kind of example of intransitive results when making pairwise comparisons from among *k* > 2 proportions. (A general answer stated symbolically suffices.)
18. What influences the accuracy of the normal-approximation procedure for constructing a confidence interval for the difference between two probabilities?

19. Explain why the interpretation of a given difference between two probabilities depends on whether both probabilities are close to 1 or 0, or both are close to .5.
20. Define *relative risk*, and explain when it is most useful.
21. What might be a better name than relative risk when this measure is applied to a category that represents a successful outcome?
22. Discuss a limitation of relative risk as an effect size.
23. For which kinds of categorizing or assignment of participants is relative risk applicable?
24. Define *prospective* and *retrospective research*.
25. Define *odds ratio* in general terms.
26. Define *odds ratio* formally.
27. To which kinds of categorization or assignment of participants is an odds ratio applicable?
28. Calculate and interpret an odds ratio for the data in Table 8.1.
29. Construct and interpret a confidence interval for the population odds ratio for the data in Table 8.1.
30. Why is an empty cell problematic for a sample odds ratio?
31. How does one test the null hypothesis that the population odds ratio is equal to 1 against the alternate hypothesis that it is not equal to 1?
32. Construct a null–counternull interval for the population odds ratio for the data in Table 8.2.
33. In which circumstance would it not be surprising that a null–counternull interval is very wide?
34. Name two common measures of the overall association between row and column variables for tables larger than $2 \times 2$.
35. For which kind of sampling are the two measures in Question 34 applicable?
36. Two or more values of the $CC$ should only be compared or averaged for tables that have what in common?
37. Two or more values of $V$ should only be compared or averaged for tables that have what in common?
38. Why should a research report always present a contingency table on whose data an estimate of effect size is reported?
39. Define the *NNT* and discuss its meaning.
40. Discuss the problem of testing the significance of an estimate of *NNT*.

# Chapter 9

# Effect Sizes
# for Ordinal Categorical Variables

## INTRODUCTION

Often one of the two categorical variables that are being related is an ordinal categorical variable, a set of categories that, unlike a nominal variable, has a meaningful order. Examples of ordinal categorical variables include the set of rating-scale categories Worse, Unimproved, Moderately Improved, and Much Improved; the set of attitudinal scale categories Strongly Agree, Agree, Disagree, and Strongly Disagree; the set of categories Applicant Accepted, Applicant on Waiting List, Applicant Rejected; and the scale from Introversion to Extroversion. The technical name for such ordinal categorical variables is *ordered polytomy*. The focus of this chapter is on some relatively simple methods for estimating an effect size in tables with two rows that represent two groups and three or more columns that represent ordinal categorical outcomes (2 × c tables). (The methods also apply to the case of two ordinal categorical outcomes. However, with fewer categories, the number of tied outcomes between the groups is more likely to increase, a matter that is discussed later in this chapter.) Table 9.1 provides an example with real data in which participants were randomly assigned to one or another treatment. Of course, the roles of the rows and columns can be reversed, so the methods also apply to comparable r × 2 tables. The clinical details do not concern us here, but we do observe that the Improved column reveals that neither Therapy 1 nor Therapy 2 appears to have been very successful. However, this result is perhaps less surprising when we note that the results were based on a 4-year follow-up study after therapy and the presenting problem (marital problems) was likely deteriorating just prior to the start of therapy. The data are from D. K. Snyder, Wills, and Grady-Fletcher (1991).

Gliner et al. (2002) provided reminders of two important points about the use of ordinal categorical scales. First, the number of categories to be used should be the greatest number of categories into which

### TABLE 9.1

### Ordinal Categorical Outcomes of Two Psychotherapies

|  | 1 | 2 | 3 |  |
|---|---|---|---|---|
|  | Worse | No Change | Improved | Total |
| Therapy 1 | 3 | 22 | 4 | 29 |
| Therapy 2 | 12 | 13 | 1 | 26 |

Note.   The data are from "Long-term effectiveness of behavioral versus insight-oriented marital therapy: A four-year follow-up study," by D. K. Snyder, R. M. Wills, and A. Grady-Fletcher, 1991, *Journal of Consulting and Clinical Psychology, 59*, p. 140. Copyright © 1999 by the American Psychological Association. Adapted with permission.

the participants can be reliably placed. Second, if the data are originally continuous it is generally not appropriate (due to a likely decrease in statistical power) to slice the continuous scores into ordinal categories. Note also that one should be very cautious about comparing effect sizes across studies that involve attitudinal scales. Such effect sizes can vary if there are differences in the number of items, number of categories of response, or the proportion of positively and negatively worded items across studies. Refer to Onwuegbuzie and Levin (2003) for further discussion.

The statistical significance of the association between the row and column variables, as well as the effect size that is used to measure the strength of that association, might vary depending on who is doing the categorizing. For example, there may not be high interobserver reliability in the categorization done by a patient, a close relative of the patient, or a professional observer of the patient. Therefore, a researcher should be appropriately cautious in interpreting the results. (Refer to Davidson, Rasmussen, Hackett, & Pitrosky, 2002, for an example of comparing effect sizes for patient-rated and observer-rated scales in generalized anxiety disorder.) A related concern has been raised about the use of a researcher's rating of the status of patients after treatment with a drug, even under double-blind conditions, in cases in which the researcher has a monetary relationship with the drug company. This and other possibly drug-favoring methodologies (Antonuccio, Danton, & McClanahan, 2003) might inflate the estimate of effect size.

Before discussing estimation of effect sizes for such data we briefly consider the related problem of testing the statistical significance of the association between the row and column variables. Suppose that the researcher's hypothesis is that one specified treatment is better than the other—a specified ordering of the efficacies of the two treatments. Such a research hypothesis leads to a one-tailed test. Alternatively, suppose that the researcher's hypothesis is that one treatment or the other (unspecified) is better—a prediction that there will be an unspecified ordering of the efficacies of the two treatments. This latter hypothesis leads to a two-tailed test. One or the other of these two *ordinal hypotheses* provides the alternative to the usual $H_0$ that posits no association between the row and column variables. An ordinal hypothesis is a hypothesis that predicts not only a difference between the two treatments in the distribution of their scores in the outcome categories (columns in this example) but a superior outcome for one (specified or unspecified) of the two treatments. These typical ordinal researchers' hypotheses are of interest in this chapter.

A $\chi^2$ test is inappropriate to test the null hypotheses at hand because the value of $\chi^2$ is insensitive to the ordinal nature of ordinal categorical variables. In this ordinal case a $\chi^2$ test can only validly test a not very useful "nonordinal" researcher's hypothesis that the two groups are in some way not distributed the same in the various outcome categories (Grissom, 1994b). Also, recall from chapter 8 that the magnitude of $\chi^2$ is not an estimator of effect size because it is very sensitive to sample size, not just to the strength of association between the variables. (The Kolmogorov–Smirnov two-sample test would be a better choice than the $\chi^2$ test for testing $H_0$ against a researcher's hypothesis of superiority of one treatment over another, but this test also has unacceptable shortcomings for this purpose; Grissom, 1994b.) Although there are other, more complex, approaches to data analysis for a $2 \times c$ contingency table with an ordinal categorical outcome variable, in this chapter we consider those that involve relatively simple measures of effect size: the point-biserial correlation (perhaps the most problematic in this case), the probability of superiority, the dominance measure, the generalized odds ratio, and the cumulative odds ratio.

## THE POINT-BISERIAL $r$ APPLIED TO ORDINAL CATEGORICAL DATA

Although we soon observe that there are limitations to this method (as is often true regarding measures of effect size), one might calculate a point-biserial correlation, $r_{pb}$ (see chap. 4), as perhaps the simplest estimate of an effect size for the case at hand. First, the $c$ column category labels are replaced by ordered numerical values, such as 1, 2, ..., $c$. For the column categories in Table 9.1 one might use 1, 2, and 3, and call these the *scores* on a $Y$ variable. Next, the labels for the row categories are replaced with numerical values, say, 1 and 2, and these are called the *scores* on an $X$ variable. One then uses any statistical software to calculate the correlation coefficient, $r$, for the now numerical $X$ and $Y$ variables.

Software output yielded $r_{pb} = -.397$ for the data in Table 9.1. When the sample sizes are unequal, as they are in Table 9.1, one can correct for the attenuation of $r$ that results from such inequality by using Equation 4.4 from chapter 4 for $r_c$, where $c$ denotes corrected. Because sample sizes are reasonably large and not very different for the data in Table 9.1, we are not surprised to find that the correction makes little difference in this case; $r_c = -.398$. The correlation is moderately large using Cohen's (1988) criteria for the relative sizes of correlations that were critiqued in chapter 4. Output also indicates that $r_{pb} = -.397$ is statistically significantly different from 0 at the $p < .002$ level, two-tailed. Note that the negative correlation indicates that Therapy 1 is better than Therapy 2. One can now conclude, subject to the limitations that are discussed later, that Therapy 1 has a statistically significant and moderately strong superiority over Therapy 2.

## CONFIDENCE INTERVAL AND NULL–COUNTERNULL INTERVAL FOR $r_{pop}$

Recall from chapter 4 that construction of an accurate confidence interval for $r_{pop}$ can be complex and that there may be no entirely satisfactory method. Therefore, researchers who report a confidence interval for $r_{pop}$ should also include such a cautionary comment in their research reports. For more details consult Hedges and Olkin (1985), Smithson (2003), and Wilcox (1996, 1997, 2003). Refer to the section on confidence intervals and null–counternull intervals in chapter 4 for a brief discussion of the improved methods for construction of a confidence interval for $r_{pop}$ by Smithson (2003) and Wilcox (2003). As an alternative to a confidence interval one might be inclined to construct instead the simple null–counternull interval for $r_{pop}$ using Equation 4.2 from chapter 4. However, as pointed out in chapter 8, a null–counternull interval for an effect size is less useful (very wide) when the estimate of the effect size is already known to be large and statistically significant, which is the case for the data in Table 9.1.

Although, from chapter 8 we know in advance that the null–counternull interval will be wide when the null hypothesis is $H_0$: $r_{pop} = 0$ and the obtained estimate of effect size is large, we proceed to use Equation 4.2 to construct a null–counternull interval for $r_{pop}$ for these data as an exercise. Because our null-hypothesized value of $r_{pop}$ is 0, the lower limit of the interval (null value) is 0. We apply the obtained $r = -.397$ to Equation 4.2, $r_{cn} = 2r / (1 + 3r^2)^{1/2}$, to find that the upper limit (counternull value) is $2(-.397) / [1 + 3(-.397^2)]^{1/2} = -.654$. Therefore, the interval runs from 0 to $-.654$.

## LIMITATIONS OF $r_{pb}$ FOR ORDINAL CATEGORICAL DATA

For general discussion of limitations of $r_{pb}$ refer to the section Assumptions of $r$ and $r_{pb}$ in chapter 4. The limitations may be especially troublesome in cases, such as the present one, in which there are very few values of the $X$ and $Y$ variables (two and three values, respectively). These data cause concerns such as the possibly inaccurate obtained $p$ levels for the $t$ test that is used to test for the statistical significance of $r_{pb}$. However, in this ordinal example there might be some favorable circumstances that possibly reduce the risk in using $r_{pb}$. First, sample sizes are reasonably large. Second, the obtained $p$ level is well beyond the customary minimum criterion of .05. Also, some studies have indicated that statistical power and accurate $p$ levels can be maintained for the $t$ test even when the $Y$ variable is dichotomous (resulting in a 2 × 2 table) if sample sizes are greater than 20 each, as they are in our example (D'Agostino, 1971; Lunney, 1970). A dichotomy is a much coarser grouping of categorical outcome than the polytomy of tables such as Table 9.1.

Regarding the $t$ test of the statistical significance of $r_{pb}$, it has been reported that even when sample sizes are as small as five the $p$ levels for the $t$ test can be accurate when there are at least three ordinal categories (Bevan, Denton, & Meyers, 1974). Also, Nanna and Sawilowsky (1998) showed that the $t$ test can be robust with respect to Type I error and can maintain power when applied to data from rating scales, but Maxwell and Delaney (1985) showed that, under heteroscedasticity and equality of means of populations, parametric methods applied to ordinal data might result in misleading conclusions. (However, in experimental research it might not be common to find that treatments change variances without changing means.) For references to many articles whose conclusions favor one or the other side of this longstanding controversy about the use of parametric methods for ordinal data, consult Nanna (2002) and Maxwell and Delaney (2004). Regarding the prospects for future development of a satisfactory method for constructing a confidence interval for the difference between the mean ratings of two groups, refer to Penfield (2003).

One might also be concerned about the arbitrary nature of our equal-interval scoring of the columns (1, 2, and 3) because other sets of three increasing numbers could have been used. Snedecor and Cochran (1989) and Moses (1986) reported that moderate differences among ordered, but not necessarily equally spaced, numerical scores that replace ordinal categories do not result in important differences in the value of $t$. However, Delaney and Vargha (2002) provided contrary results in which there was a statistically significant difference between the means for two treatments for problem drinking when the increasing levels of alcohol consumption were ordinally numerically scaled with equal spacing as 1 (abstinence), 2 (2 to 6 drinks per week), 3 (between 7 and 140 drinks per week), and 4 (more than 140 drinks per week), but there was not a statistically significant difference when the same four levels of drinking were scaled with slightly unequal spacing such as 0, 2, 3, 4. Consult Agresti (2002) for similar results that indicated the spacing is important and for further discussion of the choice of scores for the categories. For dependent variables for which there is no obvious choice of score spacing, such as the dependent variable in Table 9.1, Agresti (2002) acknowledged that equal spacing of scores is often a reasonable choice.

If, unbeknownst to the researcher, a continuous latent variable happens to underlie the scale, one would want the spacing of scores to be consistent with the differences between the underlying values. Agresti (2002) recommended the use of *sensitivity analysis* in which the results from two or three sensible scoring schemes are compared. One would hope that the results would not be very different. In any event, the results from each of the scoring schemes should be presented.

Some researchers will remain concerned about the validity of $r_{pb}$ and the accuracy of the $p$ levels of the $t$ test under the following combination of circumstances: Sample sizes are small, there are as few as three ordinal categories, there is possible skew or skew in different directions for the two groups, and there is possible heteroscedasticity. Because the lowest and/or highest extremes of the ordinal categories may not be as extreme as the actual most extreme standings of the participants with regard to the construct that underlies the rating scale, skew or differential skew may result. For example, suppose that there are respondents in one group who disagree extremely strongly with a presented attitudinal statement and respondents in the other group who agree extremely strongly with it. If the scale does not include these very extreme categories, the responses of the two groups will "bunch up" with those in the less extreme strongly disagree or strongly agree categories, respectively (which are floor and ceiling effects, as discussed in chap. 1). The consequence will be skew in different directions for the two groups as well as a restricted range of the dependent variable. Recall from chapter 4 that differential skew and restricted range of the measure of the dependent variable can be problematic for $r_{pb}$. Note that the issue of the Pearson $r_{pop}$ as a measure of only the linear component of a relationship between $X$ and $Y$ is not relevant here because the two values of the $X$ variable do not represent a dichotomized continuous variable that might have a nonlinear relationship with the $Y$ variable. Instead, the two values of the $X$ variable represent a true dichotomy such as Therapy 1 and Therapy 2 or male and female.

Finally, Cliff (1993, 1996) argued that there is rarely empirical justification for treating the numbers that are assigned to ordinal categories as having other than ordinal properties. We now turn to a less problematic effect size for ordinal categorical data, a measure for which the categories need only be ordered and the issue of the spacing of numerical scores is irrelevant.

## THE PROBABILITY OF SUPERIORITY APPLIED TO ORDINAL DATA

The part of the following material that is background information was explained in more detail in chapter 5, where the effect size called the probability of superiority was introduced in the context of a continuous $Y$ variable. Recall that the probability of superiority, $PS$, was defined as the probability that a randomly sampled member of Population a will have a score ($Y_a$) that is higher than the score attained by a randomly sampled member of Population b ($Y_b$). Symbolically, $PS = Pr(Y_a > Y_b)$. In the case of Table 9.1 a represents Therapy 1 and b represents Therapy 2, so we now call these therapies Therapy a and Therapy b. The *PS* is estimated by $\hat{p}_{a > b}$, which is the proportion of times that members of Sample a have a better outcome than members of Sample *b* when the outcome of each member of Sample a is compared to the outcome of each member of Sample b, one by one. In Table 9.1 we consider the outcome of No Change ($Y = 2$) to be better than the outcome Worse ($Y = 1$) and the outcome Improved ($Y = 3$) to be better than the outcome No Change. The number of times that the outcome for a member of Sample a is better than the outcome for the compared member of Sample b in all of these head-to-head comparisons is called the *U* statistic. (We soon consider the handling of tied scores.) The total number of such head-to-head comparisons is given by the product of the two sample sizes, $n_a$ and $n_b$. Therefore, an estimate of the *PS* is given by Equation 5.2 from chapter 5, $\hat{p}_{a > b} = U/n_a n_b$. The *PS* and its $\hat{p}_{a > b}$ estimator are not sensitive to the magnitudes of the scores that are being compared two at a time, but they are sensitive to which of the two scores is higher (better), that is, an ordering of the two scores. Therefore, the *PS* and $\hat{p}_{a > b}$ are applicable to $2 \times c$ tables in which the *c* categories are ordinal categorical. Note that numerous ties are likely when comparing two scores at a time when outcomes are categorical, even more so the smaller the effect size and the fewer the categories; consult Fay (2003). Therefore, we pay particular attention to ties in the following sections.

## WORKED EXAMPLE OF ESTIMATING THE *PS* FROM ORDINAL DATA

Before discussing the use of software for the present task we describe manual calculation. (Although a standard statistical package might provide at least intermediate values for the calculations, we describe manual calculation here because it should provide readers with a better understanding of the concept of the *PS* when applied to ordinal categorical data. Also, manual calculation requires only cell frequencies, whereas calculation using standard software might require more laborious entry of each observation.) We estimate $PS = Pr(Y_a > Y_b)$ using $S_a$ to denote the number of times that a member of Sample a has an outcome that is superior to the outcome for the compared member of Sample b. We use *T* to denote the number of times that the two outcomes are tied. A tie occurs whenever the two participants who are being compared have outcomes that are in the same outcome category (same column of Table 9.1). The number of ties arising from each column of the table is the product of the two cell frequencies in the column. Using the simple tie-handling method that was recommended by Moses, Emerson, and Hosseini (1984) and also adopted by Delaney and Vargha (2002) we allocate ties equally to each group by counting each tie as one half of a win assigned to each of the two samples. (Consult Brunner & Munzel, 2000; Fay, 2003; Pratt & Gibbons, 1981; Randles, 2001; Rayner & Best, 2001; and Sparks, 1967, for further discussions of ties.) Therefore,

$$U = S_a + .5T. \tag{9.1}$$

Calculating $S_a$ by beginning with the last column (Improved) of Table 9.1, observe that the outcomes of the four patients in the first row (now called Therapy a) are superior to those of $13 + 12 = 25$ of the patients in row 2 (now called Therapy b). Therefore, thus far $4(13 + 12) = 100$ pairings of patients have been found in which Therapy a had the superior outcome. Similarly, moving now to the middle column (No Change) of the table observe that the outcomes of 22 of the patients in Therapy a are superior to those of 12 of the patients in Therapy b. This latter result adds $22 \times 12 = 264$ to the previous subtotal of 100 pairings within which patients in Therapy a had the superior outcome. Therefore, $S_a = 100 + 264 = 364$. The number of ties arising from columns 1, 2, and 3 is $3 \times 12 = 36$, $22 \times 13 = 286$, and $4 \times 1 = 4$, respectively, so $T = 36 + 286 + 4 = 326$. Thus, $U = S_a + .5T = 364 + .5(326) = 527$. The number of head-to-head comparisons in which a patient in Therapy a had a better outcome than a patient in Therapy b, when one allocates ties equally, is 527. There were $n_a n_b = 29 \times 26 = 754$ total comparisons made. Therefore, the proportion of times that a patient in Therapy a had an outcome that was superior to the outcome of a compared patient in Therapy b, $\hat{p}_{a > b}$, (with equal allocation of ties) is $527/754 = .699$. We thus estimate that there is nearly a .7 probability that a randomly sampled patient from a population that receives Therapy a will outperform a randomly sampled patient from a population that receives Therapy b.

If type of therapy has no effect on outcome, $PS = .5$. Before citing methods that might be more robust we discuss traditional methods for testing $PS = .5$. As discussed in chapter 5, one might test $H_0$: $PS = .5$ against $H_{alt}$: $PS \neq .5$ using the Mann–Whitney $U$ test (perhaps more appropriately called, in terms of historical precedence, the Wilcoxon–Mann–Whitney test). However, as discussed in the section Assumptions in chapter 5, heteroscedasticity can result in a loss of power or inaccurate $p$ levels and inaccurate confidence intervals for the $PS$ (cf. Delaney & Vargha, 2000; Wilcox, 1996, 2001, 2003).

Only a minority of textbooks of statistics have a table of critical values of $U$ for various combinations of sample sizes, $n_a$ and $n_b$. Also, books that do include such a table (or a table for the equivalent statistic, $W_m$, that is discussed shortly) may not include the same sample sizes that were used by the researcher. Therefore, we now consider the use of software to conduct a $U$ test.

Programs of statistical software packages can be used to conduct a $U$ test from ordinal categorical data if a data file is created in which the ordinal categories are replaced by a set of any increasing positive numbers, as we already did for the columns in Table 9.1. Available software may instead provide an equivalent test using Wilcoxon's $W_m$ statistic. Software may also be using an approximating normal distribution instead of the exact distribution of the $W_m$ statistic and use as the standard deviation of this distribution (the standard error) a standard deviation that has not been adjusted for ties. (We adjust for ties later in this section.) For the data in Table 9.1 such software yields $W_m = 878$, $p = .0114$, two-tailed, using a normal approximation in which the standard error is not adjusted for ties, so the reported $p$ level is not as accurate as it could be although the reported value of $W_m$ is correct. To derive an estimate of $PS$ from this output $W_m$ is transformed to $U$ using, as in chapter 5,

$$U = W_m - \frac{n_s(n_s + 1)}{2},$$
(9.2)

where $n_s$ is the smaller of the two sample sizes or simply $n$ if $n_a = n_b$. Applying the data in Table 9.1 to Equation 9.2, the obtained $W_m = .878$ transforms to $U = 878 - [26(26 + 1)] / 2 = 527$, which is the same value for $U$ that we previously obtained using manual calculation.

When sample sizes are larger than those in a table of critical values of $U$ a manually-calculated $U$ test is often conducted using a normal approximation. (Unlike tables of critical values of $U$ or of $W_m$, tables of the normal curve appear in all books on general statistics.) For ordinal categorical data there is an old three-part rule of thumb (possible modification of which we suggest later) that has been used to justify use of the version of the $W_m$ test or $U$ test that uses the normal approximation. The rule consists of (Part 1) $n_a \geq 10$, (Part 2) $n_b \geq 10$, and (Part 3) no column total frequency $> .5N$, where $N = n_a + n_b$ (Emerson & Moses, 1985; Moses et al., 1984). According to this rule, if all of these three criteria are satisfied the following transformation of $U$ to $z$ is made, and the obtained $z$ is referred to a table of the normal curve to see if it is at least as extreme as the critical value that is required for the adopted significance level (e.g., $z = \pm 1.96$ for the .05 level, two-tailed):

$$z_u = \frac{U - .5(n_a n_b)}{s_u},$$
(9.3)

where $s_u$ is the standard deviation of the distribution of $U$ (standard error) and

$$s_u = \left[ \frac{n_a n_b (n_a + n_b + 1)}{12} \right]^{1/2}.$$
(9.4)

With regard to the minimum sample sizes that might justify use of the normal approximation, recall from chapter 5 that Fahoome (2002) found that the minimum equal sample sizes that would justify the use of the normal approximation for the $W_m$ test (equivalent to the $U$ test), in terms of adequately controlling Type I error, were 15 for tests at the

.05 level and 29 for tests at the .01 level. Therefore, until there is further evidence about minimum sample sizes for the case of using the normal approximation to test $PS = .5$ with ordinal categorical data, perhaps a better rule of thumb would be to substitute Fahoome's (2002) minimum sample sizes for those in Parts 1 and 2 in the previously described old rule.

A more accurate significance level can be attained by adjusting $s_u$ for ties. Such an adjustment might be especially beneficial if any column total contains more than one half of the total participants. This condition violates the criterion for Part 3 that was previously listed for justifying use of a normal approximation. (Because some software might not make this adjustment we demonstrate the manual adjustment.) Observe that column 2 of Table 9.1 contains $22 + 13 = 35$ of the $29 + 26 = 55$ of the total patients. Because $35/55 = .64$, which is greater than the criterion maximum of .5, we use the adjusted $s_u$, denoted $s_{adj}$, in the denominator of $z_u$ for a more accurate test,

$$ s_{adj}' = \left[ \frac{s_u\left[1 - \sum\left(f_i^3 - f_i\right)\right]}{N^3 - N} \right]^{1/2} , \qquad (9.5)$$

where $f_i$ is a column total frequency.

Beginning our calculation with Equation 9.4 for $s_u$ we find for the data in Table 9.1 that $s_u = [29(26)(29 + 26 + 1)/12]^{1/2} = 59.318$. Next, we calculate $f_i^3 - f_i$ for each of the columns 1, 2, and 3 in that order. These results are $15^3 - 15 = 3,360$, $35^3 - 35 = 42,840$, and $5^3 - 5 = 120$, respectively. Summing these last three values yields $3,360 + 42,840 + 120 = 46,320$. Placing $46,320$ into Equation 9.5 we have $s_{adj} = 59.318[1 - 46,320/(55^3 - 55)]^{1/2} = 50.385$. From Equation 9.3 with $s_{adj}$ replacing $s_u$, we now have $z_u = [527 - .5(29)(26)] / 50.385 = 2.98$. Inspection of a table of the normal curve reveals that a $z$ that is equal to 2.98 is statistically significant beyond the .0028 level, two-tailed. There is thus support for a researcher's hypothesis that one of the therapies is better than the other, and we soon find that Therapy a is the better one.

Observe first that adjusting $s_u$ for ties results now in a different obtained significance level from the value of .0114 that was previously obtained, although both levels represent significance at $p < .02$. Because our estimate of $Pr(Y_a > Y_b)$, $\hat{p}_{a>b}$, was .699, which is a value greater than the null-hypothesized value of .5, the therapy for which there is this just-reported statistically significant evidence of superiority is Therapy a. Because $U$ is statistically significant beyond the .0028 (approximately) two-tailed level, $\hat{p}_{a>b} = .699$ is statistically significantly greater than .5 beyond the .0028 two-tailed level.

When both $n_a$ and $n_b > 10$ the presence of many ties, as is true for the data in Table 9.1, has been reported to result generally in the approximate $p$ level being within 50% of the exact $p$ level (Emerson & Moses, 1985; but also consult Fay, 2003). In this example the obtained $p$ level, .0028, is so far from the usual criterion of .05 that perhaps one need not be very concerned about the exact $p$ level attained by the results. However, especially when more than half of the participants fall in one outcome column and the approximate obtained $p$ level is close to .05, a researcher might prefer to report an exact obtained $p$ level as is discussed in the paragraph after the next one.

Note that the $PS$ (and the $DM$ and $OR_{pop}$ of the next three sections) is applicable to tables that have as few as two ordinal outcome categories, although more ties are likely when there are only two outcome categories. Tables 4.1 (chap. 4) and 8.1 (chap. 8) provide examples because Participant Better versus Participant Not Better after treatment in Table 4.1 and Symptoms Remain versus Symptoms Gone after treatment in Table 8.1 represent in each case an ordering of outcomes. One outcome is not just different from the other, as would be the case for a nominal scale, but in each example one outcome can be considered to be superior to its alternative outcome. As an exercise the reader might apply the results of Table 8.1 to Equation 9.1 to verify, with regard to the superiority of Psychotherapy to Drug Therapy in that example, that the $PS$ is estimated to be .649.

An exact $p$ level for $U$ and, therefore, for testing $H_0$: $PS = .5$ against $H_{alt}$: $PS \neq .5$, can be obtained using the statistical software packages StatXact, SPSS Exact, or SAS Version 9. (Refer to Posch, 2002, for a study of the power of exact [StatXact] versions of the $W_m$ test and competing tests applied to data from $2 \times c$ tables.) Recall from chapter 5 that Fay (2002) provided a Fortran 90 program to produce exact critical values for the $W_m$ test over a wider range of sample sizes and alpha levels than can generally be found in published tables. For further discussions of the $PS$ and $U$ test in general review the The Probability of Superiority: Independent Groups and Assumptions sections in chapter 5.

Consult Delaney and Vargha (2002) for discussion of robust methods for the current case of ordinal categorical dependent variables. However, such methods might inflate Type I error under some conditions of skew. Delaney and Vargha (2002) demonstrated that these methods might not perform well when extreme skew is combined with one or both sample sizes being at or below 10. Sample sizes between 20 and 30 might be satisfactory. Wilcox (2003) provided an S-PLUS function for the Brunner and Munzel (2000) method for testing $H_0$: PS = .5 and for constructing a confidence interval for the $PS$ under conditions of heteroscedasticity, ties, or both.

Recall that from time to time in this book we recommended that researchers consider estimating and reporting more than one kind of effect size for a given set of data to gain different perspectives on the results. However, we also acknowledged a contrary opinion that holds that such reporting of estimates of multiple measures might only serve to confuse some readers. The example of estimation of the point-biserial $r_{pop}$ and the PS for data such as those in Table 9.1 are of interest in this regard. The estimate of the former was $-.398$ and the estimate of the latter was $.699$. A researcher who reports both of these values would be obliged not only to discuss the limitations of the point-biserial correlation in the case of ordinal data but also to make clear to readers the different meanings, but consistent message, of the two reported estimates of effect size. Both results support the superiority of Therapy a.

The values $-.398$ and $.699$ for the two estimates both constitute estimates of moderately large effect sizes by Cohen's (1988) criteria that were discussed in chapters 4 and 5. Also, referring to the columns for $r_{pop}$, the PS, and Cohen's (1988) $U_3$ measure of overlap in Table 5.1 of chapter 5, observe that these two values for estimates of $r_{pop}$ and the PS both correspond to a value of $U_3$ that indicates that approximately three fourths of the members of the better performing group have outcomes that are above the median outcome of the poorer performing group. (Note that it is of no concern when interpreting the results or examining the rows closest to $r_{pop} = .398$ in Table 5.1 that $r_{pb}$ was negative and the estimate of the PS was positive. Because it is a proportion the estimate of PS cannot be negative, and a value over .5 indicates superiority for Group a. A negative value for $r_{pb}$ similarly indicates that Group 1 [same as Group a] tends to score higher than Group 2. The sign of $r_{pb}$ depends on which sample's data are arbitrarily placed in row 1 or row 2, as discussed in chap. 4.) Note that those who do not find the median to be meaningful in the case of ordinal data with few categories and many ties would not want to apply $U_3$ in such cases.

Note that in the case of ordinal categorical data, due to the limited number of possible outcomes (categories) there is no opportunity for the most extreme outcomes to be shifted up or down by a treatment to a more extreme value (for which there is no outcome category). The result would be a bunching of tallies in the existing most extreme category (skew; cf. Fay, 2003), obscuring the degree of shift in the underlying variable. Such bunching can cause an underestimation of the PS, because this bunching can increase ties in an existing extreme category when in fact some of these ties actually represent superior outcomes for members of one group regarding the underlying variable. Skew resulting from such bunching can also cause $r_{pb}$ to underestimate $r_{pop}$, as was discussed in the section Assumptions of $r$ and $r_{pb}$ in chapter 4. Again, such problems can be reduced by the use of the maximum number of categories into which participants can reliably be placed and by the use of either the Brunner and Munzel (2000) tie-handling method or Cliff's (1996) method that is discussed in the next section.

## THE DOMINANCE MEASURE AND SOMERS' D

Recall from the section The Dominance Measure in chapter 5 that Cliff (1993, 1996) discussed an effect size that is a variation on the PS concept that avoids allocating ties, a measure that we called the dominance measure and defined in Equation 5.5 as $DM = Pr(Y_a > Y_b) - Pr(Y_b > Y_a)$. Cliff (1993, 1996) called the estimator of this effect size the *dominance statistic*, which we defined in Equation 5.6 as $ds = \hat{p}_{a>b} - \hat{p}_{b>a}$. When calculating the $ds$ each $\hat{p}$ value is given by the sample's value of $U/n_a n_b$ with no allocation of ties, so each $U$ is now given only by the $S$ part of Equation 9.1. The denominator of each $\hat{p}$ value is still given by $n_a n_b$. Note again that many ties are likely in the case of ordinal categorical data, which is especially true with fewer ordinal outcomes. The application of the $DM$ and the $ds$ will be made clear in the worked example in the next section.

Recall from chapter 5 that the $ds$ and $DM$ range from −1 to +1. When every member of Sample b has a better outcome than every member of Sample a, $ds = -1$. When every member of Sample a has an outcome that is better than the outcome of every member of Sample b, $ds = +1$. When there is an equal number of superior outcomes for each sample in the head-to-head pairings, $ds = 0$.

When $ds = -1$ or $+1$ there is no overlap between the two samples' distributions in the $2 \times c$ table, and when $ds = 0$ there is complete overlap in the two samples' distributions. However, because estimators of the $PS$ and the $DM$ are sensitive to which outcome is better in each pairing, but not sensitive to how good the better outcome is, reporting an estimate of these two effect sizes is not very informative for ordinal categorical data unless the $2 \times c$ (or $r \times 2$) table is also presented. For example, with regard to a table with the column categories of Table 9.1 (but not the data therein), if $\hat{p}_{a>b} = 1$ or $ds = +1$ (both indicating the most extreme possible superiority of Therapy a over Therapy b) the result could mean that (a) all members of Sample b were in the Worse column whereas all members of Sample a were in the No Change column, Improved Column, or in either the No Change or Improved columns; or (b) all members of Sample b were in the No Change column, whereas all members of Sample a were in the Improved column. Readers of a research report would want to know which of these four meaningfully different results underlying $\hat{p}_{a>b} = 1$ or $ds = +1$ had occurred. Similarly, when $\hat{p}_{a>b} = .5$ or $ds = 0$ (both indicating no superiority for either therapy), among other possible patterns of frequencies in the table the result could mean that all participants were in the Worse column, all were in the No Change column, or all were in the Improved column. One would certainly want to know whether such a $\hat{p}_{a>b}$ or $ds$ were indicating that both therapies were always possibly harmful (Worse column), always ineffective (No Change column), always effective (Improved column), or that there were some other pattern in the table.

Refer to Cliff (1993, 1996) for a discussion of significance testing for the $ds$ and construction of confidence intervals for the $DM$ for the independent-groups and the dependent-groups cases and for software to undertake the calculations. Wilcox (2003) provided an S-Plus software function for Cliff's (1993, 1996) method and, as noted in the discussion of the $DM$ in chapter 5, (Wilcox, 2003) reported tentative findings that this method controls Type I error well even when there are many ties. Consult Simonoff, Hochberg, and Reiser (1986), Vargha and Delaney (2000), and Delaney and Vargha (2002) for further discussions. The $ds$ is also known as the version of Somers' $D$ statistic (Agresti, 2002; Somers, 1962) that is applied to $2 \times c$ tables with ordinal outcomes (Cliff, 1996). An exact $p$ level for the statistical significance of Somers' $D$ is provided by StatXact and SPSS Exact.

## WORKED EXAMPLE OF THE $ds$

Calculating the $ds$ with the data in Table 9.1 by starting with column 3, and not allocating ties, we note that (as already found in the previous section) Therapy a had $S_a = 364$ superior outcomes in the $29 \times 26 = 754$ head-to-head comparisons. Therefore, $\hat{p}_{a > b} = 364/754 = .4828$. Starting again with column 3 we now find that 1 patient in Therapy b had a better outcome than $22 + 3$ patients in Therapy a, so thus far there are $1(22 + 3) = 25$ pairs of patients within which Therapy b had the superior outcome. Moving now to column 2 we find that 13 patients in Therapy b had an outcome that was superior to the outcome of 3 patients in Therapy a, adding $13 \times 3 = 39$ to the previous subtotal of 25 superior outcomes for Therapy b. Therefore, $\hat{p}_{b > a} = (25 + 39)/754 = .0849$. Thus, $ds = \hat{p}_{a > b} - \hat{p}_{b > a} = .4828 - .0849 = .398$, another indication, now on a scale from $-1$ to $+1$, of the degree of superiority of Therapy a over Therapy b.

Observe that one can check our calculation of $25 + 39 = 64$ superior outcomes for Therapy b by noting that there were a total of 754 comparisons, resulting in 364 superior outcomes ($S_a$) for Therapy a and $T = 326$ ties; so there must be $754 - 364 - 326 = 64$ comparisons in which Therapy b had the superior outcome. Note that it is a coincidence that the absolute values of the $ds$ and the previously reported corrected $r_{pb}$ (i.e., $r_c$), for the data in Table 9.1 are the same, $|.398|$. The $ds$ and $r_{pb}$ actually describe somewhat different characteristics of the data.

## GENERALIZED ODDS RATIO

Recall from the A Related Effect Size section in chapter 5 the discussion of an estimator of an effect size that results from the ratio of the two $\hat{p}$ values, the generalized odds ratio. We now apply the generalized odds ratio to the data in Table 9.1 by using the same definitions of $\hat{p}_{a > b} = U_a/n_a n_b$ and $\hat{p}_{b > a} = U_b/n_a n_b$ that were used in the previous two sections; that is, we ignore ties in calculating the two $U$ values but we use all $n_a n_b = 26 \times 29 = 754$ possible comparisons for the two denominators. Therefore, the generalized odds ratio estimate, $OR_g$, is given by

$$OR_g = \frac{\hat{p}_{a > b}}{\hat{p}_{b > a}}. \tag{9.6}$$

From the values that were calculated in the previous section we now find that $\hat{p}_{a>b}/\hat{p}_{b>a} = .4828/.0849 = 5.69$. For these data the $OR_g$ provides the informative estimate that in the population there are 5.69 times more pairings in which patients in Therapy a have a better outcome than patients in Therapy b than pairings in which patients in Therapy b have a better outcome than patients in Therapy a. The estimated parameter, $OR_{gpop} = Pr(Y_a > Y_b) / Pr(Y_b > Y_a)$, measures how many times more pairings there are in which a member of Population a has an outcome that is better than the outcome for a member of Population b than vice versa. For more discussion of generalized odds ratios consult Agresti (1984).

## CUMULATIVE ODDS RATIO

Suppose that in a $2 \times c$ table with ordinal categories, such as Table 9.2, one is interested in comparing the two groups with respect to their attaining at least some ordinal category. For example, with regard to the ordinal categories of the rating scale—Strongly Agree, Agree, Disagree, and Strongly Disagree—suppose that one wants to compare the college women and college men with regard to their attaining at least the Agree category. Attaining at least the Agree category means attaining the Strongly Agree category or the Agree category instead of the Strongly Disagree category or the Disagree category. Therefore, one's focus would be on the now combined Strongly Agree and Agree categories versus the now combined Strongly Disagree and Disagree categories. Thus, Table 9.2 is temporarily collapsed (reduced) to a $2 \times 2$ table for this purpose, rendering the odds ratio (OR) effect size for $2 \times 2$ tables of chapter 8 applicable to the analysis of the collapsed data.

A population OR that is based on combined categories is called a population *cumulative odds ratio* (population $OR_{cum}$). This effect size is a measure of how many times greater the odds are that a member of a certain group will fall into a certain set of categories (e.g., Agree and Strongly Agree) than the odds that a member of another group will fall into that set of categories. In our example we are calculating the ratio of (a) the odds that a woman Agrees or Strongly Agrees with the statement (instead of Disagreeing or Strongly Disagreeing with it) and (b) the odds that a man Agrees or Strongly Agrees with that statement (instead of

### TABLE 9.2
#### Gender Comparison With Regard to an Attitude Scale

|  | Strongly Agree | Agree | Disagree | Strongly Disagree |
|---|---|---|---|---|
| Women | 62 | 18 | 2 | 0 |
| Men | 30 | 12 | 7 | 1 |

Disagreeing or Strongly Disagreeing with it). The choice of which of the two or more categories to combine in a $2 \times c$ ordinal categorical table should be made before the data are collected. Table 9.2 presents an example of an original complete table (before collapsing it into Table 9.3) using actual data, but the labels of the response categories have been changed somewhat. The nonstatistical details of the research do not concern us here.

Collapsing Table 9.2 by combining columns 1 and 2 and by combining columns 3 and 4 produces Table 9.3. One finds $OR_{cum}$ by applying Equation 8.7 from chapter 8 to Table 9.3, $OR = f_{11}f_{22}/f_{12}f_{21}$. Observe in Table 9.3 that $f_{11} = 62 + 18 = 80, f_{22} = 7 + 1 = 8, f_{12} = 2 + 0 = 2$, and $f_{21} = 30 + 12 = 42$. As in chapter 8 we adjust each $f$ value by adding .5 to it to improve the sample $OR_{cum}$ as an estimator of $OR_{pop}$. We then use in Equation 8.7 $f_{11} = 80.5, f_{22} = 8.5, f_{12} = 2.5$, and $f_{21} = 42.5$. Therefore, the adjusted $OR_{cum}$ is $OR_{adj} = 80.5(8.5) / 2.5(42.5) = 6.44$. We have just found from the sample $OR_{adj}$ that the odds that a woman will Agree or Strongly Agree with the statement are estimated to be more than six times greater than the odds that a man will do so. However, to avoid exaggerating the gender difference that was found by $OR_{adj}$ in these data, it is also important to note in Table 9.3 that a great majority of the men Agree or Strongly Agree with the statement ($42/50 = 84\%$) but an even greater majority of the women Agree or Strongly Agree with it ($80/82 = 97.6\%$).

Any of the measures of effect size that were discussed previously in this chapter are applicable to the data in Table 9.2, subject to the previously discussed limitations. With regard to Table 9.3, if the two population odds are equal, the population $OR_{pop} = 1$. Recall from chapter 8 that a test of $H_0: OR_{pop} = 1$ versus $H_{alt}: OR_{pop} \neq 1$ can be conducted using the usual $\chi^2$ test of association. If $\chi^2$ is significant at a certain $p$ level, then $OR_{adj}$ is statistically significantly different from 1 at the same $p$ level.

The data of Table 9.3 yield $\chi^2 = 11.85, p < .001$. Readers might obtain somewhat varying, but still statistically significant, results because textbooks and different software might use somewhat different equations for $\chi^2$. Some use one or another of the equations that are modified for application to tables that have one or more cells with relatively small frequencies. Although Table 9.3 is such a table, we did not use a modified

**TABLE 9.3**

**Collapsed Version of Table 9.2**

|  | Agree or Strongly Agree | Disagree or Strongly Disagree |
|---|---|---|
| Women | $f_{11} = 80$ | $f_{12} = 2$ |
| Men | $f_{21} = 42$ | $f_{22} = 8$ |

equation because we assumed that many readers would not be accessing a modified equation. (We discuss a situation in which researchers should not use a modified equation in the next section.)

As stated in chapter 8, when cell counts are small the distribution of the supposed $\chi^2$ statistic less accurately approximates the actual $\chi^2$ distribution. Authors are inconsistent in their criteria for small cell counts. Refer to Agresti (1990, 2002) for further discussion and references for the complex problem of adjusting $\chi^2$ for small cell counts. Fisher's exact test can be conducted using StatXact, SPSS Exact, or SAS Version 9. Refer to chapter 8 for discussion and worked examples of construction of a confidence interval or a null–counternull interval for $OR_{pop}$

## THE *Phi* COEFFICIENT

Recall from chapter 4 that $phi_{pop}$ is the correlation between two dichotomous variables, such as the two variables in Table 9.3. For a final estimated effect size for the data in Table 9.3 we apply Equation 8.1 from chapter 8 to find that $phi = (\chi^2/N)^{1/2} = (11.85/132)^{1/2} = .300$, which reflects a medium strength of relationship (between gender and attitude in our example) according to Cohen's (1988) criteria. Note again that, following the recommendation of Fleiss et al. (2003), when using $\chi^2$ to calculate *phi* one should use the standard equation for $\chi^2$ instead of a version of the equation that is adjusted for small samples. Also note again that the applications of $\chi^2$ as a test statistic and *phi* as an estimator of effect size for the data of Table 9.3 assume naturalistic sampling, as described in chapter 8. We applied $\chi^2$ and *phi* to these data as a worked example under the assumption of naturalistic sampling although we cannot be certain that the author of this attitudinal research actually used naturalistic sampling. The reason for our uncertainty is that there is a large difference between the number of women (82) and the number of men (50) sampled, which would seem to be an unlikely difference when sampling from some populations. A plausible explanation for the preponderance of women would be that perhaps the research was conducted on students in a college course that attracts many more women than men. In this case we would be concerned about the nature of the population to which these results would generalize.

## A CAUTION

Some researchers and statisticians will be concerned about conducting two tests of significance for estimates of effect size on the same set of data. For example, there might be concern about proper interpretation of the $p$ level attained by a $\chi^2$ test of the significance of $OR_{cum}$ for the data of a collapsed table, such as Table 9.3, after one has already conducted a test of significance of association between the rows and columns of the original complete table, such as Table 9.2, having used any one of the methods that were previously discussed in this chapter. The simplest solution would be to compensate for giving oneself two chances to obtain a significant result from the same data by adopting a more conservative alpha level than the usual .05 level for the test of $OR_{cum}$ and for the statistical test of the estimate of effect size that is first applied to the full table. For example, one might use a Bonferroni–Dunn approach by adopting the .025 alpha level for each of the two tests. If there are going to be two tests of significance, the conservative alpha levels to be adopted for these two forthcoming tests should be chosen before data collection. Note, however, that in our case the obtained $p$ level is so small, $p < .001$, that perhaps we need not worry about this otherwise important issue this time.

## REFERENCES FOR FURTHER DISCUSSION OF ORDINAL CATEGORICAL METHODS

For further discussions of ordinal categorical methods that lead to estimation of effect sizes consult Agresti (1984, 1989, 1990, 2002), Cliff (1996), Fleiss et al. (2003), Gibbons (1985, 1993), Hildebrand, Laing, and Rosenthal (1977), Liebetrau (1983), Liu (1998), Moses et al. (1984), Randles (2001), and Wickens (1989). Consult Vargha and Delaney (2000) and Brunner and Puri (2001) for application of what we call the *PS* for ordinal categorical outcomes to the cases of between-groups and within-groups one-way and factorial designs.

## QUESTIONS

1. Define *ordinal categorical variable*, and provide an example that is not in the text.
2. What is a technical name for an ordered categorical variable?
3. State two criteria for one's choice of the number of ordinal categories to be used for the dependent variable.
4. Why should one be cautious about comparing effect sizes across studies that involve attitudinal scales?
5. What do the authors mean by an *ordinal hypothesis*?
6. Why is a $\chi^2$ test inappropriate to test an ordinal hypothesis?
7. Describe the procedure for calculating a point-biserial $r$ for a $2 \times c$ table in which the dependent variable is ordinal categorical.
8. What adjustment should be made to the procedure in Question 7 in the case of unequal sample sizes?
9. How does one interpret a negative and a positive point-biserial $r$ in tables such as Table 9.1?
10. Discuss a possible limitation of the use of the point-biserial $r$ for ordinal categorical data.

11. Discuss the problem of choosing a scale of scores to replace ordinal categories.
12. Provide, discussing your reasoning, your own choice of a possible sensible numerical scale for the example of treatment for alcoholism in the text in which the four outcome categories were abstinence, 2 to 6 drinks per week, 7 to 140 drinks per week, and more than 140 drinks per week.
13. Describe how skew in opposite directions might occur in the case of $2 \times c$ tables involving attitude scales, and why might this differential skew be problematic for the point-biserial $r$?
14. Define the probability of superiority.
15. What adjustment might improve the accuracy of an obtained significance level for a $U$ test based on the normal approximation?
16. What is the estimate of the $PS$ if there are 610 wins for therapy in head-to-head comparisons of the outcomes of 33 participants who received therapy and outcomes of 33 participants who received a placebo?
17. When is it valid, but why would it still be problematic, to apply the $PS$ to $2 \times 2$ tables?
18. Apply Equation 9.1 to the data in Table 8.1 of chapter 8.
19. Why is the negative value for the point-biserial correlation applied to Table 9.1 not inconsistent with the estimate of $PS = .699$ for those data?
20. Why might the use of too few categories cause the $PS$ to be underestimated?
21. Define *dominance measure*.
22. Why might the estimation of the $PS$ or the $DM$ not be very informative to a reader of a research report unless the underlying contingency table is also presented?
23. What is another name for *dominance statistic*?
24. Define *generalized odds ratio*.
25. Interpret a generalized odds ratio that is equal to 5.
26. Define *cumulative odds ratio*.
27. Interpret a cumulative odds ratio that is equal to 2.
28. Under which circumstance is the phi coefficient applicable to a $2 \times 2$ table that results from collapsing a larger table?
29. Calculate phi for the data in Table 9.3.
30. What is the problem, and what is the simplest solution to the problem, that arises from conducting a test of significance for an original table and then conducting another test of significance for a collapsed $2 \times 2$ version of that table?

# References

Abelson, R. P. (1995). *Statistics as principled argument*. Mahwah, NJ: Lawrence Erlbaum Associates.

Abelson, R. P., & Prentice, D. A. (1997). Contrast tests of interaction hypotheses. *Psychological Methods, 2*, 315–328.

Abu Libdeh, O. (1984). *Strength of association in the simple general linear model: A comparative study of Hays' omega-squared*. Unpublished doctoral dissertation, The University of Chicago, Chicago.

Agresti, A. (1984). *Analysis of ordinal categorical data*. New York: Wiley.

Agresti, A. (1989). Tutorial on modeling ordered categorical response data. *Psychological Bulletin, 105*, 290–301.

Agresti, A. (1990). *Categorical data analysis*. New York: Wiley.

Agresti, A. (2002). *Categorical data analysis* (2nd. ed.). Hoboken, NJ: Wiley.

Ahadi, S., & Diener, E. (1989). Multiple determinants and effect size. *Journal of Personality and Social Psychology, 56*, 398–406.

Algina, K., & Keselman, H. J. (2003) Approximate confidence intervals for effect sizes. *Educational and Psychological Measurement, 63*, 537–553.

Altman, D. G., Machin, D., Bryant, T. N., & Gardner, M. J. (2000). *Statistics with confidence: Confidence intervals with statistical guidelines* (2nd ed.). London: British Medical Journal Books.

American Psychological Association. (2001). *Publication manual of the American Psychological Association* (5th ed.). Washington, DC: Author.

Antonuccio, D. O., Danton, W. G., & McClanahan, T. M. (2003). Psychology in the prescription era: Building a firewall between marketing and science. *American Psychologist, 58*, 1028–1043.

Aspin, A. A. (1949). Tables for use in comparisons whose accuracy involves two variances separately estimated. *Biometrika, 36*, 290–293.

Auguinis, H., & Whitehead, R. (1997). Sampling variance in the correlation coefficient under indirect range restriction: Implications for validity generalization. *Journal of Applied Psychology, 82*, 528–538.

Barnett, V., & Lewis, T. (1994). *Outliers in statistical data* (3rd ed.). Chichester, England: Wiley.

Barnette, J. J., & McLean, J. E. (1999, November). *Empirically based criteria for determining meaningful effect size*. Paper presented at the annual meeting of the Mid-South Educational Research Association, Point Clear, AL.

Barnette, J., & McLean, J. E. (2002, April). *Shedding light on the eta-squared and omega-squared relationships with the standardized effect size*. Paper presented at the annual meeting of the American Educational Research Association, New Orleans, LA.

Baugh, F. (2002a). Correcting effect sizes for score reliability: A reminder that measurement and substantive issues are linked inextricably. *Educational and Psychological Measurement, 62,* 254–263.

Baugh, F. (2002b). Correcting effect sizes for score reliability. In B. Thompson (Ed.), *Score reliability: Contemporary thinking on reliability issues* (pp. 31–41). Thousand Oaks, CA: Sage.

Beal, S. L. (1987). Asymptotic confidence intervals for the difference between two binomial parameters for use with small samples. *Biometrics, 43,* 941–950.

Beatty, M. J. (2002). Do we know a vector from a scalar? Why measures of association (not their squares) are appropriate indices of effect. *Human Communication Research, 28,* 605–611.

Bedrick, E. J. (1987). A family of confidence intervals for the ratio of two binomial proportions. *Biometrics, 43,* 993–998.

Begg, C. B. (1994). Publication bias. In H. Cooper & L. V. Hedges (Eds.), *The handbook of research synthesis* (pp. 399–499). New York: Russell Sage Foundation.

Belsley, D. A., Kuh, E., & Welsch, R. E. (1980). *Regression diagnostics: Identifying influential data and sources of collinearity.* New York: Wiley.

Bergmann, R., Ludbrook, J., & Spooren, W. P. J. M. (2000). Different outcomes of the Wilcoxon–Mann–Whitney test from different statistics packages. *The American Statistician, 54,* 72–77.

Bernhardson, C. S. (1975). Type I error rates when multiple comparison procedures follow a significant F test of ANOVA. *Biometrics, 31,* 229–232.

Bevan, M. F., Denton, J. Q., & Meyers, J. L. (1974). The robustness of the F test to violations of continuity and form of treatment population. *British Journal of Mathematical and Statistical Psychology, 27,* 199–204.

Bickel, P. J., & Lehmann, E. L. (1975). Descriptive statistics for nonparametric models: II. Location. *Annals of Statistics, 3,* 1045–1069.

Bird, K. D. (2002). Confidence intervals for effect sizes in analysis of variance. *Educational and Psychological Measurement, 62,* 197–226.

Bond, C. F., Wiitala, W. L., & Richard, F. D. (2003). Meta-analysis of raw differences. *Psychological Methods, 8,* 406–418.

Bonett, D. G., & Price, R. M. (2002). Statistical inference for a linear function of medians: Confidence intervals, hypothesis testing, and sample size requirements. *Psychological Methods, 7,* 370–383.

Borenstein, M. (1994). The case for confidence intervals in controlled clinical trials. *Controlled Clinical Trials, 15,* 411–428.

Bradeley, M. T., Smith, D., & Stoica, G. (2002). A Monte-Carlo estimation of effect size distortion due to significance testing. *Perceptual and Motor Skills, 95,* 837–842.

Brant, R. (1990). Comparing classical and resistant outlier rules. *Journal of the American Statistical Association, 85,* 1083–1090.

Breaugh, J. A. (2003). Effect size estimation: Factors to consider and mistakes to avoid. *Journal of Management, 29,* 79–97.

Brown, R. A., Evans, D. M., Miller, I. W., Burgess, E. S., & Mueller, T. I. (1997). Cognitive-behavioral treatment for depression in alcoholism. *Journal of Consulting and Clinical Psychology, 65,* 715–726.

Brunner, E., & Munzel, U. (2000). The nonparametric Behrens–Fisher problem: Asymptotic theory and small-sample approximation. *Biometrical Journal, 42,* 17–25.

Brunner, E., & Puri, M. L. (2001). Nonparametric methods in factorial designs. *Statistical Papers, 42,* 1–52.

Bryk, A. S. (1977). Evaluating program impact: A time to cast away stones, a time to gather stones together. *New Directions for Program Evaluation, 1,* 32–58.

Bryk, A. S., & Raudenbush, S. W. (1988). Heterogeneity of variance in experimental studies: A challenge to conventional interpretations. *Psychological Bulletin, 104,* 396–404.

Bunner, J., & Sawilwosky, S. (2002). Alternatives to $S_w$ in the bracketed interval of the trimmed mean. *Journal of Modern Applied Statistical Methods, 1,* 176–181.

Callender, J. C., & Osburn, H. G. (1980). Development and test of a new model for validity generalization. *Journal of Applied Psychology, 65,* 543–558.

Campbell, J. M. (2004). Statistical comparison of four effect sizes for single-subject designs. *Behavior Modification, 28,* 234–246.

Carling, K. (2000). Resistant outlier rules and the non-Gaussian case. *Computational Statistics and Data Analysis, 33,* 249–258.

Carroll, J. B. (1961). The nature of the data, or how to choose a correlation coefficient. *Psychometrika, 26,* 347–372.

Carroll, R. M., & Nordholm, L. A. (1975). Sampling characteristics of Kelley's $\varepsilon^2$ and Hays' $\hat{\omega}^2$. *Educational and Psychological Measurement, 35,* 541–554.

Chan, I. S. F. (1998). Exact tests of equivalence and efficacy with a non-zero lower bound for comparative studies. *Statistics in Medicine, 17,* 1403–1413.

Chan, W., & Chan, W.-L. (2004). Bootstrap standard error and confidence intervals for the correlation corrected for range restriction: A simulation study. *Psychological Methods, 9,* 369–385.

Chen, P. Y., & Popovich, P. M. (2002). *Correlation: Parametric and nonparametric measures.* Thousand Oaks, CA: Sage.

Chernick, M. R. (1999). *Bootstrap methods: A practitioner's guide.* New York: Wiley.

Chuang-Stein, C. (2001). Testing for superiority or inferiority after concluding equivalence? *Drug Information Journal, 35,* 141–143.

Cleveland, W. S. (1985). *The elements of graphing data.* Monterey, CA: Wadsworth.

Cleveland, W. S. (Ed.). (1988). *The collected works of John W. Tukey: Vol. V. Graphics.* New York: Chapman and Hall.

Cliff, N. (1993). Dominance statistics: Ordinal analyses to answer ordinal questions. *Psychological Bulletin, 114,* 494–509.

Cliff, N. (1996). *Ordinal methods for behavioral data analysis.* Mahwah, NJ: Lawrence Erlbaum Associates.

Cohen, J. (1973). Eta-squared and partial eta-squared in fixed factor ANOVA designs. *Educational and Psychological Measurement, 33,* 107–112.

Cohen, J. (1988). *Statistical power analysis for the behavioral sciences* (2nd ed.). New York: Academic Press.

Cohen, J. (1994). The earth is round ($p < .05$). *American Psychologist, 49,* 997–1003.

Cohen, J., Cohen, P., West, S. G., & Aiken, L. S. (2003). *Applied multiple regression/correlation analysis for the behavioral sciences* (3rd ed.). Mahwah, NJ: Lawrence Erlbaum Associates.

Cohn, L. D., & Becker, B. J. (2003). How meta-analysis increases statistical power. *Psychological Methods, 8,* 243–253.

Colditz, G. A., Miller, J. N., & Mosteller, F. (1988). Measuring gain in the evaluation of medical technology: The probability of a better outcome. *International Journal of Technology Assessment in Health Care, 4,* 637–642.

Cook, R. D., & Weisberg, S. (1982). *Residuals and influence in regression.* New York: Chapman and Hall.

Cooper, H. M. (1989). *Integrating research: A guide for literature reviews.* Thousand Oaks, CA: Sage.

Cooper, H., & Findley, M. (1982). Expected effect sizes: Estimates for statistical power analysis in social psychology. *Personality and Social Psychology Bulletin, 8,* 168–173.

Cooper, H., & Hedges, L. V. (Eds.). (1994). *The handbook of research synthesis.* New York: Russell Sage Foundation.

Cornfield, J. (1956). A statistical problem arising from retrospective studies. In J. Neyman (Ed.), *Proceedings of the Third Berkeley Symposium on Mathematical Statistics and Probability* (Vol. 4, pp. 135–148). Berkeley: University of California Press.

Cortina, J. M., & Nouri, H. (2000). *Effect sizes for ANOVA designs.* Thousand Oaks, CA: Sage.

Cribbie, R. A., & Keselman, H. J. (2003a). The effects of nonnormality on parametric, nonparametric, and model comparison approaches to pairwise comparisons. *Educational and Psychological Measurement, 63,* 615–635.

Cribbie, R. A., & Keselman, H. J. (2003b). Pairwise multiple comparisons: A model testing approach versus stepwise procedures. *British Journal of Mathematical and Statistical Psychology, 56,* 167–182.

Crits-Christoph, P., Tu, X., & Gallop, R. (2003). Therapists as fixed versus random effects—some statistical and conceptual issues: A comment on Siemer and Joormann. *Psychological Methods, 8,* 518–523.

Crow, E. L. (1991). Response to Rosenthal's comment "How are we doing in soft psychology?" *American Psychologist, 46,* 1083.

Cumming, G., & Finch, S. (2001). A primer on the understanding, use, and calculation of confidence intervals that are based on central and noncentral distributions. *Educational and Psychological Measurement, 61,* 532–574.

D'Agostino, R. B. (1971). A second look at analysis of variance on dichotomous data. *Journal of Educational Measurement, 8,* 327–333.

Darlington, M. L. (1973). Comparing two groups by simple graphs. *Psychological Bulletin, 79,* 110–116.

Davidson, J. R. T., Rasmussen, J., Hackett, D., & Pitrosky, B. (2002). Effect size comparisons of patient and observer rated scales in generalized anxiety disorder, using the venlafaxine ER dataset. *European Neuropsychopharmacology, 12,* 346–347.

Davies, L., & Gather, U. (1993). The identification of multiple outliers. *Journal of the American Statistical Association, 88,* 782–792.

Davison, A. C., & Hinkley, D. V. (1997). *Bootstrap methods and their applications.* Cambridge, England: Cambridge University Press.

Dayton, C. M. (2003). Information criteria for pairwise comparisons. *Psychological Methods, 8,* 61–71.

De Carlo, L. T. (1997). On the meaning and use of kurtosis. *Psychological Methods, 2,* 292–307.

Delaney, H. D., & Vargha, A. (2002). Comparing several robust tests of stochastic equality with ordinally scaled variables and small to moderate sized samples. *Psychological Methods, 7,* 485–503.

Diaconis, P., & Efron, B. (1983). Computer-intensive methods in statistics. *Scientific American, 248*(5), 116–130.

Dixon, W. J., & Massey, F. J. (1983). *Introduction to statistical analysis* (4th ed.). New York: McGraw-Hill.

Dodd, D. H., & Schultz, R. F. (1973). Computational procedures for estimating magnitude of effect for some analysis of variance designs. *Psychological Bulletin, 79*, 391–395.

Doksum, K. A. (1977). Some graphical methods in statistics. A review and some extensions. *Statistica Neerlandica, 31*, 53–68.

Dunlap, W. P. (1999). A program to compute McGraw and Wong's common language effect size indicator. *Behavior Research Methods, Instruments, & Computers, 31*, 706–709.

Dwyer, J. H. (1974). Analysis of variance and the magnitude of effects: A general approach. *Psychological Bulletin, 81*, 731–737.

Efron, B., & Tibshirani, R. J. (1993). *An introduction to the bootstrap.* New York: Chapman and Hall.

Emerson, J. D., & Moses, L. E. (1985). A note on the Wilcoxon–Mann–Whitney test for 2 × k ordered tables. *Biometrics, 41*, 303–309.

Emerson, J. D., & Stoto, M. A. (1983). Transforming data. In D. C. Hoaglin, F. Mosteller, & J. W. Tukey (Eds.), *Understanding robust and exploratory data analysis* (pp. 97–127). New York: Wiley.

Ezekiel, M. (1930). *Methods of correlational analysis.* New York: Wiley.

Fahoome, G. (2002). Twenty nonparametric statistics and their large-sample approximations. *Journal of Modern Applied Statistical Methods, 2*, 248–268.

Fan, X. (2001). Statistical significance and effect size in education research: Two sides of a coin. *Journal of Educational Research, 94*, 275–282.

Fay, B. R. (2002). JMASM4: Critical values for four nonparametric and/or distribution-free tests of location for two independent samples. *Journal of Modern Applied Statistical Methods, 2*, 489–517.

Fay, B. R. (2003). *A Monte Carlo computer study of the power properties of six distribution-free and/or nonparametric statistical tests under various methods of resolving tied ranks when applied to normal and nonnormal data distributions.* Unpublished doctoral dissertation, Wayne State University, Detroit, MI.

Feingold, A. (1992). Sex differences in variability in intellectual abilities: A new look at an old controversy. *Review of Educational Research, 62*, 61–84.

Feingold, A. (1995). The additive effects of differences in central tendency and variability are important in comparisons between groups. *American Psychologist, 50*, 5–13.

Feinstein, A. R. (1998). P-values and confidence intervals: Two sides of the same unsatisfactory coin. *Journal of Clinical Epidemiology, 61*, 355–360.

Fern, F. E., & Monroe, K. B. (1996). Effect-size estimates: Issues and problems in interpretation. *Journal of Consumer Research, 23*, 89–105.

Feske, U., & Goldstein, A. J. (1997). Eye movement desensitization and reprocessing treatment for panic disorder: A controlled outcome and partial dismantling study. *Journal of Consulting and Clinical Psychology, 65*, 1026–1035.

Fidler, F., Thomason, N., Cumming, G., Finch, S., & Leeman, J. (2004). Editors can lead researchers to confidence intervals, but can't make them think. *Psychological Science, 15*, 119–126.

Fidler, F., & Thompson, B. (2001). Computing correct confidence intervals for ANOVA fixed- and random-effects effect sizes. *Educational and Psychological Measurement, 61*, 575–604.

Fisher, R. A. (1925). *Statistical methods for research workers*. London: Oliver & Boyd.

Fleiss, J. L. (1986). *The design and analysis of clinical experiments*. New York: Wiley.

Fleiss, J. L. (1994). Measures of effect size for categorical data. In H. Cooper & L. V. Hedges (Eds.), *The handbook of research synthesis* (pp. 245–260). New York: Russell Sage Foundation.

Fleiss, J. L., Levin, B., & Paik, M. C. (2003). *Statistical methods for rates and proportions* (3rd ed.). New York: Wiley.

Fligner, M. A., & Policello, II, G. E. (1981). Robust rank procedures for the Behrens–Fisher problem. *Journal of the American Statistical Association, 76,* 162–168.

Fowler, R. L. (1987). A general method for comparing effect magnitudes in ANOVA designs. *Educational and Psychological Measurement, 47,* 361–367.

Fox, J. (1999). *Applied regression analysis, linear models, and related methods*. Thousand Oaks, CA: Sage.

Frick, R. W. (1995). A problem with confidence intervals. *American Psychologist, 50,* 1102–1103.

Frigge, M., Hoaglin, D. C., & Iglewicz, B. (1989). Some implementations of the boxplot. *The American Statistician, 43,* 50 –54.

Gart, J. J., & Nam, J. (1988). Approximate interval estimation of the ratio of binomial parameters: A review and corrections of skewness. *Biometrics, 44,* 323–338.

Gart, J. J., & Thomas, D. G. (1972). Numerical results on approximate confidence limits for the odds ratio. *Journal of the Royal Statistical Society (Series B), 34,* 441–447.

Gibbons, J. D. (1985). *Nonparametric statistical inference* (2nd ed.). New York: Dekker.

Gibbons, J. D. (1993). *Nonparametric measures of association*. Thousand Oaks, CA: Sage.

Gigerenzer, G., & Edwards, A. (2003, September 27). Simple tools for understanding risk: From innumeracy to insight [Electronic version]. *British Medical Journal, 327,* 741–744. Retrieved March 10, 2004, from http://bmj.bmjjournals.com/cgi/content/full/327/7417/741

Gillett, R. (2003). The metric comparability of meta-analytic effect size measures. *Psychological Methods, 8,* 419–433.

Glass, G. V., & Hopkins, K. D. (1996). *Statistical methods in psychology and education* (3rd ed.). Boston: Allyn & Bacon.

Glass, G. V., McGaw, B., & Smith, M. L. (1981). *Meta-analysis in social research*. Thousand Oaks, CA: Sage.

Gleser, L. J. (1996). Comment on "Bootstrap Confidence Intervals." *Statistical Science, 11,* 219–221.

Gliner, J. A., Morgan, G. A., & Harmon, R. J. (2002). The chi-square test and accompanying effect size indices. *Journal of the American Academy of Child and Adolescent Psychology, 41,* 1510–1512.

Goldberg, K. M., & Iglewicz, B. (1992). Bivariate extensions of the boxplot. *Technometrics, 34,* 307–320.

Goodman, L. A. (1964). Simultaneous confidence limits for cross-product ratios in contingency tables. *Journal of the Royal Statistical Society (Series B), 26,* 86–102.

Goodman, L. A. (1969). How to ransack social mobility tables and other kinds of cross-classification tables. *American Journal of Sociology, 75,* 1–40.

Gorecki, J. A. (2002). *A meta-analysis of the effectiveness of antidepressants compared to placebo.* Unpublished master's thesis, San Francisco State University, San Francisco.

Grice, G. R. (1966). Dependence of empirical laws upon the source of experimental variation. *Psychological Bulletin, 66,* 488–499.

Grissom, R. J. (1994a). Probability of the superior outcome of one treatment over another. *Journal of Applied Psychology, 79,* 314–316.

Grissom, R. J. (1994b). Statistical analysis of ordinal categorical status after therapies. *Journal of Consulting and Clinical Psychology, 62,* 281–284.

Grissom, R. J. (1996). The magical number .7 ± .2: Meta-meta analysis of the probability of superior outcome in comparisons involving therapy, placebo, and control. *Journal of Consulting and Clinical Psychology, 64,* 973–982.

Grissom, R. J. (2000). Heterogeneity of variance in clinical data. *Journal of Consulting and Clinical Psychology, 68,* 155–165.

Grissom, R. J., & Kim, J. J. (2001). Review of assumptions and problems in the appropriate conceptualization of effect size. *Psychological Methods, 6,* 135–146.

Gross, J. S. (1985). *Weight modification and eating disorders in adolescent boys and girls.* Unpublished doctoral dissertation, University of Vermont, Burlington.

Haase, R. F., Waechter, D. M., & Solomon, G. S. (1982). How significant is a significant difference? Average effect size of research in counseling psychology. *Journal of Counseling Psychology, 29,* 58 –65.

Haddock, C. K., Rindskopf, D., & Shadish, W. R. (1998). Using odds ratios as effect sizes for meta-analysis of dichotomous data: A primer on methods and issues. *Psychological Methods, 3,* 339–353.

Hampel, F. R., Ronchetti, E. M., Rousseeuw, P. J., & Stahel, W. A. (1986). *Robust statistics: The approach based on influence functions.* New York: Wiley.

Hand, D. J. (1992). On comparing two treatments. *The American Statistician, 46,* 190–192.

Hand, D. J., Daly, F., Lunn, A. D., McConway, K. J., & Ostrowski, E. (1994). *A handbook of small data sets.* London: Chapman and Hall.

Harlow, L. L., Mulaik, S. A., & Steiger, J. H. (Eds.). (1997). *What if there were no significance tests?* Mahwah, NJ: Lawrence Erlbaum Associates.

Harrell, F. E., & Davis, D. E. (1982). A new distribution-free quantile estimator. *Biometrika, 69,* 635–640.

Hauck, W. W., & Anderson, S. (1986). A comparison of large-sample confidence interval methods for the difference of two binomial probabilities. *The American Statistician, 40,* 318–322.

Hays, W. L. (1994). *Statistics for psychologists* (5th ed.). Fort Worth, TX: Hartcourt Brace.

Hedges, L. V. (1981). Distribution theory for Glass's estimator of effect size and related estimators. *Journal of Educational Statistics, 6,* 107–128.

Hedges, L. V. (1982). Estimation of effect size from a series of independent experiments. *Psychological Bulletin, 92,* 490–499.

Hedges, L. V., & Friedman, L. (1993). Gender differences in variability in intellectual abilities: A re-analysis of Feingold's results. *Review of Educational Research, 63,* 94–105.

Hedges, L. V., & Nowell, A. (1995). Sex differences in mental test scores, variability, and numbers of high-scoring individuals. *Science, 269,* 41–45.

Hedges, L. V., & Olkin, I. (1984). Nonparametric estimators of effect size in meta-analysis. *Psychological Bulletin, 96,* 573–580.

Hedges, L. V., & Olkin, I. (1985). *Statistical methods for meta-analysis*. San Diego, CA: Academic Press.

Hekmat, H. (1973). Systematic versus semantic desensitization and implosive therapy: A comparative study. *Journal of Consulting and Clinical Psychology, 4*, 202–209.

Hess, B., Olejnik, S., & Huberty, C. J. (2001). The efficacy of two improvement over chance effect sizes for two-group univariate comparisons under variance heterogeneity and nonnormality. *Educational and Psychological Measurement, 61*, 909–936.

Hildebrand, D. K., Laing, J. D., & Rosenthal, H. (1977). *Analysis of ordinal data*. Thousand Oaks, CA: Sage.

Hoaglin, D.C., Mosteller, F., & Tukey, J. W. (Eds.). (1983). *Understanding robust and exploratory data analysis*. New York: Wiley.

Hoaglin, D. C., Mosteller, F., & Tukey, J. W. (Eds.). (1985). *Exploring data tables, trends, and shapes*. New York: Wiley.

Hogarty, K. Y., & Komrey, J. D. (2001, April). *We've been reporting some effect sizes: Can you guess what they mean?* Paper presented at the annual meeting of the American Educational Research Association, Seattle, WA.

Hou, C.-D., Chiang, J., & Tai, J. J. (2003). A family of simultaneous confidence intervals for multinomial proportions. *Computational Statistics and Data Analysis, 43*, 29–45.

Howell, D. C. (1997). *Statistical methods for psychology* (4th ed.). Boston: Duxbury.

Hsu, J. C. (1996). *Multiple comparisons: Theory and methods*. New York: Chapman and Hall.

Hsu, L. M. (2004). Biases of success rate differences shown in binomial effect size displays. *Psychological Methods, 9*, 183–197.

Huberty, C. J. (2002). A history of effect size indices. *Educational and Psychological Measurement, 62*, 227–240.

Hunter, J. E., & Schmidt, F. L. (1994). Correcting for sources of artifactual variance across studies. In H. Cooper & L. V. Hedges (Eds.), *The handbook of research synthesis* (pp. 323–338). New York: Russell Sage Foundation.

Hunter, J. E., & Schmidt, F. L. (2004). *Methods of meta-analysis* (2nd ed.). Thousand Oaks, CA: Sage.

Huynh, C. I. (1989). *A unified approach to the estimation of effect size in meta-analysis*. Paper presented at the Annual Meeting of the American Educational Research Association, San Francisco, CA. (ERIC Document Reproduction Service Clearinghouse No. ED306248)

Hyndman, R. J., & Fan, Y. (1996). Sample quantiles in statistical packages. *The American Statistician, 50*, 361–365.

Izenman, A. J. (1991). Recent developments in nonparametric density estimation. *Journal of the American Statistical Association, 86*, 205–224.

Jacoby, W. G. (1997). *Statistical graphics for univariate and bivariate data*. Thousand Oaks, CA: Sage.

Jones, L. V., & Tukey, J. W. (2000). A sensible formulation of the significance test. *Psychological Methods, 5*, 411–414.

Kempthorne, O., & Folks, L. (1971). *Probability, statistics, and data analysis*. Ames, IA: Iowa State University Press.

Kendall, P. C., & Grove, W. M. (1988). Normative comparisons in therapy outcome. *Behavioral Assessment, 10*, 147–158.

Kendall, P. C., Marss-Garcia, A., Nath, S. R., & Sheldrick, R. C. (1999). Normative comparisons for the evaluation of clinical significance. *Journal of Consulting and Clinical Psychology, 67*, 285–299.

Keppel, G. (1991). *Design and analysis: A researcher's handbook* (3rd ed.). Englewood Cliffs, NJ: Prentice-Hall.

Keren, G., & Lewis, C. (1979). Partial omega squared for ANOVA designs. *Educational and Psychological Measurement, 39,* 119–128.

Keselman, H. (1975). A Monte Carlo investigation of three estimates of treatment magnitude: Epsilon squared, eta squared, and omega squared. *Canadian Psychological Review, 16,* 44–48.

Keselman, H. J., Cribbie, R. A., & Wilcox, R. R. (2002). Pairwise multiple comparison tests when data are nonnormal. *Educational and Psychological Measurement, 62,* 420–434.

Keselman, H. J., Huberty, C. J., Lix, L. M., Olejnik, S., Cribbie, R. A., Donahue, B., Kowalchuk, R. K., Lowman, R. L., Petoskey, M. D., Keselman, J. C., & Levin, J. R. (1998). Statistical practices of educational researchers: An analysis of their ANOVA, MANOVA and ANCOVA analyses. *Review of Educational Research, 68,* 350–386.

Keselman, H. J., Othman, A. R., Wilcox, R. R., & Fradette, K. (2004). The new and improved two-sample t test. *Psychological Science, 15,* 47–51.

Keselman, H. J., Wilcox, R. R., & Lix, L. M. (2003). A generally robust approach to hypothesis testing in independent and correlated groups designs. *Psychophysiology, 40,* 586–596.

Keselman, H. J., Wilcox, R. R., Othman, A. R., & Fradette, K. (2002). Trimming, transforming statistics, and bootstrapping: Circumventing the biasing effects of heteroscedasticity and nonnormality. *Journal of Modern Applied Statistical Methods, 2,* 288–309.

Kirk, R. E. (1996). Practical significance: A concept whose time has come. *Educational and Psychological Measurement, 56,* 746–759.

Kirk, R. E. (2001). Promoting good statistical practices: Some suggestions. *Educational and Psychological Measurement, 61,* 213–218.

Kleinknecht, R. A., Dinnel, D. L., Kleinknecht, E. E., Hiruma, N., & Hirada, N. (1997). Cultural factors in social anxiety: A comparison of social phobia symptoms and *taijin kyofusho. Journal of Anxiety Disorders, 11,* 157–177.

Kline, R. B. (2004). *Beyond significance testing: Reforming data analysis methods in behavioral research.* Washington D.C., American Psychological Association.

Knapp, T. R. (2002). Some reflections on significance testing. *Journal of Modern Applied Statistical Methods, 1,* 240–242.

Knapp, T. R. (2003). Was Monte Carlo necessary? *Journal of Modern Applied Statistical Methods, 2,* 237–241.

Knapp, T. R., & Sawilowsky, S. S. (2001). Constructive criticisms of methodological and editorial practices. *The Journal of Experimental Education, 70,* 65–69.

Kraemer, H. C. (1983). Theory of estimation and testing of effect sizes: Use in meta-analysis. *Journal of Educational Statistics, 8,* 93–101.

Kraemer, H. C., & Andrews, G. (1982). A non-parametric technique for meta-analysis effect size calculation. *Psychological Bulletin, 91,* 404–412.

Kraemer, H. C., & Thiemann, S. (1987). *How many subjects? Statistical power analysis in research.* Thousand Oaks, CA: Sage.

Krueger, J. (2001). Null hypothesis significance testing: On the survival of a flawed method. *American Psychologist, 56,* 16–26.

Kruskal, W. H. (1957). Historical notes on the Wilcoxon unpaired two-sample test. *Journal of the American Statistical Association, 52,* 356–360.

Laird, N. M., & Mosteller, F. (1990). Some statistical methods for combining experimental results. *International Journal of Technology Assessment in Health Care, 6,* 5–30.

Lambert, M. J., & Bergin, A. E. (1994). The effectiveness of psychotherapy. In A. E. Bergin & S. L. Garfield (Eds.), *Handbook of psychotherapy and behavior change* (4th ed., pp. 143–189). New York: Wiley.

Laupacis, A., Sackett, D. L., & Roberts, R. S. (1988). An assessment of clinically useful measures of the consequences of treatment. *New England Journal of Medicine, 318,* 1728–1733.

Lax, D. A. (1985). Robust estimators of scale: Finite sample performance in long-tailed symmetric distributions. *Journal of the American Statistical Association, 80,* 736–741.

Lehmann, E. L. (1975). *Nonparametrics: Statistical methods based on ranks.* San Francisco: Holden-Day.

Levin, J. R., & Robinson, D. H. (1999). Further reflections on hypothesis testing and editorial policy for primary research journals. *Educational Psychological Review, 11,* 143–155.

Levin, J. R., & Robinson, D. H. (2003). The trouble with interpreting statistically nonsignificant effect sizes in single-study investigations. *Journal of Modern Applied Statistical Methods, 2,* 231–236.

Levine, T. R., & Hullett, C. R. (2002). Eta squared, partial eta squared, and misreporting of effect size in communication research. *Human Communication Research, 28,* 612–625.

Levy, P. (1967). Substantive significance of significant differences between two groups. *Psychological Bulletin, 67,* 37–40.

Liebetrau, A. M. (1983). *Measures of association.* Thousand Oaks, CA: Sage.

Lipsey, M. W. (1990). *Design sensitivity: Statistical power for experimental research.* Thousand Oaks, CA: Sage.

Lipsey, M. W. (2000). Statistical conclusion validity for intervention research. In L. Bickman (Ed.), *Validity and social experimentation* (pp. 101–120). Thousand Oaks, CA: Sage.

Lipsey, M. W., & Wilson, D. B. (1993). The efficacy of psychological, educational, and behavioral treatments: Confirmation from meta-analysis. *American Psychologist, 48,* 1181–1209.

Lipsey, M. W., & Wilson, D. B. (2001). *Practical meta-analysis.* Thousand Oaks, CA: Sage.

Liu, Q. (1998). An order-directed score test for trend in ordered 2 × k tables. *Biometrics, 54,* 1147–1154.

Lix, L. M., Cribbie, R., & Keselman, H. J. (June, 1996). *The analysis of completely randomized univariate designs.* Paper presented at the annual meeting of the Psychometric Society, Banff, Alberta, Canada.

Lunneborg, C. E. (1999). *Data analysis by resampling: Concepts and applications.* Pacific Grove, CA: Duxbury.

Lunneborg, C. E. (2001). Random assignment of available cases: Bootstrap standard errors and confidence intervals. *Psychological Methods, 6,* 402–412.

Lunney, G. H. (1970). Using analysis of variance with a dichotomous dependent variable: An empirical study. *Journal of Educational Measurement, 7,* 263–269.

Mancini, G. B. J., & Schulzer, M. (1999). Reporting risks and benefits of therapy by the use of the concepts of unqualified success and unmitigated failure. *Circulation, 99,* 377–383.

Mann, H. B., & Whitney, D. R. (1947). On a test of whether one of two random variables is stochastically larger than the other. *Annals of Mathematical Statistics, 18,* 50–60.

Markus, K. A. (2001). The converse inequality argument against tests of statistical significance. *Psychological Methods, 6,* 147–160.

Martell, R. F., Lane, D. M., & Emrich, C. (1996). Male–female differences: A computer simulation. *American Psychologist*, *51*, 157–158.

Martín Andrés, A., & Herranz Tejedor, I. (2003). Unconditional confidence interval for the difference between two proportions. *Biometrical Journal*, *45*, 426–436.

Martín Andrés, A., & Herranz Tejedor, I. (2004). Exact unconditional non-classical tests on the difference of two proportions. *Computational Statistics and Data Analysis*, *45*, 373–388.

Matsumoto, D., Grissom, R. J., & Dinnel, D. L. (2001). Do between-culture differences really mean that people are different? A look at some measures of cultural effect size. *Journal of Cross-Cultural Psychology*, *32*, 478–490.

Maxwell, S. E. (1998). Longitudinal designs in randomized group comparisons: When will intermediate observations increase statistical power? *Psychological Methods*, *3*, 275–290.

Maxwell, S. E. (2004). The persistence of underpowered studies in psychological research: Causes, consequences, and remedies. *Psychological Methods*, *9*, 147–163.

Maxwell, S. E., Camp, C. C., & Arvey, R. D. (1981). Measures of strength of association: A comparative examination. *Journal of Applied Psychology*, *66*, 525–534.

Maxwell, S. E., & Delaney, H. D. (1985). Measurement and statistics: An examination of construct validity. *Psychological Bulletin*, *97*, 85–93.

Maxwell, S. E., & Delaney, H. D. (2004). *Designing experiments and analyzing data: A model comparison perspective* (2nd ed.). Mahwah, NJ: Lawrence Erlbaum Associates.

McGraw, K. O. (1991). Problems with the BESD: A comment on Rosenthal's "How are we doing in soft psychology?" *American Psychologist*, *46*, 1084–1086.

McGraw, K. O., & Wong, S. P. (1992). A common language effect size statistic. *Psychological Bulletin*, *111*, 361–365.

McKean, J. W., & Schrader, R. M. (1984). A comparison of methods for studentizing the sample median. *Communications in Statistics-Simulation and Computation*, *13*, 751–773.

McNemar, Q. (1962). *Psychological statistics* (3rd ed.). New York: Wiley.

Mee, R. W. (1990). Confidence intervals for probabilities and tolerance regions based on a generalization of the Mann–Whitney statistic. *Journal of the American Statistical Association*, *85*, 793–800.

Meeks, S. L. & D'Agostino, R. B. (1983). A note on the use of confidence limits following rejection of a null hypothesis. *The American Statistician*, *37*, 134–136.

Micceri, T. (1989). The unicorn, the normal curve, and other improbable creatures. *Psychological Bulletin*, *105*, 156–166.

Mohr, D. C. (1995). Negative outcomes in psychotherapy: A critical review. *Clinical Psychology: Science and Practice*, *2*, 1–27.

Morris, S. B., & DeShon, R. P. (2002). Combining effect size estimates in meta-analysis with repeated measures and independent-groups designs. *Psychological Methods*, *7*, 105–125.

Moses, L. E. (1986). *Think and explain with statistics*. Reading, MA: Addison-Wesley.

Moses, L. E., Emerson, J. D., & Hosseini, H. (1984). Analyzing data from ordered categories. *New England Journal of Medicine*, *311*, 442–448.

Mosteller, F., & Chalmers, T. C. (1992). Some progress and problems in meta-analysis of clinical trials. *Statistical Science*, *7*, 227–236.

Mueller, C. G. (1949). Numerical transformations in the analysis of experimental data. *Psychological Bulletin, 46,* 198–223.

Murphy, B. P., (1976). Comparison of some two sample means tests by simulation. *Communications in Statistics-Simulation and Computation, B5*(1), 23–32.

Murphy, K. R., & Myors, B. (2003). *Statistical power analysis: A simple and general model for traditional and modern hypothesis tests.* Mahwah, NJ: Lawrence Erlbaum Associates.

Murray, L. W., & Dosser, D. A. (1987). How significant is a significant difference? Problems with the measurement of magnitude of effect. *Journal of Counseling Psychology, 34,* 68–72.

Nanna, M. J. (2002). Hoteling's $T^2$ vs. the rank transformation with real Likert data. *Journal of Modern Applied Statistical Methods, 1,* 83 –99.

Nanna, M. J., & Sawilowsky, S. S. (1998). Analysis of Likert scale data in disability and medical rehabilitation research. *Psychological Methods, 3,* 55–56.

Newcombe, R. G. (1998). Interval estimation for the difference between independent proportions: Comparison of eleven methods. *Statistics in Medicine, 17,* 873–890.

Nickerson, R. S. (2000). Null hypothesis significance testing: A review of an old and continuing controversy. *Psychological Methods, 5,* 241–301.

Norusis, M. J. (1995). *SPSS 6.1 Guide to data analysis.* Englewood Cliffs, NJ: Prentice Hall.

Nouri, H., & Greenberg, R. H. (1985). Meta-analytic procedures for estimation of effect sizes in experiments using complex analysis of variance. *Journal of Management, 21,* 801–812.

O'Brien, P. C. (1988). Comparing two samples: Extensions of the *t*, rank-sum, and log-rank tests. *Journal of the American Statistical Association, 83,* 52–61.

O'Grady, K. E. (1982). Measures of explained variance: Cautions and limitations. *Psychological Bulletin, 92,* 766–777.

Olejnik, S., & Algina, J. (2000). Measures of effect size for comparative studies: Applications, interpretations, and limitations. *Contemporary Educational Psychology, 25,* 241–286.

Olejnik, S., & Algina, J. (2003). Generalized eta and omega squared statistics: Measures of effect size for some common research designs. *Psychological Methods, 8,* 434–437.

Onwuegbuzie, A. J., & Levin, J. R. (2003). Without supporting evidence, where would measures of substantive importance lead? *Journal of Modern Applied Statistical Methods, 2,* 133–151.

Othman, A. R., Keselman, H. J., Wilcox, R. R., Fradette, K., & Padmanabhan, A. R. (2002). A test of symmetry. *Journal of Modern Applied Statistical Methods, 1,* 310–315.

Ozer, D. J. (1985). Correlation and the coefficient of determination. *Psychological Bulletin, 97,* 307–315.

Parker, S. (1995). The "difference of means" may not be the "effect size." *American Psychologist, 50,* 1101–1102.

Pedersen, W. C., Miller, L. C., Putcha-Bhagavatula, A. D., & Yang, Y. (2002). Evolved sex differences in sexual strategies: The long and the short of it. *Psychological Science, 13,* 157–161.

Penfield, R. D. (2003). A score method of constructing asymmetric confidence intervals for the mean of a rating scale item. *Psychological Methods, 8,* 149–163.

Perry, K. T., & Stoline, M. R. (2002). A comparison of the D'Agostino $S_u$ test to the triples test for testing symmetry versus asymmetry as a preliminary test to testing the equality of means. *Journal of Modern Applied Statistical Methods, 1,* 316–325.

Plake, B. S., Impara, J. C., & Spies, R. A. (Eds.). (2003). *The fifteenth mental measurements yearbook.* Lincoln, NB: Buros Institute.

Posch, M. (2002). Asymptotic and exact tests in $2 \times c$ ordered categorical contingency tables. *Journal of Modern Applied Statistical Methods, 1,* 167–175.

Pratt, J. W. (1964). Obustness (sic) of some procedures for the two-sample location problem. *Journal of the American Statistical Association, 59,* 665–680.

Pratt, J. W. (1968). A normal approximation for binomial, F, beta, and other common related tail probabilities, I. *Journal of the American Statistical Association, 63,* 1457–1483.

Pratt, J. W., & Gibbons, J. D. (1981). *Concepts of nonparametric theory.* New York: Springer-Verlag.

Preece, P. F. W. (1983). A measure of experimental effect size based on success rates. *Educational and Psychological Measurement, 43,* 763–766.

Prentice, D. A., & Miller, D. T. (1992). When small effects are impressive. *Psychological Bulletin, 112,* 160–164.

Ramsey, P. H. (1980). Exact Type I error rates for robustness of Student's *t* test with unequal variance. *Journal of Educational Statistics, 5,* 337–350.

Randles, R. H. (2001). On neutral responses (zeros) in the sign test and ties in the Wilcoxon–Mann–Whitney test. *The American Statistician, 55,* 96–101.

Raudenbush, S. W., & Bryk, A. S. (1987). Examining correlates of diversity. *Journal of Educational Statistics, 12,* 241–269.

Rayner, J. C. W., & Best, D. J. (2001). *A contingency table approach to nonparametric testing.* Boca Raton, FL: Chapman & Hall/CRC.

Reed III, J. F. (2003). Solutions to the Behrens-Fisher problem. *Computer Methods and Programs in Biomedicine, 70,* 259 –263.

Reichardt, C. S., & Gollob, H. E. (1997). When confidence intervals should be used instead of statistical tests, and vice versa. In L. L. Harlow, S. A. Mulaik, & J. H. Steiger (Eds.), *What if there were no significance tests?* (pp. 259–284). Mahwah, NJ: Lawrence Erlbaum Associates.

Rice, M. E. (1997). Violent offender research and implications for the criminal justice system. *American Psychologist, 52,* 414–423.

Richardson, J. T. E. (1996). Measures of effect size. *Behavior Research Methods, Instruments & Computers, 28,* 12–22.

Roberts, J. K., & Henson, R. K. (2003). Not all effects are created equal: A rejoinder to Sawilowsky. *Journal of Modern Applied Statistical Methods, 2,* 226–230.

Robinson, D. H., & Levin, J. R. (1997). Reflections on statistical and substantive significance, with a slice of replication. *Educational Researcher, 26,* 21–26.

Röhmel, J. & Mansmann, U. (1999). Unconditional non-asymptotic one-sided tests for independent binomial proportions when the interest lies in showing non-inferiority and/or superiority. *Biometrical Journal, 41,* 149–170.

Ronis, D. L. (1981). Comparing the magnitude of effects in ANOVA designs. *Educational and Psychological Measurement, 41,* 993–1000.

Rosenberger, J. L., & Gasko, M. (1983). Comparing location estimators: Trimmed means, medians, and trimeans. In D. C. Hoaglin, F. Mosteller, & J. W. Tukey (Eds.). *Understanding robust and exploratory data analysis* (pp. 297–336). New York: Wiley.

Rosenthal, R. (1991a). Effect sizes: Pearson's correlation, its display via the BESD, and alternative indices. *American Psychologist, 46,* 1086–1087.

Rosenthal, R. (1991b). *Meta-analytic procedures for social research.* Thousand Oaks, CA: Sage Press.

Rosenthal, R. (2000). Effect sizes in behavioral and biomedical research. In L. Bickman (Ed.), *Validity and social experimentation* (pp. 121–139). Thousand Oaks, CA: Sage.

Rosenthal, R., Rosnow, R. L., & Rubin, D. B. (2000). *Contrasts and effect sizes for Behavioral Research.* Cambridge, England: Cambridge University Press.

Rosenthal, R., & Rubin, D. B. (1982). A simple general purpose display of magnitude of experimental effect. *Journal of Educational Psychology, 74,* 166–169.

Rosenthal, R., & Rubin, D. B. (1994). The counternull value of an effect size: A new statistic. *Psychological Science, 5,* 329–334.

Rudas, T. (1998). *Odds ratios in the analysis of contingency tables.* Thousand Oaks, CA: Sage.

Sackett, D. L., Strauss, S. E., Richardson, W. S., Rosenberg, W., & Haynes, R. B. (2000). *Evidence based medicine: How to practice and teach EBM* (2nd ed.). Edinburgh: Churchill Livingtone.

Sánchez-Meca, J., Marín-Martínez, F., & Chacón-Moscoso, S. (2003). Effect-size indices for dichotomized outcomes in meta-analysis. *Psychological Methods, 8,* 448–467.

Santner, T. J., & Snell, M. K. (1980). Small-sample confidence intervals for $p_1 - p_2$ and $p_1/p_2$ in $2 \times 2$ contingency tables. *Journal of the American Statistical Association, 75,* 386–394.

Satterthwaite, F. E. (1946). An approximate distribution of estimates of variance components. *Biometrics Bulletin, 2,* 110–114.

Sawilowsky, S. S. (2002). A measure of relative efficiency for location of a single sample. *Journal of Modern Applied Statistical Methods, 1,* 52–60.

Sawilowsky, S. S. (2003). Trivials: The birth, sale, and final production of meta-analysis. *Journal of Modern Applied Statistical Methods, 2,* 242–246.

Sawilowsky, S. S., & Blair, R. C. (1992). A more realistic look at the robustness and type II error properties of the *t* test to departures from population normality. *Psychological Bulletin, 111,* 352–360.

Sawilowsky, S. S., & Fahoome, G. (2003). *Statistics through Monte Carlo simulation with Fortran.* Rochester Hills, MI: Journal of Modern Applied Statistical Methods.

Sawilowsky, S. S., & Markman, B. S. (2002). Using the t test with uncommon sample sizes. *Journal of Modern Applied Statistics, 1,* 145–146.

Sawilowsky, S. S., & Yoon, J. S. (2002). The trouble with trivials (p > .05). *Journal of Modern Applied Statistics, 1,* 143–144.

Schmidt, F. L., & Hunter, J. E. (1996). Measurement error in psychological research: Lessons from 26 research scenarios. *Psychological Methods, 1,* 199–223.

Schmidt, F. L., Le, H., & Ilies, R. (2003). Beyond alpha: An empirical examination of the effects of different sources of measurement error on reliability estimates for measures of individual differences constructs. *Psychological Methods, 8,* 206–224.

Schmidt, N. (1996). Statistical significance testing and cumulative knowledge in psychology: Implications for training of researchers. *Psychological Methods, 1,* 115–129.

Schulzer, M., & Mancini, G. B. J. (1996). 'Unqualified success' and 'unmitigated failure': Number-needed-to-treat related concepts for assessing treatment efficacy in the presence of treatment induced adverse effects. *International Journal of Epidemiology, 25,* 704–712.

Schwertman, N. C., Owens, M. A., & Adnan, R. (2004). A simple more general boxplot method for identifying outliers. *Computational Statistics and Data Analysis, 47,* 165–174.

Serfling, R. J. (1980). *Approximation theorems of mathematical statistics.* New York: Wiley.

Serlin, R. C. (2002). Constructive criticism. *Journal of Modern Applied Statistical Methods, 1,* 202–227.

Serlin, R. C., Wampold, B. E., & Levin, J. R. (2003). Should providers of treatment be regarded as a random factor? If it ain't broke, don't fix it: A comment on Siemer and Joorman (2003). *Psychological Methods, 8,* 524–534.

Shaffer, J. P. (2002). Multiplicity, directional (Type III) errors, and the null hypothesis. *Psychological Methods, 7,* 356–369.

Siegel, S., & Castellan, N. J. (1988). *Nonparametric statistics for the behavioral sciences* (2nd ed.). New York: McGraw-Hill.

Siemer, M., & Joormann, J. (2003a). Power and measures of effect size in analysis of variance with fixed versus random nested factors. *Psychological Methods, 8,* 497–517.

Siemer, M., & Joormann, J. (2003b). Assumptions and consequences of treating providers in therapy studies as fixed versus random effects: Reply to Crits-Christoph, Tu, and Gallop (2003) and Serlin, Wampold, and Levin (2003). *Psychological Methods, 8,* 535–5441.

Silverman, B. W. (1986). *Density estimation for statistics and data analysis.* New York: Chapman and Hall.

Simonoff, J. S., Hochberg, Y., & Reiser, B. (1986). Alternative estimation procedures for Pr(X < Y) in categorical data. *Biometrics, 42,* 895–907.

Skinner, B. F. (1958). Teaching machines. *Science, 128,* 969–977.

Skipka, G. (2003). *The likelihood ratio test for order restricted hypotheses in non-inferiority trials.* Unpublished doctoral dissertation. Göttingen University, Göttingen, Germany.

Smith, M. L., & Glass, G. V. (1977). Meta-analysis of psychotherapy outcome studies. *American Psychologist, 32,* 752–760.

Smithson, M. (2001). Correct confidence intervals for various regression effect sizes and parameters. *Educational and Psychological Measurement, 61,* 605–632.

Smithson, M. (2003). *Confidence intervals.* Thousand Oaks, CA: Sage.

Snedecor, G. W., & Cochran, W. G. (1989). *Statistical methods* (8th ed.). Ames, IA: Iowa State University Press.

Snyder, D. K., Wills, R. M., & Grady-Fletcher, A. (1991). Long-term effectiveness of behavioral vs. insight-oriented marital therapy: A 4-year follow-up study. *Journal of Consulting and Clinical Psychology, 59,* 138–141.

Snyder, P., & Lawson, S. (1993). Evaluating results using corrected and uncorrected effect size estimates. *Journal of Experimental Education, 61,* 334–349.

Somers, R. H. (1962). A new asymmetrical measure of association for ordinal variables. *American Sociological Review, 27,* 799–811.

Sparks, J. N. (1967). *Effects of inapplicability of the continuity condition upon the probability distributions of selected statistics and their implications for research in education* (Final Rep. No. RIE SYN71840). University Park: Pennsylvania State University.

Sprent, P. (1998). *Data driven statistical methods.* London: Chapman and Hall.

Staudte, R. G., & Sheather, S. J. (1990). *Robust estimation and testing.* New York: Wiley.

Steiger, J. H. (1999). *STATISTICA power analysis.* Tulsa, OK: StatSoft.

Steiger, J. H. (2004). Beyond the F test: Effect size confidence intervals and tests of close fit in the analysis of variance and contrast analysis. *Psychological Methods, 9,* 164–182.

Steiger, J. H., & Fouladi, R. T. (1997). Noncentrality interval estimation and the evaluation of statistical methods. In L. L. Harlow, S. A. Mulaik, & J. H. Steiger (Eds.), *What if there were no significance tests?* (pp. 221–257). Mahwah, NJ: Lawrence Erlbaum Associates.

Storer, B. E., & Kim, C. (1990). Exact properties of some exact test statistics for comparing two binomial proportions. *Journal of the American Statistical Association, 85,* 146–155.

Strahan, R. F. (1991). Remarks on the binomial effect size display. *American Psychologist, 46,* 1083–1084.

Susskind, E. C., & Howland, E. W. (1980). Measuring effect magnitude in repeated measures ANOVA designs: Implications for gerontological research. *Journal of Gerontology, 35,* 867–876.

Thompson, B. (1993). The use of statistical significance tests in research: Bootstrap and other alternatives. *Journal of Experimental Education, 61,* 361–377.

Thompson, B. (1999, April). *Common methodology mistakes in educational research, revisited, along with a primer on both effect sizes and the bootstrap.* Paper presented at the annual meeting of the American Educational Research Association, Montreal, Canada.

Thompson, B. (2002). What future quantitative social science research could look like: confidence intervals for effect sizes. *Educational Researcher, 31,* 25–32.

Thompson, K. N., & Schumacker, R. E. (1997). An evaluation of Rosenthal and Rubin's binomial effect size display. *Journal of Educational and Behavioral Statistics, 22,* 109–117.

Timm, N. H. (2004). Estimating effect sizes in exploratory experimental studies when using a linear model. *The American Statistician, 58,* 213–217.

Tomarken, A. J., & Serlin, R. C. (1986). Comparison of ANOVA alternatives under variance heterogeneity and specific noncentrality structures. *Psychological Bulletin, 99,* 90–99.

Trenkler, D. (2002). Quantile-boxplots. *Communications in Statistics-Simulation and Computation, 31,* 1–12.

Tryon, W. W. (2001). Evaluating statistical difference, equivalence, and indeterminacy using inferential confidence intervals: An integrated alternative method of conducting null hypothesis statistical tests. *Psychological Methods, 6,* 371–386.

Vargha, A., & Delaney, H. D. (2000). A critique and improvement of the CL common language effect size statistics of McGraw and Wong. *Journal of Educational and Behavioral Statistics, 25,* 101–132.

Vaske, J. J., Gliner, J. A., & Morgan, G. A. (2002). Communicating judgments about practical significance: Effect size, confidence intervals and odds ratios. *Human Dimensions of Wildlife, 7,* 287–300.

Vaughan, G. M., & Corballis, M. C. (1969). Beyond tests of significance: Estimating strength of effects in selected ANOVA designs. *Psychological Bulletin, 72,* 204–213.

Venables, W. (1975). Calculation of confidence intervals for noncentrality parameters. *Journal of the Royal Statistical Society (Series B)*, 37, 406–412.

Walker, E. L. (1947). *Factors in vernier acuity and distance discrimination.* Unpublished doctoral dissertation, Stanford University, Stanford, CA.

Wampold, B. E., & Serlin, R. C. (2000). The consequences of ignoring a nested factor on measures of effect size in analysis of variance. *Psychological Methods*, 5, 425–433.

Watson, J. S. (1985). Volunteer and risk-taking groups are more homogeneous on measures of sensation seeking than control groups. *Perceptual and Motor Skills*, 61, 471–475.

Weisz, J. R., Weiss, B., Han, S. S., Granger, D. A., & Morton, T. (1995). Effects of psychotherapy with children and adolescents revisited: A meta-analysis of treatment outcome studies. *Psychological Bulletin*, 117, 450–468.

Welch, B. L. (1938). The significance of the difference between two means when the population variances are unequal. *Biometrika*, 29, 350–362.

Werner, M., Stabenau, J. B., & Pollin, W. (1970). TAT method for the differentiation of families of schizophrenics, delinquents, and normals. *Journal of Abnormal Psychology*, 75, 139–145.

Weston, T., & Hopkins, K. D. (1998). *Testing for homogeneity of variance: An evaluation of current practice.* Unpublished manuscript, University of Colorado at Boulder.

Wickens, T. D. (1989). *Multiway contingency tables analysis for the social sciences.* Mahwah, NJ: Lawrence Erlbaum Associates.

Wiener, R. L., & Gutek, B. (1997). Sexual harassment [Special issue]. *Psychology, Public Policy, and Law*, 5(3).

Wilcox, R. R. (1987). New designs in analysis of variance. *Annual Review of Psychology*, 38, 29–60.

Wilcox, R. R. (1995). Comparing two independent groups via multiple quantiles. *The Statistician*, 44, 91–99.

Wilcox, R. R. (1996). *Statistics for the social sciences.* San Diego, CA: Academic Press.

Wilcox, R. R. (1997). *Introduction to robust estimation and hypothesis testing.* San Diego, CA: Academic Press.

Wilcox, R. R. (2001). *Fundamentals of modern statistical methods: Substantially improving power and accuracy.* New York: Springer-Verlag.

Wilcox, R. R. (2002). Multiple comparisons among dependent groups based on a modified one-step M-estimator. *Biometrical Journal*, 44, 466–477.

Wilcox, R. R. (2003). *Applying contemporary statistical techniques.* San Diego, CA: Academic Press.

Wilcox, R. R., Charlin, V. L., & Thompson, K. L. (1986). New Monte Carlo results on the robustness of the ANOVA $F$, $W$, and $F^*$ statistics. *Communications in Statistics-Simulation and Computation*, 15, 933–943.

Wilcox, R. R., & Keselman, H. J. (2002a). Power analysis when comparing trimmed means. *Journal of Modern Applied Statistical Methods*, 1, 24–31.

Wilcox, R. R., & Keselman, H. J. (2002b). Within groups multiple comparisons based on robust measures of location. *Journal of Modern Applied Statistical Methods*, 1, 281 –287.

Wilcox, R. R., & Keselman, H. J. (2003a). Modern robust data analysis: Measures of central tendency. *Psychological Methods*, 8, 254–274.

Wilcox, R. R., & Keselman, H. J. (2003b). Repeated measures one-way ANOVA based on a modified one-step M-estimator. *British Journal of Mathematical and Statistical Psychology, 56,* 1–13.

Wilcox, R. R., & Muska, J. (1999). Measuring effect size: A non-parametric analog of $\omega^2$. *British Journal of Mathematical and Statistical Psychology, 52,* 93–110.

Wilcoxon, F. (1945). Individual comparisons by ranking methods. *Biometrics, 1,* 80–83.

Wilde, M. C., Boake, C., & Sherer, M. (1995). Do recognition-free recall discrepancies detect retrieval deficits in closed-head injury? An exploratory analysis with the California Verbal Learning Test. *Journal of Clinical and Experimental Neuropsychology, 17,* 849–855.

Wilk, M. B., & Gnanadesikan, R. (1968). Probability plotting methods for the analysis of data. *Biometrika, 55,* 1–17.

Wilkinson, L., & APA Task Force on Statistical Inference. (1999). Statistical methods in psychology journals: Guidelines and explanations. *American Psychologist, 54,* 594–604.

Wilson, D. B., & Lipsey, M. W. (2001). The role of method in treatment effectiveness: Evidence from meta-analysis. *Psychological Methods, 6,* 413–429.

Wright, S. T. (1946). *Spacing of practice in verbal learning and the maturation hypothesis.* Unpublished master's thesis, Stanford University, Stanford, CA.

Yuen, K. K. (1974). The two sample trimmed t for unequal population variances. *Biometrika, 61,* 165–170.

Zimmerman, D. M. (1996). Some properties of preliminary tests of equality of variances in the two-sample location problem. *The Journal of General Psychology, 123,* 217–231.

Zimmerman, D. M., & Zumbo, B. D. (1993). Rank transformations and the power of the Student t test and Welch t´ test for non-normal populations with unequal variances. *Canadian Journal of Experimental Psychology, 47,* 523–539.

# Author Index

237

# Subject Index

## A

American Psychological Association (APA), 5
*Publication Manual of the American Psychological Association*, 24
APA Task Force on Statistical Inference, 8, 24, 62, 78, 236
*American Psychologist*, 6
Assumptions,
  effect sizes, 9–10
  F test, 10
  t test, 10
  violations in real data, 10–14
Attitudinal scales, see also Rating scale data
  problems in comparing effect sizes, 201

## B

Biased estimators of effect size, 6
Binomial Effect Size Display (BESD), 87–91
  and dichotomizing, 90
  limitations, 89–91
  and median split, 90
  and phi coefficient, 87–88
  and success percentages, 88–90
  and uniform margins, 89–90
Binomial variables, 171
Biweight midvariance, 59
Biweight standard deviation,
  as standardizer, 59

Bonett-Price method, 40
Bonferroni-Dunn adjustment, 56
  in factorial ANOVA, 161
  within-group multiple comparisons, 135
Bootstrapping, 42–43
Boxplots 18–19, 114
  quantile-boxplot, 114
*British Medical Journal*, 188

## C

Capitalizing on chance, 56
Case-control research, 185
Categorical variables, 170–171
Causal efficacy ratio, 84
Cause size, 84
Chi-square test, 170, 173–175
  adjusted and unadjusted, 174–175, 190–191
Classificatory factors, 139
Coefficient of determination, 91–95
  curvilinearity and skew, 94–95
  interpretation, 91–95
  multiple, 95
  reasons for disfavor, 92–95
  underestimation of practical significance, 93–94
Coefficient of nondetermination, 93
Cohen's $d_s$, 54
Cohen's $f$, 120
  unbiased estimator, 122
Cohen's $U_3$, 108–109
Cohort research, 185–186
Common Language Effect Size Statistic, 105–106